Women and Change at the U.S.-Mexico Border

Women and Change
at the U.S.-Mexico Border

MOBILITY, LABOR, AND ACTIVISM

Doreen J. Mattingly and Ellen R. Hansen, EDITORS

The University of Arizona Press Tucson

The University of Arizona Press
© 2006 The Arizona Board of Regents
Manufactured in the United States of America

11 10 09 08 07 06   6 5 4 3 2 1

Library of Congress Cataloging-in-Publication Data
Women and change at the U.S.–Mexico border /
Doreen J. Mattingly and Ellen R. Hansen, editors.
     p. cm.
     Includes bibliographical references and index.
     ISBN-13: 978-0-8165-2528-7 (hardcover : alk. paper)
     ISBN-10: 0-8165-2528-5 (hardcover : alk. paper)
     1. Women — Mexican-American Border Region — Social conditions. 2. Women —
Mexican-American Border Region — Economic conditions. 3. Women — Employment
— Mexican-American Border Region. 4. Women political activists — Mexican-
American Border Region. I. Mattingly, Doreen J., 1962– II. Hansen, Ellen R.
HQ1464.M59 W66 2006
305.40972'1 — dc22   2006005717

For the women of the border

Contents

Acknowledgments   ix

1   Women at the Border: Foundations and Frameworks   3
    Ellen R. Hansen and Doreen J. Mattingly

PART ONE Women's Mobility

2   The Unsettling, Gendered Consequences of Migration for
    Mexican Indigenous Women   19
    Elizabeth Maier

3   Women's Daily Mobility at the U.S.–Mexico Border   36
    Ellen R. Hansen

4   Abortion in a Transborder Context   53
    Norma Ojeda

PART TWO Labor and Empowerment in the Border Region

5   The Changing Gender Composition of the Maquiladora
    Workforce along the U.S.–Mexico Border   73
    Susan Tiano

6   The Roots of Autonomy through Work Participation in the
    Northern Mexico Border Region   91
    Ana Bergareche

7   Domestic Service and International Networks of Caring
    Labor   103
    Doreen J. Mattingly

PART THREE Activist Women Changing the Border

   8 Mexican Women's Activism in New Mexico Colonias   125
      Rebecca Dolhinow

   9 Styles, Strategies, and Issues of Women Leaders at the
      Border   142
      Irasema Coronado

  10 Border Women's NGOs and Political Participation in
      Baja California   159
      Silvia López Estrada

  11 "Making Believe" and "Willing Partners" in Academics'
      Activism in the U.S.–Mexico Borderlands   178
      Patricia Manning, with Janice Monk and Catalina Denman

      Notes   195
      Bibliography   205
      About the Contributors   225
      Index   229

Acknowledgments

Many people contributed to this volume who will never know how important they were to its completion. We are deeply grateful to Chris Szuter, Allyson Carter, and the staff at the University of Arizona Press, who have been a delight to work with and unfailingly enthusiastic. Furthermore, their hard work and careful scholarship have made the book possible. For help with the practicalities of putting the manuscript together, we thank Beth, Amanda, Alicia, and Jacque for their time and patience. Several papers in this volume were presented at the 2004 Annual Meeting of the Association of American Geographers in Philadelphia, Pennsylvania. The volume benefited significantly from the comments and suggestions of the conference audience.

Ellen would like to thank her supportive family, who has always been proud of her work and has made the path smoother. Good friends have provided her with listening ears and hearts and practical necessities such as a place to stay and a full table, especially Laurie, Leslie, Mimi, Barb, Connie, Stephen, Kim, Margaret, Jon, and Joel. She also thanks her colleagues at Emporia State University for ongoing support.

Doreen would like to thank the Department of Women's Studies at San Diego State University for the support and collegiality. She is also grateful to her family and friends who have sustained body and soul through this and many other projects.

The editors and publisher gratefully acknowledge the following for permission to reproduce copyrighted material: Blackwell Publishing for Doreen J. Mattingly. 2001. The home and the world: Domestic service and international networks of caring labor. *Annals of the Association of American Geographers* 91 (2): 370–86.

Women and Change at the U.S.-Mexico Border

I Women at the Border

FOUNDATIONS AND FRAMEWORKS

Ellen R. Hansen and Doreen J. Mattingly

One enduring quality of feminist scholarship about the border region is the portrayal of women as active agents influencing the world around them, rather than as passive victims of forces beyond their control. The central concern of this volume is the agency of women in the border region, in the context of the structural constraints of the local and transnational locations. Women's relationships to change at the border take a variety of forms. The mobility, labor, and activism suggested by the three section divisions refer to different areas of women's lives in which they change, and are changed by, the border context. Women move physically across and around the border on a daily and longer-term basis. Through their physical mobility, women create transnational lives that overcome the barriers created by the international boundary reinforced by governments on both sides. Women's paid and unpaid labor is shaped by both the economic structure of the border and women's capabilities. The conditions of women's work illuminate the ongoing interplay between structure and agency; work can empower women, but at the same time, it can marginalize or exploit them. Activism refers to the ways women organize to bring change to their communities, at times setting the agenda and at times responding to larger structural changes. The impact of these chapters makes clear the vital roles that women play in changing the U.S.–Mexico border region as they shape their own lives.

In addition to emphasizing women's agency, this book contributes in other ways to a dynamic tradition of feminist scholarship. The chapters all put women's experiences and women's stories at the heart of the investigations. The chapters included here treat gender as a changing social construct and acknowledge the great variation within the category "woman." By definition, border regions are places of cultural diversity and, therefore, of multiple gender ideologies (Anzaldúa 1987; Vila 2003b; Wright 2003).

For women in the border region, different cultural constructs of gender shape the ideological terrain they negotiate. The chapters in this book illustrate the opportunities and obstacles presented by the region's multiple gender ideologies.

At a superficial level, the border creates differences between "Mexican" and "American" peoples and cultures. Look beyond the surface, however, and the binary crumbles into a multitude of experiences and interpretations of those categories (Fregoso 2003; Vila 2000, 2003a). The chapters in the book do not assume the validity of the Mexican/American binary; instead, they illuminate the cultural mosaic that actually shapes women's lives at the border.

One of the interesting things about studying the border is that it provides a window into the ways women's lives cross boundaries, in both a physical and a metaphorical sense. Women living near the U.S.–Mexico border cross for a variety of reasons, including work, shopping, socializing, and collaborative activities. Simultaneously, women's lives are also shaped by transnational social processes, ideologies, and discourses (Castillo and Tabuenca Córdoba 2002). In particular, cross-border immigrants maintain attachments to people and institutions in their places of origin (Mahler 2003). The contributors to this volume exemplify these cross-border patterns in their own lives. All of the authors have traveled and worked in both Spanish- and English-speaking countries, most have lived on both sides of the border, and many have published in both languages. Transnational authorship is one of the distinguishing and valuable characteristics of this volume.

Conceptualizing the Border

"The U.S.–Mexican border *es una herida abierta* [is an open wound] where the third world grates against the first and bleeds" (Anzaldúa 1987, 3). The border creates a geographical binary, with the space divided into two national territories. But even as governments pour resources into the enforcement of the physical boundary, people overcome the division as they appropriate, shift, and ignore the presence of the border in their daily lives (Velez-Ibáñez 1996). The division of space into separate countries is not easily mapped onto people's lives; the categories "Mexican" and "American" often obscure more than they reveal.

Defining borders can be a difficult endeavor. At the most basic level, a border is a political boundary between two countries. Even that basic statement is laden with implications of complex political and social relations; no border can be so simply defined. Borders are best understood as processes that are socially constructed and maintained by a variety of actors (Ackelson 2003). Although we discuss the border as a region, it is a zone without fixed boundaries. As the chapters in this volume show, the geographical extent of the border's influence varies widely, and it is not possible to map a cohesive border region that captures all the meanings of the border. Despite these conceptual complexities, the U.S.–Mexico border is important as the specific geographical context of people's lives — the space within which women's agency takes shape.

The physical border dividing the United States and Mexico is about two thousand miles long and spans a diversity of landscapes and settlements. From the Pacific Coast to the cities of El Paso and Ciudad Juárez, it is formed by the political line drawn by the Treaty of Guadalupe Hidalgo; for the rest of its extent to the east, it is formed by the Rio Grande/Río Bravo (see fig. 1.1). The case studies in this book take place in the urban areas along the western half of the border. Human settlement along the border is primarily urban, formed by twin cities from San Diego–Tijuana on the west to Brownsville-Matamoros on the east (Arreola and Curtis 1993). With the exception of the San Diego–Tijuana twin cities, the largest populations are found on the Mexico side of the border. The cities on the U.S. side tend to be among the lowest income in the United States, whereas the cities on the Mexico side are high income relative to the rest of the country. In all U.S. border cities except for San Diego, the Latino population is a majority; on the Mexico side, ethnic diversity is often higher at the border than in cities of the interior due to significant in-migration from other parts of Mexico, and Central and South America.

Economic and political patterns are other significant parts of the border context that shape women's lives. Because the border is unique in dividing the first world from the third world, it has been altered by economic globalization and the dominance of neoliberal ideology and institutions. The passage of the Border Industrialization Program in 1965 made northern Mexico a pioneer in export-led industrialization — in many ways a laboratory for neoliberal experimentation. Although initially proposed as a solution to male unemployment, the majority of workers in the

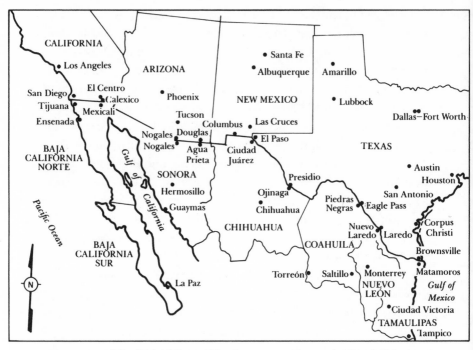

FIGURE 1.1 The U.S.–Mexico border region. Drawn by Linda Marston. *Source:* Oscar J. Martínez, *Troublesome Border.* Tucson: University of Arizona Press, 1988.

new maquiladora factories were women, making it also an important site in the feminization of the labor force (Standing 1999). The passage of the North American Free Trade Agreement (NAFTA) in 1994 changed the export-led industrialization of the border from a niche economy to the focal point of Mexican industrialization. The maquiladora industry grew to employ over one million people by the turn of the century with the factories concentrated in the three largest border cities—Tijuana, Ciudad Juárez, and Matamoros. Since 2000, both the absolute number of export-manufacturing workers in border states and the proportion of employees who are women have declined (Tiano, this vol.).

The border creates a zone of economic contrast where some highly mobile commuters live on one side and work on the other. The expanding transnational economy promotes the economic migration of peoples across most national borders, including the one between Mexico and the

United States. In addition to creating low-wage manufacturing jobs, the neoliberal economic model has also reduced government spending on social services. On both sides of the border, governments have cut public funding for social programs and shifted responsibility (without funding) for many basic needs to local communities. In Mexico, as in other middle- and low-income debtor nations, cuts in government funding for social services have been required by Structural Adjustment Programs as part of debt refinancing (McCaughan 1993). In the United States, welfare reform and other policies have reduced social spending, often by targeting non-citizens, particularly immigrants from Mexico (Chang 2000; Harris 1995; Hondagneu-Sotelo 1997).

In both Mexico and the United States, the reduction of government funding for social services has had the greatest impact on already impoverished families and placed additional demands on women's unpaid labor (Baden 1997). Reduced government social support has increased pressure on working people and moved many into new forms of political participation. An additional irony of U.S. cuts is that they limit support for the social reproduction of immigrant women who are employed primarily in service occupations, where they support the social reproduction of U.S. citizens (Chang 2000; Mattingly, this vol.). Economic crisis and displacement of rural people have exacerbated the push from the south, while the continued demand for low-wage labor pulls workers north.

Since the decade of the 1980s ended, NAFTA has encouraged cross-border business, and the U.S.–Mexico border has become more prominent in international relations and U.S. and Mexican foreign policy. At the same time, the U.S. government has sought to seal the border against undocumented migrants, altering patterns of migration across the border and mobility in the border region. Government policies have disrupted patterns of daily mobility for border residents who have crossed the international line for generations; for international migrants, they have discouraged return visits and therefore promoted longer stays in the United States (Andreas and Biersteker 2003). The juxtaposition of expanding free trade and limits on human mobility have created what Andreas (2003, 4) calls "both a borderless economy and a barricaded border." The border region remains a diverse, dynamic, and divided region, with countless formal and informal international interactions.

The U.S.–Mexico border has also been an important site for feminist academic scholarship. For many of us, the 1987 publication of *Women on the U.S.–Mexico Border: Responses to Change*, edited by Vicki L. Ruiz and Susan Tiano, marked the beginning of a conversation. A collection of articles analyzing diverse aspects of women's lives in the border region, the book played a foundational role in feminist scholarship of this important region. It pioneered a growing and increasingly dynamic body of scholarly literature about women's lives in the border region and was one of a few books published in the 1980s that showed the human face of the changes wrought by increasing manufacturing and militarization occurring at the border. Ruiz and Tiano accurately noted in their introduction "border scholars either ignore women entirely or rely on well-worn stereotypes" (1987, 4). In the intervening years, writing on women and gender in the borderlands has multiplied across the disciplines.

The humanities have seen a flowering of research and publications on gender and border culture. A host of historical monographs (e.g., D. González 1999; Gordon 1999; Heyman 1991; Hurtado 1999) all contribute to our understanding of the interconnections between gender, race, class, and place and of the important role that gender roles and sexual relations have played in the process of nation building. In cultural studies, a rich literature has applied notions of border crossing and borderlands as powerful metaphors in both critiquing dominant culture and tracing a myriad of resistances and remakings of meaning and community (e.g., Hicks 1991; Saldívar 1997). Feminist scholarship has been central to the emerging field of border studies, and many of the most significant works in the genre highlight gender as a dimension in oppression, identity, and resistance (Alonzo 1995; Anzaldúa 1987; Castillo and Tabuenca Córdoba 2002; Fregoso 2003; Price 2004; Salvídar-Hull 2000). Indeed, the contributions of these feminist writers have created an analytical framework that makes gender roles and relations central to analysis of the numerous encounters of diverse people in the border region.

Social science research on women at the border has also expanded dramatically. The tensions among women's oppression, empowerment, politics, and identity in feminist scholarship have remained a focus of feminist scholarship into the present. In the last decade and a half, the lives of women employed in border maquiladoras have been documented in several outstanding books (Cravey 1998; Iglesias Prieto 1997; Peña 1997; Salzinger 2003; Tiano 1994) and numerous articles. Apart from the established debate on women's work in maquiladoras, social science research has recently addressed many other aspects of women's lives in the border region, from employment in a range of occupations (Castillo et al. 1999; Staudt 1998) to activism and social justice (Staudt and Coronado 2002), health care and sexuality (Luibhéid 2002), language (N. González 2001), rape and militarization (Falcón 2001), representation and urban development (Wright 2001), and migration (Hondagneu-Sotelo 1994a; Zavella 2002). A recent edited volume (Vila 2003a) presents a collection of essays by social scientists exploring many aspects of contemporary life at the border, including labor, militarization, representations of women's and men's lives, and international politics.

The central theme of this book is the interplay between the external forces at the border that shape women's lives and women's individual and collective actions. The chapters are grouped into three sections dealing with women's daily and longer-term mobility, women's employment, and women's political activism. They are tied together by the themes of empowerment, the tension between agency and socioeconomic structures, and the gendered nature of social processes, particularly mobility.

Women's Mobility

Like all social processes, geographic mobility is gendered (Hanson and Pratt 1995; Pessar and Mahler 2003; Rosenbloom 1993). Men and women tend to have different patterns and experiences of movement at all scales, from the local to the international. Mobility is shaped by, and in turn shapes, what it means to be a man or a woman within different cultures. One theme in the growing literature on gender and migration is the potential for women to find emancipation and empowerment through labor migration and the associated loosening of traditional patriarchal relations (Grasmuck and Pessar 1991; Hondagneu-Sotelo 1994b; Kibria 1993). Yet many have found this emancipation relative to migrant men to be insignificant, as it occurs in the context of marginalization of the migrant group as a whole.

In chapter 2, "The Unsettling, Gendered Consequences of Migration for Mexican Indigenous Women," Elizabeth Maier draws on life narratives of Mexican indigenous women living in the border region to discuss the paradoxical effect of migration on women's lives. In the first half of the chapter, Maier carefully documents the myriad of added work pressures on women's lives that result from leaving traditional indigenous communities for resettlement as low-wage workers in heterogeneous border cities. In the second part of the chapter, Maier shifts her focus and examines the ways that the unsettling experiences of immigration and employment also provide a space for the empowerment of indigenous immigrant women. Immigration, she argues, challenges tradition, including patriarchal gender traditions. These migrant communities "have marked new social geographies where Mexican Native women can gradually reinvent themselves, stretching the margins of women's entitlements, engaging in new relational experiences, and (re)configuring notions of self." Thus, integration into a global economy is both unsettling traditional communities and women's lives and unsettling some of the traditional patriarchal forces that have oppressed women.

A second way that mobility is gendered is through the division of labor. Women and men tend to hold different jobs and have different family responsibilities, which affects patterns of both daily travel and migration (Christensen 1993; Hanson and Pratt 1995). In chapter 3, "Women's Daily Mobility at the U.S.–Mexico Border," Ellen Hansen shows the gendering of everyday movement among women on both sides of the border. Her interviews in Douglas, Arizona, U.S.A., and Agua Prieta, Sonora, Mexico, reveal that daily mobility for women on both sides of the border is shaped by their roles in the household and the communities. Specifically, women's lower likelihood of having a car and their responsibility for children lead to time-consuming and complex daily mobility patterns. New government policies implemented since 9/11 create further constraints, particularly as increased border-crossing times require women and families to adjust already tight schedules as they go about their daily activities. Hansen finds that women are among those most impinged on by the barricaded border, even as they are also among those who benefit most from the borderless economy.

Although the border region presents challenges and constraints for women, the proximity of different economic and political landscapes also presents border women with exceptional opportunities. Hansen's chapter includes examples of women regularly crossing the border to take advantage of opportunities for work, children's education, or shopping. Norma Ojeda, in chapter 4, "Abortion in a Transborder Context," takes up the issue of crossing the border for opportunities on the other side, weaving together women's daily mobility between San Diego, California, U.S.A., and Tijuana, Mexico, with the cultural context and health-care services at the border. Focusing on the controversial and emotionally charged issue of obtaining abortions, Ojeda's study analyzed movements and attitudes of Hispanic and non-Hispanic women from both sides of the border as they sought abortion services in San Diego. Ojeda found that the "social and cultural factors associated with the women's choice to abort . . . are linked in one way or another to the mosaic of opportunities offered by the U.S.–Mexico international border and the diversity and social complexity of a space where the Mexican and the American cultures are interwoven and coexist in a unique border culture."

While chronicling distinctions between Mexico and the United States, Ojeda moves beyond a simple distinction between "Mexicans" and "Americans," instead grouping respondents from both sides of the border into three groups based on reported ethnicity (Hispanic and non-Hispanic) and the language used to complete a survey. This categorization captures some of the fluidity of border identities and reveals complex variations in women's sexuality and attitudes towards abortion.

Labor and Empowerment in the Border Region

Women's labor provides a valuable vantage point for analyzing the interplay between economic structure and individual agency, as well as the tension between oppression and empowerment. Many studies have concluded that women's employment in export processing is best seen as a double-edged sword, offering women economic autonomy but insufficient wages to rise out of poverty (e.g., K. Ward and Pyle 1995). This tension between empowerment and oppression in the context of globalization is the focus of the three studies in this section on women's employment in the border region.

In chapter 5, "The Changing Gender Composition of the Maquiladora Workforce along the U.S.–Mexico Border," Susan Tiano uses empirical data on manufacturing employment in Mexican border cities to examine three alternative theories/scenarios about industrialization's gendered impacts. They are (1) the integration thesis, which argues industrialization benefits women by absorbing them into the formal labor force;

(2) the exploitation thesis, which argues capitalism takes advantage of patriarchal relations to create a low-wage labor force; and (3) the marginalization thesis, which argues that industrialization prefers male workers and therefore relegates women to the margins of employment. Tiano uses the three theses to reflect on changes in employment in border maquiladoras since the late 1990s, an era when both overall employment and the proportion of women in the workforce have declined. While the case of Mexican maquiladora employment has long seemed like a classic example of the exploitation thesis, Tiano's research suggests the actual case may be more complex, and that the pattern of feminization in export manufacturing may well be changing. Nevertheless, her macro-level research shows how women continued to be marginalized and exploited by the global economy.

A different approach to the relationship between employment and women's empowerment is found in chapter 6, "The Roots of Autonomy through Work Participation in the Northern Mexico Border Region," by Ana Bergareche. She explores the factors that influence whether employment contributes to women's autonomy, and therefore to their empowerment. To understand autonomy, Bergareche broadens her scope from the workplace to women's intimate lives, on the premise that women's ability to free themselves from sexual violence is a meaningful manifestation of autonomy. Her interviews with women in Cuidad Juárez show that the factors most important in women's ability to transform social constraints into growth experiences are their positive spiritual beliefs and support networks with other women. Bergareche's chapter contributes to a fuller understanding of the relationship between employment and women's experiences of empowerment and autonomy in many areas of their lives. By showing that age influenced how women found autonomy through work, the chapter also contributes to our understanding of the diversity of women's experiences in the border region. Among older women, especially migrants with little education, spirituality was the key intervening factor. For younger women, in contrast, support networks were crucial.

The question of differences among women in terms of empowerment and employment is developed further by Doreen Mattingly in chapter 7, "Domestic Service and International Networks of Caring Labor." In this chapter, she examines the strategies used by two groups of working mothers in San Diego: immigrant domestic workers and the professional women who employ them. The chapter illustrates how the gender divisions of household labor place pressures and constraints on working women, but that the women differ in the ways they manage their "double days." While professional women pay for additional assistance, the immigrant domestic workers they employ must rely on the unpaid labor of female family members, a difference that perpetuates inequalities between the two sets of households. The chapter also shows that both groups of women are active agents, constructing a new geography of social reproduction, changing the border context, and contributing to further migration of women from Mexico to the United States.

Activist Women Changing the Border

In the words of Marianne Marchand, global restructuring is "effectively creating a triple burden for women: engaging in productive labour to contribute to the household income, facing an increasing burden in terms of reproductive labour because the state has been reducing its responsibility in terms of social welfare, as well as participating in community level organizing in order to improve immediate living conditions" (2002, 113–14). At the same time that it has increased the burden of poor women, however, the privatization of social services has created space for binational cooperation and for women to take on new roles as activists and community leaders (Naples 2002). Women find spaces of empowerment and positive transformation amid the massive structural changes shaping the border region, and they organize to challenge and resist the changes of global restructuring.

As in other geographical contexts, women's organizing and activism in the border region span the geographic scale from the local to the global. Given the transnational nature of structural processes today, much opposition to global economic change is also transnational in nature. This is true along the border, where local conditions and problems often cross from one side to the other. One example of this is the spread of the *colonia*. A residential form developed in Latin America and growing north of the border, colonias in the United States are immigrant neighborhoods of substandard housing with few services; they are transnational communities in every sense of the word. The expansion of colonias and the development of non-governmental organizations (NGOs) to manage them are both manifestations of the neoliberal influence of the United States on both sides of the border.

Women on both sides of the border have found positions of empowerment from which to effect positive transformation amid the massive and ongoing structural changes shaping the border region. The emergence of women community activists and leaders is tied to their household gender roles. Activism is seen by some women as a natural outgrowth of their roles as caretakers within the family. In chapter 8, "Mexican Women's Activism in New Mexico Colonias," for example, Rebecca Dolhinow reports on interviews with women leaders in colonia communities in New Mexico. Through an examination of women's discussions about gender roles, as well as observations of interactions, Dolhinow argues that gender itself is transnational in colonias, as women negotiate between traditional expectations that assign women to the roles of wives and mothers and the responsibilities of leadership in their communities. Most of the women activists retain responsibility for household management and child care and therefore have limited time for community activism. Yet their gender roles not only constrain the time and other resources available to them but, perhaps because they spend more time than men in the colonias, have also created opportunities for women to develop as community leaders in struggles for services and other improvements. Not surprisingly, Dolhinow found that women who emerge as leaders are either single or in unusually egalitarian relationships. The border setting of the colonias shapes distinct patterns of constraints and opportunities for women, as the immigrant households transplant gender ideologies into a new context. The physical space of the colonia creates an opportunity for women's leadership, but the opportunity is available only to those in positions to renegotiate traditional gender roles. Women responded to structural changes on the U.S. side by taking active parts in efforts to improve their communities.

Dolhinow's chapter focuses on low-income households in the United States. South of the border, Mexican women activists of various socioeconomic standing are described in chapter 9, "Styles, Strategies, and Issues of Women Leaders at the Border." Irasema Coronado describes how women activists began their work. Some became activists in response to perceived needs in their own low-income communities, but women of higher socioeconomic class levels also responded to religious duty or because they were members of political parties. Coronado documents the underreported work of activist women, particularly those seeking services for residents of *colonias populares*. Drawing on both interviews and ethnographic work, she conveys a sense of the way women activists operate within the context of Mexican politics. While the focus of Coronado's research is Mexican border cities, the influence of U.S. donors and international agencies on the structure of activism is also apparent in the work of activists who form autonomous organizations.

The final two chapters, by Silvia López Estrada and Patricia Manning, deal with collaborative efforts by women. Both document the ways women's groups and NGOs have allowed women to organize their efforts in collective action for change. Both also focus on organizations that transcend lines of class and nationality and create transnational spaces of cooperation. The formation of autonomous NGOs by Mexican women activists is the particular focus of Silvia López Estrada in chapter 10, "Border Women's NGOs and Political Participation in Baja California." Like Coronado, López Estrada draws on interviews and ethnographic work in her research. López Estrada presents a picture of a diverse set of Mexican women's activist organizations, analyzing them in the context of the border region, Mexican feminism, and the changing nature of government. The chapter is of particular interest because it shows how the gaps left by the neoliberal state have created a space that women have filled. For example, as part of its reforms aimed at reducing federal power, the city of Tijuana formed a Subcommittee of Women's Affairs, which a coalition of NGOs was able to use to influence legislation and to create several institutes and centers, including a battered women's shelter.

In chapter 11, "'Making Believe' and 'Willing Partners' in Academics' Activism in the U.S.–Mexico Borderlands," Patricia Manning presents the most explicit investigation of binational cooperation. She does this through a discussion of her work in two transnational organizations: the Transborder Consortium for Research and Action on Gender and Reproductive Health at the U.S.–Mexico Border and Mujer Sana~Healthy Woman. Her personal experience with these collaborative projects provides her with the material for a detailed discussion of the difficulties and rewards of transnational activism. This example shows the border as a dynamic place where the prevalent political trend against the authority of the Mexican government and in favor of global neoliberalism creates new spaces for women's organization and influence.

Common Threads: Gender, Empowerment, and Change

The chapters in this volume are linked by the portrayal of women as agents of change, whether they are physically moving across or along the border, working in paid and unpaid labor, or participating in movements to bring social change and justice. They are leaders as well as students, participants, and observers. Women on both sides of the border are taking advantage of opportunities to further efforts to gain autonomy, to create new paths and challenge traditions, and to empower themselves and their communities. In every sense of the word, they are movers.

Part One **Women's Mobility**

2 The Unsettling, Gendered Consequences of Migration for Mexican Indigenous Women

Elizabeth Maier

This chapter is about the changing lives of indigenous immigrant women[1] from Mexico's poorer southern states who currently live and work in the agro-industrial regions of Baja California, Mexico, and the U.S. state of California. New roles imposed by immigration and residential relocation, more diverse economic opportunities for women, educational benefits for young girls, generational shifts in values and practices, and the criminalizing of some culturally accepted patriarchal practices (such as those linked to parent-arranged, adolescent marriages or domestic violence) suggest a growing tendency toward a new sense of self-awareness and self-esteem among Native Mexican immigrant women. Newly discovered notions of entitlement, as subjects of rights and laws, gradually contest traditional post–Spanish Conquest indigenous beliefs and practices of female subordination.

As in other societies, many indigenous cultures rest on rigorously patriarchal family and community regimens that tend to exclude women from community decision-making bodies, while anchoring their power within the family to vigilant, male endorsement. The conventionally fixed frontiers of gender identity also have historically limited women's access to formal education, bilingual skills, and economic autonomy. Arranged marriages, though in decline today, continue to constitute a significant way of contracting marriages, traditionally representing parental decision in the matrimonial commitments of their daughters and sons.[2] Peasant cultures have historically symbolized children as family wealth. Considered active participants in agrarian economies, each child assures two more able hands to toil on the land or to do housework. Immigration has transformed the social significance of children, while also influencing the number of offspring that younger couples desire. It has also denoted adjustments in gender roles and relations, while broadening women's social and economic participation and highlighting their cultural contributions to family and community. In this chapter, I contend that immigration sets the stage for an emergent sense of entitlement and citizenship among indigenous women, both within and outside the confines of ethnically based communities.[3] As one woman put it: "We have more rights, now. We defend ourselves. There are ways to take care. We can go out now, move about, and still be respected. Before, we didn't speak. I didn't even talk to my sister or my cousin without feeling that I could be hit. I had no voice. Now I even have friends. My world is open now. Before, the world was closed."[4]

Gendering Ethnicity and Migration

Moving on in the Global World

Migration has been acknowledged as one of the defining aspects of globalization[5] (Bhabha 1994; Sassen 1998). The last half of the twentieth century set off a worldwide demographic shake-up that has shifted the weight of the population burden from rural to urban environments, while forging endless migratory circuits between developing and developed regions. Over time, the dimensions and characteristics of migration have changed. It has become increasingly massive, as specific economic actors from deprived regions are excluded from the new economic blueprint and pushed into a modern, semi-nomadic workforce reshuffling. Migration from Mexico to the United States has become more dangerous, as border vigilance intensifies, pushing people toward risky routes, while survival stakes are raised for growing numbers of aspirants. Human vulnerability has increased, as avalanches of disenfranchised people pattern new middle passages of unprotected transit, in order to finally obtain an insecure niche in the lowest socioeconomic echelons of receiving societies. Cultural diversity brands the twenty-first century, bearing witness to complex processes of dislocation and relocation that challenge feelings of belonging and identity, and modifying notions of self, daily routines, and life's expectations (Bhabha 1994; Kearney 1991; Sassen 1998).

The pain of dislocation marks individual and collective development, constituting part of the sentimental order that accompanies the migrant experience. A twenty-two-year-old trilingual Mixtec college student in California conjured up those memories, stating:

It was dark when we left our home. We walked into the night, over the hills, until we got to the place where we caught the bus. The only sound we heard as we walked were the dogs barking. It was as if they were trying to advise the townspeople that some of their loved ones, some of their own, were leaving. But no one heard. They were all sleeping. How could they know? When we got on the bus, my sisters and I looked around at our town to say goodbye for the last time. It was as if someone was ripping away something very dear to us. We didn't know where we were going, that we were going to another country. We didn't know that it was to have a better life. We didn't have any idea.

Ethnicity, Poverty, and Migration

Indigenous migration is entrenched within this global framework. Exodus from the poorer southern states to the north of Mexico and to the United States has been contingent on national and international public policies that during the past decade have reconfigured rural Mexico. Land privatization resulting from the constitutional revision of the Agrarian Reform Act (Article 27) in 1993, farm-subsidy deregulation of basic grain production, financial loan ineligibility for peasant farmers, drastic reductions of federal social welfare budgets and consequent diminished access to previous social-service support systems, reduced world-market agricultural prices, conservation of farm subsidies in the developed nations, and overly competitive agricultural importations have all forced Native Mexicans' flight from ancestral homelands.[6] Both inside and outside their country of origin, indigenous (im)migrants are frequently perceived as "alien others": unknown, unwanted, threatening, and even dangerous (Huntington 1998). If, as Sassen (1998) contends, place is central to unraveling the makings of globalization, identity embodies another privileged geography for dissecting the rearrangements of individuals and communities, fostered by technological and economic restructurings (Bhabha 1994).

With the inauguration of the U.S. Bracero Program of the 1940s, the contemporary outpouring of indigenous emigration from Mexico's southern regions began carving out a permanent route to the agricultural labor markets of the Californias. Initially, modern emigration from Mexican Native communities was based on a relief system, where fathers returning home during the rainy season to work in their own fields were replaced in faraway, industrialized agricultural camps by their oldest sons (Arizpe 1975). With time, they were replaced by their younger brothers, and these were replaced by those even younger, while the 1950s marked a collateral, rural-urban, circular migratory current of young indigenous girls, employed as domestic workers in the homes of the urban rich and newly consolidated middle-class families. Thus, at first males chronicled a rural-rural migratory pattern, while young females registered a rural-urban tendency, both exhibiting a circular migratory trend that took them from hometowns to labor markets and back again.

This early sexual division of (e)migration paved the multiple paths of the actual indigenous diaspora, originally anchored in traditional gender representations that associated agricultural production with masculinity and duties linked to domestic reproduction with femininity.[7] The advent of the 1980s, however, witnessed a growing number of indigenous families permanently settling in California, United States, and Baja California, Mexico (Kearney 1991, 1995; Velasco Ortiz 2002). Mounting transterritorial and transnational emigration[8] compressed ecological, political, religious, personal, but essentially economic, motives into an unintentional, globalized strategy of cultural resistance: a survival strategy that has resituated culture within the borders of displacement, remapped identity within extended territories, and annexed belonging to a community scattered in multiple directions.[9] The border region that bounds Baja California, with its estranged other half in California, has marked a preferential route from indigenous communities of origin to agricultural labor markets. Both transnational and internal (im)migration energizes the Mexican side of the border, while fashioning new multicultural landscapes in many of the cities and agro-industrial niches of the borderlands.

Networking to Survive

Migrant networks, established over the years, funnel this growing surge of migration to specific settlement communities, where previously relocated relatives and neighbors reside. These networks serve as symbolic bridges that transfuse the pulse of hometown life into the veins of new community settlements. They help craft the conditions in which culture-oriented communities are reorganized and a sense of belonging reestablished. As such, they are fundamental to the preservation of ethnic identity in extra-territorial contexts (Velasco Ortiz 2002). Migrant networks ease *cushion* adaptation in unknown socioeconomic and cultural environments. They are cultural support systems wrapped around gender-based social divisions that orient recent arrivals as to how to satisfy basic needs, administer natural resources, find employment, or contact *coyotes* for crossing the border.

Geographic, social, and cultural unfamiliarity with receiving societies, illiteracy, and language limitations compound the challenges of displacement. As a thirty-three-year-old Mixtec farmworker and artisan, mother of three children, described:

> My mother told me that we were going to Baja California, without knowing, without having familiarity. We didn't even have covers with us, or anything. We only had fear. There were relatives there. They sent us a letter with an address. We arrived there without even knowing how, just with the address written in the letter. We tried to ask the bus driver — we didn't speak much Spanish, only Mixtec — and he told us where to go. We had to sleep in the streets. We walked so long that my shoes broke. There was great suffering. We had nowhere to stay at first. But the letter finally got us there. Then we built a little tent of plastic to live in. When we finally arrived and saw our relatives, I was so happy, because then I knew that we had support, that we weren't alone anymore.

Gendered Networking

Gender organizes indigenous migrant networks, as it arranges all migratory experiences (Hondagneu-Sotelo 1994b). Dislocation and relocation are facilitated by culturally specific sexual divisions of labor that traditionally allot gendered tasks to men and women.[10] This social stratification of displacement greases the wheels of exodus, marshalls transit, and administrates resettlement.[11] Though women — and children — progressively participate in salaried work, a basic labor division still assigns most reproductive chores to women in Native Mexican settlement communities. Cooking, marketing, housework, washing clothes, dishwashing, child care, health care, religiosity, and family integration and consolidation are still considered women's vocations. Present female participation in traditional (mainly) male-associated agricultural production has not as yet deconstructed the conviction that female domestic and family responsibilities represent an essentially natural way of arranging daily routines. In indigenous settlements in Baja California, women frequently have double and triple workdays, attending to housework, child care, physically demanding salaried work, and craft production and its commercialization in local tourist sites.

A thirty-eight-year-old Mixtec farmworker, mother of seven, explained:

> I get up early, around four in the morning, to make tortillas and a little bit of lunch for everyone. It takes me an hour to do the tortillas and another hour for lunch. Now that my older daughters are married, I only have to make food for five people. When I finish, I go to work in the fields all day, from six in the morning to four o'clock. After work, I wash the dishes from breakfast, put them away, and make the beds. My boys are grown now, but they don't like to make the beds or sweep. I always tell them to help me out. But they don't like to. They just get up, leave their clothes in a mess on the floor and go to school. They don't pay any attention. I think that they're ashamed to do that kind of work. They come home early from school, and I tell them that they should wash their socks or do something else. The truth is that I can't do everything. But they don't do it. They're boys.

Added work embedded in the tradition of migrant network solidarity is another extension of the workday for indigenous immigrant women. Hostess functions entail extra washing, shopping, cooking, and cleaning, as overcrowded quarters and increased daily labor accompany hospitality. While gender defines the experience of hospitality, it also determines the degree of additional housework that migrant networks impose on hostesses. Male guests are labor-intensive for hostesses, whereas female guests (alone, or in a couple) ease work by sharing tasks. More female hands lighten the domestic burden for both hostesses and visitors. Over the last two decades, statistics confirming the flight of full families from southern, rural, indigenous communities to the agricultural areas of northern Mexico, or of wives and children reuniting with male heads of family already residing in the United States, suggest host families in settlement communities are essential to the reproduction of migrant networks. Women, through their traditional roles in family functioning and nurturing, play a vital part in sustaining, reinforcing, and expanding these networks.

In most of the settlement sites of northern Mexico, rickety housing serves as lodging for two, three, or four families united in the venture of survival. Five or six children sleep sideways in the same bed, couples share quarters with their offspring, running water is frequently unavailable, electricity is not always accessible, and income is insufficient to cover the families' most immediate needs. However, the standard of living conditions for (im)migrants is related to the temporality of (im)migration, as well as the reception context. Enormous differences exist between the tentative quarters of agricultural camps (or the foxholes dug into hills bordering the agricultural fields in Southern California, where many indigenous migrant farmworkers are forced to dwell for lack of affordable housing), and the permanent housing of settlement communities in either country. Permanent residency—whether documented or not—usually accompanies better living conditions in both Mexico and the United States.[12] While apartment space is a costly premium in California's housing market, basic services (electricity and running water) are generally available, as is domestic infrastructure such as refrigerators, stoves, and, occasionally, washing machines. In the Mexican settlement communities, on the other hand, accessing basic services usually is the product of long and complex processes of social agency, involving community organization and mobilization (see chapters by Dolhinow and by Coronado, this vol.). Most immigrant families have stoves, but not all own refrigerators. In general, living conditions in Mexican squatter neighborhoods are notoriously inadequate, but for the majority of families they are less precarious than in the migrant camps.

Narratives of the migrant camps evoke a profound sense of suffering and resentment. A forty-six-year-old Chinantec farmworker, mother of nine children, recalled living conditions upon her arrival, saying:

> He came before to San Quintin, and then sent for us. It rained a lot and was very windy there. At first, we lived in a kind of tent. Later on he built a wood-framed room, which we covered with a piece of plastic. We all ate and slept there. Once a big storm came. We left the babies home so they wouldn't get sprayed with 'liquid'.[13] When we got back,

they were soaked. Everything was wet. The plastic had blown away, and lots of water came in. The kids got sick, but there wasn't a doctor or a clinic nearby. Home remedies were all there was.

Living Conditions, Tradition, and the Burdens of Poverty for Women

Contrasting living conditions denote differential workloads for women. Electricity and running water ease housework, reducing the amount of time and energy used for chores. Preparing meals on a stove, rather than an open fire, also cuts time and effort. Collecting firewood, watching a pot simmer over long hours, and constantly inhaling firewood smoke adds hours to the workday and impacts health. Refrigerating food diminishes time needed for marketing, while improving economic efficiency through planning meals and recycling leftovers. Hand washing clothes is another time-demanding and labor-intensive activity for women. Nonetheless, the older generation of indigenous immigrants (forty-five or more years old), dedicated exclusively to housework and child care, often prefer labor-intensive modes of domestic work rather than time-saving, electrodomestic use. A Mixtec mother of ten, residing in a semi-rural community on the outskirts of Maneadero, Baja California, generally cooks on an open fire, although she owns a stove. "The food tastes better that way," she claims, suggesting that tradition is perhaps the secret of flavor. Another indigenous immigrant woman living with her husband and eleven children in a two-bedroom California apartment washes all the family's clothes in the bathtub, despite having access to a washing machine. The intersection of technological access, cultural practice, and new claims on daily schedules appears to influence the use of domestic technology. For the younger generation of indigenous women who attend school and/or work in income-generating activities, access to electro-domestics guarantees use. With significantly higher literacy and educational levels, and bilingual skills, modern domestic technology—if available—eases the busy schedules of active, younger lives. Dialectically, domestic technology facilitates new modes of participation in socioeconomic slots that traditionally were not part of women's ways or terrains. This identity spin-off emphasizes the historical and adaptable nature of gender and the flexibility of tradition itself.

A trilingual, Mixtec community-rights activist, U.S. citizen, married and the mother of two, living in California, laughed as she concluded:

> As girls we had to walk with our heads down on the streets of my hometown. We couldn't look directly at older people because it was considered disrespectful. You were expected to smile, but not too much. You weren't supposed to be friendly to just anyone. A good girl had to be very serious, and walk very straight. Some of these ideas stuck with me. But now, as a wife and mother, I do things very differently from the way my father and brothers thought I would turn out. They thought that I would work in the store that they were going to have. But I have a better future now. I work in defense of my people as a community promoter. I tell them about their rights, that they should earn minimum wage, that they should have running water. I represent them with local institutions. My grandmother doesn't know what I do. But if she did, she surely would say, "This girl is totally crazy!"

Stretching Traditions: Indigenous Migration and the Rearranging of Gender

Tradition, as Giddens (2003) points out, is a malleable endeavor that adjusts to circumstance and time, continuously being revised and reinvented. Immigration challenges tradition, relocating it within broader, unrelated contexts that influence its forms and its contents. The relocation of culture authorizes a review of tradition, as new circumstances intercede in refashioning customary practices and beliefs, while re-shaping ways of perceiving relationships, responsibilities, and rights. Enmeshed in the complex process of indigenous immigration, gender is particularly prone to readjustments and rearrangement. Newfound niches of female socioeconomic activity, together with the evolving demise of arranged marriages, second-generation access to sexual education and family planning, bilingual and trilingual proficiency, increased schooling for girls, and the emergence of some women professionals all suggest an ongoing blurring of the strict sexual divisions of hometown community life.

These rearrangements of gender frontiers bear witness to a process of gradual re-representation of the feminine in the collective imagination of Native societies. Though traditional gender patterns have undeniably

sustained indigenous dislocation and relocation, tradition itself becomes
rattled as women penetrate previously exclusive male domains. The gender modifications considered in this text, however, appear to surpass the
shift that late modernity has imposed on the public/private dichotomy.
Rather, they seem to be located at the very heart of the patriarchal web: in
the realm of self-delimitation, self-recognition, and self-value;[14] in the
camp of decision making and agency; and in the domain of power and
empowerment. They are suggestive modifications, more than irrefutable
conversions. Nonetheless, present gender rearrangements seem to indicate a more profound, up-and-coming cultural shake-up, given that gender roles and relations mold the very forms and contents of tradition.

Male "permissions" allotted to Mixtec women, for all aspects of their
daily functioning, are considered by Velasco Ortiz (2002) to be the prime
symbolic representation of male power over female lives. Traditionally,
women require male approval for all their endeavors. They need permission to go out, to visit relatives, to use family planning methods, to give
birth in hospitals, to participate in community activities, church events,
and political happenings: permission to study, to marry, and to work. In
most Mexican indigenous communities, male permissions delimit the
frontiers of female lives. Exclusive, male sociopolitical representation
within indigenous communities, and male mediation between women
and the outside world, traditionally tend to insulate women from community deliberation, political agency, selected personal relationships, and
intercultural exchange.

Growing family dislocation, however, and the increasing ethnicization
of agricultural wage labor, both in Mexico and the United States, have
marked new social geographies where Mexican Native women can gradually reinvent themselves, stretching the margins of women's entitlements,
engaging in new relational experiences, and (re)configuring notions of
self. For indigenous families, paid farm labor has normally been a family
affair, organized around the patriarchal principles of male authority and
social intermediation. Publicly, women walked a few steps behind men,
worked under male authority, limited communication to other members
of their family, obeyed male instructions, and did not control their own
salaries. Traditionally, male heads-of-household represented hegemonic
economic subjects, entitled to collect all family wages and oversee family
economics. With the mounting migration of the 1990s, permanent immi-

gration constantly on the rise, consolidation of extra-territorial communities, and intensified intercultural exchanges, indigenous women slowly are shaking off this ubiquitous male surveillance, as they increasingly become autonomous labor subjects.

For the women of the older generation, declining patriarchal scrutiny corresponds to aging and the time of their life cycle when they are no longer objects of desire or subjects of biological reproduction. Most women over forty-five are permitted by their husbands to seek employment individually. This lends to innovative experiences in which women learn to deal with new situations and relations without male mediation. One could say that this stage of their lives prepares them for later assuming even greater family responsibility, as aging men become ill or die. This is particularly true as older male partners suffer the combined effects of aging and a life of malnutrition, overwork, and, in many cases, excessive consumption of alcohol. The "risks of masculinity," as de Keijzer (1997) incisively refers to Mexican male deaths due to violence, cirrhosis, or heart attacks, are inevitably exacerbated by poverty. As older women enter the workforce in their own names, they are socially recognized as economic subjects. Not only do they contribute directly to family economies, but they also have access to loans, sponsor family projects (such as housing construction or small businesses), and may even assume primary roles in supervision of family affairs.[15]

Younger Women and New Entitlements

Younger women reared and educated in settlement communities register notable differences from the older generations' pervasive dependency on male authority. Often, they become independent labor subjects at an early age. They contract their own jobs, work without male supervision, negotiate relations with co-workers, develop friendships with other girls, mediate encounters with males, and collect their own salaries.[16] They have access to more diversified employment opportunities, though still in mostly lower-echelon slots. Many younger indigenous women work in the maquiladoras of Tijuana, Ensenada, Maneadero, or Mexicali. Others do paid domestic work or are employed as clerks in local stores. Most daughters of immigrant families are enrolled in high school, others are studying technical skills, and some are registered for university careers.

They have a better understanding of mestiza culture, exhibit greater participation in intercultural institutions, and display more complexity and determination in the formulation of claims.

One of the most insistent claims shared by these young women in relation to traditional community governance codes, often referred to as "uses and customs," concerns the right to choose their marriage partners.[17] Matrimonial choice increasingly substitutes for the parentally arranged marriages of original communities. Traditionally, marriages are arranged between the families of the couple. The agreement is sealed by payment of a dowry to the girl's parents, symbolically acknowledging family investment in her maintenance and recognizing her social worth. Though parents are the contracting parties, often the boy—or man—selects the girl after observing her valued characteristics. Dedication to work, obedience, humility, sweetness, and politeness are the qualities that forge a girl's reputation and make her a desirable spouse. For the older generation, it was not uncommon for a girl to be unaware of her parents' choice before her wedding day. Once the terms of the arrangement are established between parties, the girl is expected to comply with that decision as a sign of respect. Respect is at the heart of the sentimental ethos that structures indigenous communities, administering social relations and strengthening community cohesion. As Besserer (1999) indicates, being disrespectful, particularly to the symbolically empowered, is traditionally considered an inappropriate attitude within community life.

In that regard, a fifty-one-year-old Mixtec farmworker, a widow and the mother of five, residing in Baja California reminisced:

> I married very young. I was just fourteen. I had no idea what sex was. I didn't have my period yet or breasts. No one told me about anything. I didn't know anything. I just played, because I was still a child. The day of the wedding, I was a little afraid just wondering who he was and thinking what my life would be like. When we got to the church, I kept turning around looking for the boy. But there wasn't anyone there, no one but an old man. Anyway, I saw him as an old man. When the ceremony began, I realized that I was supposed to marry this old man. I just cried and cried. I couldn't stop crying. He was thirty, then, and I was only fourteen. I was so afraid. I was just a girl. I didn't know anything about anything.

Domestic
violence

Interviewees associate greater domestic violence with arranged marriages. Having little or no say in the marital selection that parents assign them sets the stage for the emergence of a female non-subject — totally dependant on male authority, power, decisions, and actions to mold the direction of her own life course — and determines the quality of her everyday existence. Traditionally, most Mexican indigenous women have lacked entitlement to true community citizenship and protection. Until recently, exclusive male participation in community government and judicial bodies limited women's voice and defense. In that sense, accentuated male hegemony in community and family governance left women little recourse in their hometowns when confronted with physical, sexual, or psychological abuse. According to many interviewees, all-male judicial committees that interpret traditional community law, determine infringement, and fix penalties tend to be gender-biased in their decision making, generally favoring the man over a woman's claims of violence. Gender solidarity among men, whether unconscious or manifest, results in the reproduction of patterns of violence towards women by minimizing the gravity of the situation and excusing aggressive male behavior as understandable and, in many cases, even justifiable. Some women indicated that men accused of wife-beating resolved their cases by inviting the judicial committee to share a beer, thus repaying the offense to the community.

A thirty-six-year-old Triqui community leader, living in Baja California, married three times and the mother of four, recalled earlier marital experiences that helped her to redefine a more acceptable relationship for her:

> They "sold" me at thirteen to an older man. His family didn't give me food or clothes. He hit me. There was always violence. . . . The good thing, though, is that in our town men like to fight, and when I was sixteen my husband got killed in a fight. My mother-in-law says that I should live with my brother-in-law. They took my kid away. I left. I just went alone, without anyone, without parents. I didn't know where I was going. I was alone and didn't speak Spanish. I left without having ever known any other world. What could I do? I found another man. The same thing happened. He hit me so hard that I was in the hospital. . . . "That's it," I said to myself, "no more fear!" We have to open our eyes. With the guy I'm with now, I also suffer sometimes.

Sometimes we fight, but I tell him: "It's true, there are times I'm not home much. There's so much I have to do. And you know I have hands. I have feet. I have eyes. I can work. I can live. Maybe I can even live better without a husband!" We need to teach the young people this. I have a few daughters, and I want to protect them. I agree with our customs, but not so young. Not any more.

Over the past two decades, growing poverty has also often played a role in parental marriage arrangements, modifying traditional considerations of well-being for the daughters in favor of monetary ones linked to family survival strategies. Some of the interviewees mentioned extremely poor families that had given up their daughters in exchange for money, because they could no longer afford to feed them. Within these extreme situations, necessity often weighs more than the traditionally required good reputation of the boy (or man) and his family, ultimately making the daughter's physical and psychological well-being contingent upon the character and conduct of the man who pays to marry her.

In receiving societies, in contrast, the influence of women's rights movements has emphasized the need to denounce and eradicate domestic violence, paying special attention to violence against women and children. Local police and legal institutions have newly organized areas that offer battered women legal, medical, and psychological support and alternatives. Some indigenous immigrants to Baja California felt, as many non-indigenous women also do, that government programs do not fully protect and assist women who experience violence. Others, however, considered official sanctions against male abuse to be one of the most valued collateral benefits of immigration. This slowly emerging notion of women's entitlement to rights and protection constitutes the essence of a newly developing exercise of female citizenship among indigenous immigrant women.

Today, many of the younger immigrant women who have finished primary and/or secondary school control their own salaries, study technical or professional careers, and defend their right to choose their partners. Feeling entitled to love (and then marriage) coincides with the sentimental paradigms of receiving societies. In these new cultural contexts, arranged marriages with under-aged girls are punishable by law, and many indigenous men spend time in jail for customary practices.[18] Members of the younger, more educated generation are increasingly choosing their marriage partners. Not only in trans-territorial communities, but also in communities of origin, arranged marriages are becoming a tradition in transition. Some authors even contend that love is the glue of indigenous transnationalization, bonding separated couples, dispersed families, and dislocated identities (Besserer 1999). For young indigenous women, however, entitlement is still a contentious issue, permeated by everyday individual, family, and community negotiations. Pulled between traditional expectations, internalized cultural representations, and new claims for larger parcels of individuality and autonomy, young women are struggling to carve out new representations of female identity. Like primary and secondary school teachers thirty years ago, these young indigenous professionals represent a new female figure in the collective imagination of their communities.

As such, indigenous immigration not only refers to a social geography that houses the dislocation of culture but also represents the unraveling of the web that interconnects gender and culture. As immigration reshapes gender identities and relationships and influences adjustments of cultural practices and beliefs, the link between specific models of gender relations and defined cultural ways of understanding the world and living everyday life becomes more apparent. Changes in one of those dimensions impose re-accommodations on the other, for gender and culture intersect intimately to create particular ways of being men and women, organizing society, and making sense of life. As one of the California Mixtec college students put it: "When I visited [my hometown] this summer, most people were very nice. Some people saw me as a foreigner, as if I didn't have the same morals anymore, as if I had broken all the rules; a girl that's been around, who isn't worth much because she's traveled a lot; a girl with other ideas in her head."

Concluding Considerations

As the global marketplace reorganizes world production, (im)migration crafts preferential survival strategies for those excluded from the new blueprint of economic opportunities. Indigenous (e)migration from economically depressed regions to dynamic national and international labor markets exemplifies present-world tendencies toward fashioning a displaced, ethnicized, vulnerable workforce of menial laborers to replace the more specialized local workers of more developed areas.[19] A sexual division of labor arranges indigenous migration. Exodus and relocation hinge on gendered tasks that facilitate the daily and generational reproduction of these culture-specific, dislocated, working-class families. As relocation re-shapes everyday life, it also revises culturally rooted gender inscriptions that from birth have molded male and female bodies into socially accept-able models of men and women. Changes in labor relations, productive patterns, reproductive ideals, environment, community organization, and living conditions make new demands on time and space. While notions of family, community, and individuality are gradually being resignified, values and goals are reformulated, and new claims of subjectivity, auton-omy, and respect for girls' and women's human rights are emerging. Con-tested judicial paradigms have invalidated some traditionally accepted gender practices of certain indigenous communities (such as arranged marriages with very young girls and intra-family violence toward women) because legal conventions of societies often criminalize these practices. Migration has undoubtedly transformed indigenous women's lives and identity. Fluency or growing competency in Spanish (and/or English, if in the United States); access to progressively higher levels of education and more advanced technical skills; availability of family planning; the emergence of a female, indigenous labor subject who controls her own sal-ary; increased diversity in wage employment; and (in many cases) female-headed, migrant-circuit households all suggest significant shifts in the collective recognition and revaluation of women's roles in the reproduc-tion of family, community, and ethnicity.

Relocation unsettles ethnic reproduction. Receiving societies' eco-nomic, social, and cultural contexts encroach on indigenous women's traditional role as cultural transmitters, representing competitive cultural paradigms that offer to ease adaptation and facilitate socioeconomic mo-bility, particularly for younger generations. The ethnicization of economic and social stratification in receiving societies, accentuated by relentless and unforgiving episodes of discrimination, embody the ubiquitous rac-ism that has delimited Native Mexican identity since colonial times. For many indigenous mothers (and fathers), the seductive lure of cultural anonymity contests the routine and unabashed rejection of indigenous culture and identity (*oaxaquita*, *indito*, "dirty people") by Mexican and non-Mexican receiving societies. In that sense, the present-day vast exodus that is draining ancestral communities represents a double-edged sword for ethnic survival. On the one hand, it has become a globalized venture of cultural resistance; at the same time, it has threatened to fracture and dislodge the very symbols, practices, values, and beliefs that traditionally have constituted ethnic identity. In that sense, the significance of women's changing roles in family and community, in this renegotiation of identity and belonging, appears to go to the heart of the intersection of gender and ethnicity, interrogating the articulation and mutual re-enforcement of gender hierarchies and cultural practices and reproduction.

As such, (im)migration's contradictory influence on indigenous women's lives should not be disregarded. Though (im)migration has empowered them by revising their social roles and significance, while forging historically unprecedented female representations with new claims to rights and citizenship, women's entrance into traditionally masculine social geographies as wage earners and heads-of-household has meant heavier workloads and longer workdays. Periodic or continuous male absence, due to abandonment or diversified family-survival strategies based on combined migration endeavors, overburdens women with much of the responsibility for decision making, household management, community commitments, and wage labor, as well as their traditional domestic chores and family nurturing. As women take on tasks and roles that, just a generation ago, were associated with masculinity, men are not undergoing as significant a reorganization of their own traditional gender confines. Housework and childrearing are still almost exclusively thought to be women's work by both men and women. Needless to say, Native Mexican immigrant women's longer, harder, and more diversified workloads marshal new strengths, proficiencies, and claims, along with economic and psychological challenges. With lessened patriarchal vigilance and economic tutelage, and decreased female isolation and dependency, indigenous immigrant women have begun to renegotiate the disenfranchisement that has shaped women's lives in home communities.

3 Women's Daily Mobility at the U.S.–Mexico Border

Ellen R. Hansen

Daily mobility reveals connections between people and the places we live: it illuminates the everyday problems we face and the strategies we employ to meet regular needs and fulfill desires. Mobility reflects the importance of spatial structures and shows how urban form constrains or facilitates opportunities. In any urban setting, mobility is significantly influenced by transportation, employment, children and child care, and education. It is also gendered and affected by class and ethnicity. Additional issues emerge to complicate the picture at the U.S.–Mexico border.

In this chapter, I first discuss how women's daily mobility illustrates gender roles and relations in the context of the neighboring cities of Douglas, Arizona, U.S.A., and Agua Prieta, Sonora, Mexico. The second half of the chapter considers how measures implemented at the border to increase national security since the terrorist attacks of September 11, 2001, will affect women's mobility. Time is one of the major constraints on daily activities; security measures that increase time requirements will further complicate women's already full schedules. Women's patterns of mobility are complex, reflecting women's multiple reproductive and productive responsibilities and conflicting demands on their time. Mobility is critical for men as well, but this study and others indicate that compared to women, men tend to have simpler daily mobility patterns and greater control over private vehicles. Focusing on women's mobility reveals the nature of relationships within the household and community and can suggest possible solutions to people for whom negotiating transportation is problematic.

Studying the U.S.–Mexico Border

National borders can be described as "processes which are constructed and sustained by the material, sociological, and discursive practices and projects of the state, sub-state actors, and the international system" (Ackelson

2003, 577). Defining the border as process emphasizes its changing nature and the multidirectional and multilevel flow of relationships. Although the central governments of the United States and Mexico impose national policies that shape the larger context, the decisions of sub-state actors contribute to the social construction of the border; these local agents are the focus of this study.

In the late twentieth century, a commonly heard refrain in the popular media characterized international borders as disappearing anachronisms of a less-globalized past. During the same period, however, many governments have dedicated increasing resources to enforcing and protecting borders, making their physical presence even more visible. The U.S. government continues to pump billions of dollars into immigration control and the war on drugs, especially since the terrorist attacks of 9/11 (Andreas 2003; Dunn 1996; Nevins 2002). These policies have resulted in what Andreas (2003, 4) calls "both a borderless economy and a barricaded border" which is "both more blurred and more sharply demarcated than ever before."[1]

Throughout its history, the U.S.–Mexico border has been selectively closed and opened (Herzog 1990; O. Martínez 1988). Government actions, from Mexico's Border Industrialization Program beginning in the 1960s to the North American Free Trade Agreement (NAFTA) in 1994 and current negotiations for a Free Trade Agreement of the Americas (FTAA), have encouraged cross-border business ties. Migration from the interior of the country to Mexican border cities has simultaneously caused rapid population growth and changed the nature of social ties in border communities. More cross-border links are based on recently established economic relationships rather than on personal, cultural, or historical ties.

One ongoing goal of any state is to maintain territorial integrity and control of borders (Nevins 2002; Saint-Germain 1998). National security is perceived by many as "a concern of high-level officials in the nation's capital and something best left to the nation's armed forces, which are largely segregated from civilian life. There are few daily reminders of this policy area in everyday life" (Saint-Germain 1998, 61). Even at the border, many residents rarely or never cross to the other side; they choose to ignore the border and the city on the other side. From experience I know that one can live at or near the border and give very little thought to its presence, its militarization, the problems of securing the border, or any of the many issues related to economic relations, national security, and territorial integrity. The reality for those who must deal with the barricaded border, however, is that it is not disappearing but has become increasingly visible and physical in ways that have significant impacts on the people who live on both sides of it.

This chapter is based on research I conducted in 1996–97 in the border cities of Douglas, Arizona, and Agua Prieta, Sonora. In those pre–9/11 days, Immigration and Naturalization Service (INS)[2] restrictions and controls were focused on capturing drug smugglers or undocumented immigrant workers (Andreas 2003; Andreas and Snyder 2000; Dunn 1996; Nevins 2002; Spener and Staudt 1998). In Douglas, residents were hopeful that increased Border Patrol efforts and a new border fence would deter illegal immigrants and would prevent criminals from sneaking across the border to commit crimes.

After 9/11, the United States implemented an array of new security measures, including more inspections and surveillance of those entering the United States (Andreas 2003; Arizona-Mexico Commission 2004; Border Governors' Conference 2002; Department of Homeland Security n.d.). In border communities, one of the most immediate effects of the new security measures was slowed crossing times, from annoying but manageable delays into nearly insurmountable barriers to carrying out daily tasks (Ackelson 2003; Border Governors' Conference 2002; Cortez 2003; Nathanson and Lampell 2001). For women who cross the border regularly, lengthened crossing times intensify already complex and full daily schedules.

I began my research with two basic questions. First, what factors shape border women's mobility on a daily, weekly, or longer basis? And second, how do residence at the border and women's perceptions of the border affect their cross-border mobility? Changes since 9/11 have added a third and ongoing question that will be explored in this chapter: how might the advent of the "war on terror" affect women's mobility at the local level? Women's movements doubtless will continue to change as a direct result of border policy changes and in response to other factors in the border region and beyond.

Women's Mobility

Women's daily routines are made up of complicated and precisely timed arrangements that reflect the major factors shaping daily mobility: employment, child care, and transportation. Studies of women and daily mobility have in general focused on the journey to work and commuting times, primarily in large metropolitan areas in North America and in Europe (Hansen 1999). Studies of third world women's mobility have focused on time use (Araya 2003; Warner 1995) and on longer-term movements, particularly rural-to-urban or international migration. Research on women's mobility at the U.S.–Mexico border has examined border crossing by women working as domestic servants (Mattingly 1999a; V. Ruiz 1987; Solórzano-Torres 1987), for other economic motives (Alegría 1990; Heyman 1991; Pavlakovic and Kim 1990; O. Ruiz 1998), for medical care (Ojeda, this vol.; Pope 2001), or attempting to cross illegally (Price 2004).

The journey to work is an important type of daily movement for women in the United States and Mexico, particularly as women in both countries make up increasing percentages of the labor force. As greater numbers of women work outside the home, they continue to bear major responsibility for child care and daily household maintenance. As a result, they often must negotiate complex schedules with other household members, relatives, and friends. Research indicates that women make choices and compromises regarding employment outside the home that may be more important to them than the costs of commuting (Araya 2003; Christensen 1993; K. England 1993). Pratt and Hanson (1991) showed that the daily space-time constraints of women's household duties influence the kinds of jobs they seek and their participation in paid labor outside the home. Liz Bondi writes that "women tend to adapt their paid employment to accommodate traditional gender divisions within the home" (1993, 242), including child care and daily household management. Dependence on public transportation, walking to the workplace, and making linked trips — for example, dropping a child at a babysitter, stopping to check on elderly parents, or doing grocery shopping on the way to or from the workplace — all place additional demands on working women's time (Rosenbloom 1993).

Women who work at home and therefore do not deal with commuting to a workplace often face greater limits to mobility because of the multiple responsibilities of work, child care, and domestic tasks (Christensen 1993, 62–63). To deal with space-time constraints, women may intensify their in-home work efforts by performing multiple tasks simultaneously. Such intensification results in overlapping of paid employment with unpaid domestic labor: for example, when women who work in their homes watch their children at the same time (Araya 2003; Christensen 1993; Flora 1994). These situations may result in women feeling trapped in their homes, dependent on others to accomplish everyday tasks.

Women's Mobility in Douglas and Agua Prieta

Women on both sides of the border plan and negotiate daily movements in response to key factors such as the demands of employment and child care, access to transportation, and urban form. In addition to these factors, cross-border movements are also influenced by the larger context of changing national security priorities, which affect women's daily mobility in ways unique to border cities. Time constraints are a major consideration for women everywhere as they arrange their days to meet obligations of children, work, and household tasks. Increased crossing times at the U.S.–Mexico border ports of entry make women's already complex schedules even more of a challenge, especially for those who have limited transportation options. This issue is addressed in the last part of this chapter.

The Study Sites

Douglas, Arizona, is a former mining-dependent town that historically offered jobs primarily for men. The city's stable population and slow economic growth have implications for short- and long-term mobility. People drive to larger urban centers to find goods, services, and opportunities not available in Douglas. The city is small in population but sprawls across the desert; no public transportation exists, so low-income, non-car-owning residents depend on friends, relatives, or expensive taxis. Douglas offers limited opportunities for young people and many leave as soon as they graduate from high school to find jobs, higher education, or entertainment elsewhere.

In contrast, Agua Prieta, Sonora, experienced rapid population growth in the 1980s and 1990s in response to employment opportunities in the maquiladora industry. The city has not been able to keep up with the growing demand for public services and its infrastructure is inadequate. Agua Prieta has a low-cost, quasi-public bus transportation system, however, that serves much of the city and is well used.

The two cities have developed with many of the structural features described as typical for border cities by Arreola and Curtis (1993), and urban form is a factor in respondents' mobility. On the U.S. side, for example, businesses locate close to the port of entry for the convenience of Mexican customers. Similarly, on the Mexico side, pharmacies and tourist shops locate as close as possible to the port of entry to attract U.S. customers. The industrial park in Agua Prieta is sited to provide efficient and convenient access to the commercial border crossing, not to maquiladora workers. The industrial park was initially located in the center of town, but Agua Prieta has expanded southwards so the factories are now farther north relative to the low-cost housing where most maquiladora workers live.

In Douglas and Agua Prieta, the journey to work is not a long-distance commute. Rather, commuting times are shaped by border-crossing waits, different transportation options on either side of the border, and by cultural practices and traditions specific to the border location. These will be discussed in the sections that follow.

Methodology

In order to discover how employment, child care, and transportation affect women's mobility at the U.S.–Mexico border, I interviewed one hundred women, fifty in each city. I chose respondents who were eighteen years of age or older in either Douglas or Agua Prieta. I used snowball sampling and walked door-to-door to find the study participants, starting with two focus groups in Douglas. These non-scientific sampling methods were appropriate to this study, as I was not aiming to generalize from a representative group to the larger population but rather was examining patterns of mobility. I hoped to find women in the two cities who were affected by a wide variety of factors and whose behavior could illustrate a range of responses and strategies. I interviewed in both cities in order to compare patterns of mobility across the political border among women connected or distanced by history, culture, and socioeconomic factors.

Women on each side, of course, did not comprise homogenous groups (table 3.1). On both sides of the border, respondents have many commonalities; at the same time, they are divided by more than the international boundary. They include older and younger women, low-income and relatively high-income women, single mothers, women in nuclear

TABLE 3.1 Characteristics of the Study Population
(fifty in each city)

	Douglas, Arizona, U.S.A.	Agua Prieta, Sonora, Mexico
Ethnicity		
Anglo	12	0
Hispanic	35	44
Native American	2	4
Other	1	2
Marital status		
Married/Civil union	25	37
Single/Divorced/Widowed	25	13
Education		
No formal education	0	3
Primary	7	22
High school/GED	4	7
Some college	24	10
College degree	13	8
Household composition		
Single	5	2
Single mother w/children	7	5
Nuclear	22	33
Extended	15	10
Households with children under 18 years of age	29	36

families, very well-educated women and some with no formal schooling, women with physical disabilities, and women at different stages in the life course, whose priorities varied widely.

Major Influences on Women's Daily Mobility

Child Care and Employment

Most of the respondents worked outside the home and the majority had children. Their mobility was shaped by the need to coordinate these two critical aspects of daily life with other household responsibilities. Over two-thirds of the respondents participated in income-generating activities, either through self-employment in family-owned businesses or as full-time or part-time employees of other businesses. Most of the employed women had children under the age of seventeen in their households (80 percent in Douglas and 61 percent in Agua Prieta). About two-thirds of respondents were solely responsible for child care in their households, and their mobility was shaped around their work schedules and their children's needs. Many of the women worked part-time in order to be at home with their children, but many had full-time work schedules and also took their children in many directions throughout the day. Child-care responsibilities resulted in creative ways of dealing with space and time conflicts. In some cases spouses, other household members, and other relatives and friends participated in child care. The presence of a husband or other relative in the household sometimes provided vital help to employed women with children but usually did not eliminate daily multiple trips for many women.

In these two relatively small cities, most employment opportunities outside the home are clustered in distinct areas; therefore, women's and men's workplaces often are located close to each other, if not in the same building. For example, several Agua Prieta respondents were employed in the same maquiladora as spouses and other household members, and other couples worked together in a family-owned store or office. With few exceptions, the respondents who had paid employment outside the home lived within two or three miles of their workplace. For those who drove to work, therefore, their journey-to-work time was affected more by their responsibilities for transporting children and accomplishing tasks related to running the household than it was by distance from the workplace.

Multiple trip making (Rey et al. 1995; Rosenbloom 1995) is a pattern of mobility distinct to employed women with children. A common routine practiced by women of both cities is illustrated by a young couple with one child in Douglas. The respondent had a part-time job in downtown Douglas. Her husband worked less than a mile away near the port of entry. Each morning the husband drove, stopping first to leave the couple's two-year-old daughter with a babysitter, next dropping the respondent at her office, then driving the last mile to his workplace. He returned to pick up the respondent at lunchtime, when she finished working for the day, and then drove back to his workplace, where she took over driving, leaving him at his job. On her way home she collected her daughter from the babysitter, did grocery shopping and other errands, or visited family members. Late in the afternoon, she drove to the port of entry to pick up her husband, who then drove the family home. Not only did this family have a complicated routine, the husband always drove when he was in the car, which meant frequent switching of drivers.

Women made multiple trips in Agua Prieta as well, though these were complicated by the fact that fewer women had access to vehicles and more depended on other means of transportation. Some respondents' husbands drove them to work, others took the bus or walked. Some maquiladoras in Agua Prieta offered bus services to employees, but most of the workers I spoke to preferred to walk. The buses were often late and their circuitous routes often took longer than walking, even though walking resulted in more time-consuming schedules. One respondent walked an extra half hour on the way to and from work to drop her baby at a babysitter's home on her way to the factory. Agua Prieta's buses did not meet her needs, and the company bus did not stop near the babysitter's house. She often shopped at a grocery store on her way home, carrying her baby as well as her purchases.

One woman in Agua Prieta had a commute of at least forty-five minutes made up of linked trips on her way to work every day. She drove her daughters to school in Douglas each morning, crossing and re-crossing the border on her way to her office in Agua Prieta. In the afternoon, she crossed the border again to pick up the children, often shopping in Douglas for groceries and doing other errands, afterwards returning to Agua Prieta to the family-owned business she operated with her husband. She was fortunate among women in Agua Prieta to have sole access to her own car during the day. It is certain that her schedule has been significantly impacted by increased waiting times at the border in both directions and will continue to be as long as her family chooses to educate the children in the United States.

Whether women cared for their own children, hired child care, or relied on family members to babysit, child-care needs resulted in some of the most complicated schedules and severe constraints on mobility reported by respondents. Those who were employed outside the home and had very young children especially faced mobility constraints. Those with full-time jobs outside the home continued to require child-care help in the afternoons when children were out of school, and many made employment decisions based on the needs of their children.

Transportation and Mobility

It seems obvious that transportation is key to mobility, but how is access to transportation gendered, and what is unique about the border setting? Having a car of one's own opens up opportunities and possibilities to women, especially in the western United States where cities grew large in the age of the automobile and spread out horizontally, rather than vertically. Even though the cities of Douglas and Agua Prieta are relatively small, many residents live far enough from workplaces, shopping areas, and services that those who do not have access to private vehicles face challenges and obstacles to mobility. Women in Agua Prieta have the advantage of the public transportation system, and although people complain about the buses, which are not air-conditioned and usually are full of dust from the city's dirt roads, ridership is high. Douglas, in contrast, has paved streets but no public transportation, leaving low-income households with few options for transportation aside from relying on other households, friends, or taxis.

In both towns, the majority of respondents had access to a vehicle: 86 percent in Douglas and 64 percent in Agua Prieta. Frequently, however, men used the family car for transportation to the workplace, so no one else in the household had access to it during the day. On both sides of the border, fewer women had driver's licenses than men in their households did. They stated a variety of reasons for this: some said their husbands would not allow them to learn; others said they preferred that others drive; one had a suspended license. Some said their husbands usually drove when they went someplace together; several said they chose to wait until their husbands were available to drive them. Whatever their reasons for not driving, women were more often dependent on men in their households for transportation.

Access to, and control over, a vehicle make women's daily movements more convenient but frequently created more complicated arrangements and trips. Women with cars often provided transportation to friends and relatives without cars, resulting in even more time constraints on their schedules. For example, one respondent in Douglas who lived with her husband's extended family spent most days at her part-time job and driving the household's one car back and forth to everyone's jobs and school. All but one household member worked outside the home, and the respondent drove the other five to work and to classes, adjusting her own part-time hours to fit the schedules of others in the household. This woman was the most mobile of all respondents yet had little independent control over her daily schedule.

Transportation and mobility patterns also reflect the economic level of the household. For example, one Agua Prieta respondent and her husband were both self-employed and owned cars. Her busy schedule was possible because she also employed a full-time housekeeper-babysitter who managed the house and watched the couple's two young children during the day. The oldest child went to school, both parents to separate offices, and they all ate lunch at home together every day. At the time of our interview, the respondent was helping her cousin get to work, home for lunch, back to work, and home at the end of the day while the cousin's car was out of commission. None of these destinations was far from the others, but the respondent spent a good portion of her day driving herself, her children, and her cousin to and from home, school, and work. Her husband stayed at his workplace and usually did not transport the children or other family members. This respondent's economic status allowed her to pay for full-time household help and reliable transportation. Because she was self-employed, her schedule was flexible, something she valued highly as it provided family time during the day.

Multiple trips were facilitated in Douglas and Agua Prieta by the relatively small size of the cities. The short distances between places allowed women to arrange their days to include trips to many different destinations with relative ease, though women whose access to private vehicles was limited had to plan their travel carefully and accomplish much on each trip. They made linked trips, *aprovechando el viaje* (making the most of each ride). Most managed to arrange transportation to the places they needed to go, thereby generating multiple trip making by those relatives or friends who gave them rides. These examples indicate that multiple trip-making in Douglas and Agua Prieta often reflects cultural values along with gender roles. Though multiple trips and linked trips filled women's days with travel through the cities and to the other side, they also fulfilled important family functions while reinforcing gender roles in the household, as the women took care of child care and maintaining social connections between households.

Cross-Border Mobility

The complicated arrangements described above are not unique to households at the border, of course. The border location adds complicating factors and additional hurdles for those who cross the border frequently, including time constraints and interactions with border officials from both sides. Respondents who crossed frequently included mothers in Agua Prieta whose children attended school in Douglas and women whose businesses required them to cross the border. Family relations, medical services, and shopping also drew respondents from both sides across the border in both directions. All of these movements are conditioned by the responsibilities in women's lives that I refer to as the critical factors affecting their mobility and by the changing socioeconomic context. The remainder of this chapter focuses on cross-border movements in pre–9/11 days, then addresses how changing national security measures since 9/11 will likely affect women's daily mobility at the border.

Nearly all the women in the study group crossed the border at least occasionally (table 3.2). Most of the Douglas respondents who crossed frequently were Hispanic: half were Mexican citizens who resided in the United States and most of the rest were Hispanic U.S. citizens, most of whom maintained close ties with relatives in Agua Prieta. Border-crossing frequency varied widely also, depending on place of residence. Respondents from Douglas crossed the border much less frequently than those from Agua Prieta did: 42 percent of respondents from Douglas crossed less than once per month, while 64 percent of those from Agua Prieta crossed once a week or more. Only one of the respondents in Agua Prieta did not want a border-crossing card, which allows border residents to cross at will. Mexican respondents considered the cost and effort required to obtain the crossing card worthwhile and valued it as an amenity of border residence.

The most common motive for crossing the border from either direction was to shop. Many respondents from Agua Prieta did most or all of the household grocery shopping in Douglas. They preferred the products in Douglas's grocery stores to what was available in Agua Prieta. Many respondents from Douglas crossed regularly to buy prescription drugs, and some bought specialty foods available only in Mexico.

TABLE 3.2 Border-Crossing Frequency (percent)

	Douglas, Arizona, U.S.A.	Agua Prieta, Sonora, Mexico
Never	10	22
Less than once/year	4	0
Less than once/month	28	2
1–2 times/month	36	12
1–2 times/week	14	30
3–7 times/week	8	30
More than once/day	0	4

Respondents on both sides mentioned many other reasons they crossed the border, including health care (doctors and dentists), visiting family and friends, and patronizing beauty salons. Respondents from Agua Prieta also attended classes in Douglas, did their banking, and used the post office.

Strong family ties are common among residents of Douglas and Agua Prieta, and some respondents maintained significant social networks in both places. I initially supposed that cross-border social and familial connections would be an important determinant of the frequency and duration of trips across the border. I found, however, that some women who knew no one on the other side made frequent trips across, and many who had friends or relatives on the other side never visited them. Social connections certainly draw people across the line, but 43 percent of respondents in Douglas and 29 percent in Agua Prieta who had relatives or friends on the other side did not cite visiting as a primary motive for crossing the border.

Most respondents crossed the border for economic rather than social reasons. As Agua Prieta's population grew rapidly in the 1980s and 1990s, the influx of newcomers resulted in a growing percentage of the city's population having few social ties across the border. In the past, relations between neighboring cities at the border depended greatly on personal ties of families and shared histories (Kiy and Kada 2004; Ortíz-González 2004). For the populations of the two cities as a whole, cross-border connections are increasingly based on economics and decreasingly on historical and family ties. This situation is changing the nature of cross-border connections and in turn is changing the nature of the relationships between the neighboring cities and their residents.

Effects of Post-9/11 Policies on
Cross-Border Mobility

The border represents a sometimes unpredictable barrier for residents. The barrier represents an opportunity cost, as increased time spent waiting to cross is lost to other tasks. Border residents or visitors can now check the Internet to find out how long the wait is at any particular time of day. Various websites regularly update waiting times to help people plan when to cross, in hopes of easing the lines.[3] In the remainder of this chapter, I discuss how women at the border have adjusted their already complex schedules to take into account the new security policies established after the terrorist attacks of September 11, 2001.

After 9/11, the U.S. government implemented various security measures intended to defend its national borders from infiltration by terrorists. The government established the U.S. Visitor and Immigrant Status Technology (U.S.–VISIT) program, which requires all visitors to the United States to be photographed and fingerprinted upon entry. The new system had obvious implications for the busy ports of entry in places like San Diego and El Paso, but also for smaller places such as Douglas. At peak crossing times, corresponding with rush-hour traffic on both sides of the border, the wait to get through the car lanes at even a relatively small port of entry can be up to an hour or more as U.S. Customs officials question each carload entering the United States.

The Department of Homeland Security (DHS) has implemented the U.S.–VISIT program in the fifty busiest inland ports of entry and at numerous seaports and airports (Department of Homeland Security website n.d.). When the system was introduced to the public in late 2003, a government official said the process of fingerprinting each border crosser was a simple process that would take "maybe twenty to thirty seconds" (Waterman 2003). The response from border communities was (predictably) vociferous outrage. Even adding twenty to thirty seconds to each individual crossing the border could cause huge delays, especially at peak crossing times in the mornings and afternoons and on weekends. In response, the U.S. government installed scanners at some ports to quickly read computerized crossing cards to avoid crossing slowdowns. According to recent reports, however, it appears the scanners will be used only to check the authenticity of suspicious cards or persons and U.S. Customs inspectors will continue manual examinations of other cards (Bustos 2004). Predictably, again, the response from border communities was disappointment because individual manual inspection was one of the problems that the new laser visas were to have eliminated.

Border communities have demanded special services for frequent crossers at busy ports of entry in order to avoid long delays as entrants were being interviewed, photographed, and fingerprinted. The government responded with the Secure Electronic Network for Travelers Rapid Inspection (SENTRI) system, which allows frequent travelers to use an alternative crossing lane and an electronic crossing card. So far, SENTRI and other fast-crossing programs are in place only at one port of entry in El Paso and two in San Diego. Officials predicted that the people who would be most likely to sign up for the program would be maquiladora managers and executives who live in the United States and work at the factories in Mexico, and Mexican parents who take their children to U.S. schools every day (Turf 2004). Even though it was specifically designed to speed crossing times for regular crossers, the SENTRI system has come under fire because it has, instead, increased wait times at the ports of entry where it has been implemented (Spagat 2005).

What are the implications of these measures for women's mobility? Long delays at ports of entry in all border cities have affected everything from agriculture to education to trade. Women are involved in all aspects of daily life at the border that take people across to the other side and are therefore affected by all the measures to increase security at the ports of entry as they go about their daily activities. Women who already have full schedules will find their schedules even tighter as they deal with longer wait times at the border. Mexican women who take their children across the border to attend school in the United States must allow for increased waiting time in the mornings and afternoons. Time to shop will also be reduced by longer wait times at the port of entry. Decreased shopping has affected businesses on both sides of the border, though numbers of vehicles crossing into the United States have increased steadily since 2002 (Arizona-Mexico Commission 2004; San Ysidro Chamber of Commerce n.d.). The Border Governors' Conference reported that increased security measures "crippled trade and commerce, depressing local border economies" (2002, 1; see also Ackelson 2003; Andreas 2003; Nathanson and Lampell 2001). Women are among the small- and large-business owners who were immediately affected by the slowdown in cross-border traffic, which would have a significant impact on their businesses and their households. In Mexico, women still make up large percentages of workers in the electronics and textiles maquiladoras, and any slowdown in production and export caused by increased security measures would affect their employment. This would have a ripple effect through their households and communities that would also affect the U.S. border cities, where declining incomes among Mexican workers always negatively impact local businesses.

Commercial farms in the United States depend on farmworkers — women and men — who legally cross the border to work in the fields every day. People from both sides who work on the other have seen their schedules disrupted by unpredictably longer crossing times (Andreas 2003, Arizona-Mexico Commission 2004; Border Governors' Conference 2002; Border Trade Alliance 2003; Nathanson and Lampell 2001). In some areas, this means thousands of people waiting in longer lines to cross the border twice daily.

Not surprisingly, some types of cross-border traffic declined after the new security measures were implemented, including tourists and other so-called non-essential visitors. The Border Governors' Conference estimated that personal vehicle crossings dropped by 27 to 33 percent along the border, while wait times to cross increased at all ports of entry (2002, 2–3). Peter Andreas (2003, 10) estimates that "[c]ross-border trade, which had been running at about $670 million, fell by an average of 15 percent in the weeks following the attacks. Most severely affected were electronics, textiles, chemicals, and Mexican factories supplying just-in-time parts to U.S. auto companies." For small and large businesses on both sides that depend on tourists and other visitors, all of these border crossings are far from nonessential and any slowdown has a significant impact on their success.

Conclusions

One of the central objectives of this research was to ask how patterns of mobility reflect structural differences, similarities, and connections among and between women in Douglas and Agua Prieta. Patterns of mobility vary yet reveal many commonalities that reflect women's multiple, gendered roles as income-earners, mothers, daughters, business owners, consumers, and participants in community activities. Women on both sides of the border negotiate the socioeconomic and physical structures of the two cities. They depend on family members and friends, they make linked trips and multiple trips throughout the day, and they prioritize family relations and accommodate them by creating complex daily travel schedules. These patterns hold true for women across socioeconomic groups and at different stages of the life course.

Feminist scholars have extended the literature of mobility to include the more complicated mobility patterns of women, the constraints they face based on gendered obligations of reproductive labor in the household and productive labor inside and outside the home, the occupational and geographical segregation of employed women, and differences based on ethnicity and class in addition to gender. This research has shown that certain commonalities act to shape women's mobility in smaller cities as well as in the larger metropolitan areas where most research has been carried out. These include the critical factors identified here: children and child care, employment, household management, and transportation. On a daily basis, women juggle these multiple responsibilities. Even as some women gain financial independence through employment or business ownership, men continue to dominate in certain areas that affect women's mobility. Some men do participate in child care and household management, but in this study, none assumed major responsibility. Men continue to control the family vehicle and to drive when the family travels together.

As is obvious from the information presented here, the new security measures will add to the time constraints women already face. Even those who do not regularly cross the border are affected by the increased surveillance and inspections that have slowed crossing. Many businesses have been hard hit by the slowdown in cross-border traffic, investments have slowed, and business is lost. In the literature of the border since 9/11, I have not encountered research on the gendered nature of the effects of new security policies. This is an area for further research, as gender roles continue to evolve in both countries, and women's opportunities and the barriers to their progress are affected by the changing international context at the U.S.–Mexico border.

4 Abortion in a Transborder Context

Norma Ojeda

The border between Mexico and the United States makes up a unique transborder context in which the first world and the third world meet and interact to create a society that is distinct from that of either Mexican or U.S. society. Among its other characteristics, the border is marked by the fact that it offers a broad mosaic of economic, social, and cultural options from which the population that lives on both sides of the border can choose. Women's reproductive health-care options are of particular interest in the study of border women's lives. The proximity of the two countries with important differences in both their understanding of women's reproductive rights and their legal systems creates alternative women's reproductive health-care services. One alternative is the practice of abortion. Abortion in Mexico is a legally prosecutable crime, while in the United States the voluntary interruption of pregnancy is a constitutional right, although access is limited. The U.S.–Mexico transborder context creates a social space in which a part of the female population residing in Mexico is able to cross the border into the United States to seek various health-care services, including safe abortion. Additionally, the border is a space marked by a high degree of demographic and cultural diversity and by a social complexity that cannot be ignored. Border culture influences women's everyday lives, their gender, their sexuality and reproduction, and the choices that they make in that regard.

The present study is a descriptive analysis of abortion among border women, taking the San Diego–Tijuana transborder context as a specific case. It includes women residing on the two sides of the border who commute back and forth between the two countries. San Diego and Tijuana make up a metropolitan area within which the populations residing on both sides of the international boundary line interact (Herzog 1990). These are regular interactions, and they are a part of everyday life for various female population subgroups. The study focuses on the different patterns of abortion among Hispanic border women living in San Diego–Tijuana. For this purpose, ethnic-linguistic subgroups of women are identified as a proxy to the complexity of border culture in this particular U.S.–Mexico transborder context. Special interest is paid to the Mexico resident women who cross the border to have abortions in San Diego.

Legal Status of Abortion

The study of abortion in Mexico's northern border region (or anywhere else in the rest of the country) is a difficult undertaking because of problems obtaining information on the issue. Abortion in Mexico is a legally prosecutable crime with some exceptions that can vary among the country's different federated states. The Mexican border state of Baja California is the focus of our study, and in this case, the penal code and penal procedures in place establish that abortion shall not be punishable when it is (1) a negligent abortion—that is, when it is the result of negligent conduct by the pregnant woman; (2) an abortion where the pregnancy is the result of a rape or artificial insemination carried out against the pregnant woman's will, as long as the abortion is performed within the first ninety days of gestation and a complaint regarding the act has been filed; (3) a therapeutic abortion, where in the opinion of the attending physician the pregnant woman's life is in danger unless an abortion is performed (Ojeda 2003, 4–5). Notwithstanding these exceptions, the legal practice of abortion is very limited for social, cultural, and even political reasons, as demonstrated in the "Paulina Case" that took place in Baja California in 1999 and was widely reported in the Mexican and international press (Poniatowska 2000).[1]

Another factor that makes the study of abortion in Mexico difficult is the near impossibility of measuring the illegal practice of voluntary abortions, as they are not registered in relevant hospital and public records. Illegal abortions take place in two ways. Some take place in clandestine establishments and are not reported to the relevant health authorities. Other abortion cases show up at public and private hospital emergency rooms claiming to be spontaneous abortions and are recorded as miscarriages. These in reality are abortions that were previously induced, at times by non-medical persons or by the pregnant women themselves. These practices mean that the country's hospital records are not a trustworthy source of information for the study of voluntarily induced abortions in Mexico. In the face of these difficulties, one alternative is to study the practice of abortion among Mexican women abroad, especially in the U.S.–Mexico border region. In the United States, the voluntary interruption of pregnancy has been a constitutional right since the 1973 Supreme Court ruling in the case of *Roe v. Wade* (Tribe 1990). This has made it possible for women living in the United States to seek abortion under safe medical conditions, although access is limited and increasingly under restrictions. Safe medical abortions are also available for women who decide to travel to the United States to seek one. A part of the female population residing in Mexican territory is able to cross the border into the United States to seek various health services, including abortion. These women are able to have an abortion, free from legal harassment and in a social environment where abortion is understood as part of women's reproductive rights. Thus, contiguity between Mexico and the United States at those points where Mexican border cities are located makes it possible for a select group of Mexican women to have access to safe abortion.[2]

The Transborder Context: San Diego–Tijuana

The border region creates a social and cultural context that is distinct from either Mexican or U.S. society. Contrasting and sometimes conflicting lifestyles emerge as alternatives to the respective national cultural models. In light of this, it is useful to understand the behavior of borderlanders as part of a larger whole that has been called a border culture (O. Martínez 1997). Border culture is seen as a particular cultural system that takes shape and emerges in a specific geographic and social context and that acquires its own identity. Women at the border are exposed to the coexistence of various gender and family systems that are interwoven into a unique culture that is the "border culture" and that combines cultural elements of both societies in a hybrid manner, without replicating either one. Border culture means that there is a complex system of social norms and values that influence different groups of women to a greater or lesser degree. This is the case as much in their everyday lives as in the way in which they view themselves, their gender condition, their sexuality and reproduction, and the options that they have in that regard.

Despite the existence of a border culture over its nearly two thousand miles, the border is not a homogeneous region. There are important differences between border communities as expressed in variation in economic and social development and in distinct local features that are adopted in each specific border context. San Diego and Tijuana, with their combined population of 2,493,077 inhabitants in 2000 (Pick et al. 2001), stand out among the border's twin cities. This pair of cities is one of the most contrasting and complex border contexts. The economic structure of these two border cities is marked by its dynamism and high degree of diversity compared to other twin border cities. The tourism industry is important in both cities. These two cities, considered separately and as a whole, have a high degree of demographic and cultural diversity. This diversity is greater in San Diego, although it is also a reality in Tijuana. Native-born and immigrant populations coexist in the San Diego–Tijuana region, having widely ranging periods of residence in the border and coming from numerous countries.

The complexities of the San Diego–Tijuana border region are expressed in different ways. A long history of migration between both countries has left its imprint on the border and has given rise to the formation of extensive social networks linked by blood, marriage, and social bonds in transborder families (Ojeda 1994). This type of family frequently includes persons born in both countries with different immigration status, citizens of one or another country, and/or persons with dual citizenship who have been socialized in both countries to a greater or lesser degree. In addition, the asymmetrical conditions of economic power between one side of the border and the other give rise to border commuters: workers who live on one side of the border but work on the other (Herzog 1990). The daily north-south and south-north movement of goods, services, and people searching for opportunities, better living conditions, or emotional relations are also part of this border space. These relationships and interchanges take place regardless of the existence of the international dividing line between the two nation-states involved (Ojeda 1994).

From this perspective, it is pertinent to understand the permeable nature of the border in order to approach the study of induced abortions among the population of Mexican women. One of the features of border life is crossing to the "other side" looking for what cannot be found or is of lesser quality on "this side." The population's transborder movements in search of health services take place in both directions on the border. For example, residents of Mexico cross over to San Diego, among other reasons, to obtain prenatal health care or to give birth (Social Science Research Laboratory, San Diego State University 2001). For their part, U.S. residents frequently cross over to the Mexican side seeking dental and eye care, among other services (Hansen 1999). This is a part of border life for many women.

Crossing to the other side to have an abortion is also a part of border life for many women. In fact, this has been the case for several generations, although the crossings have not always taken place in the same direction. Up until 1973, when abortion was converted into a constitutional right in the United States and became available in the state of California, the flow of crossings was from north to south. This was a practice that lasted several generations and is described by Donald Ball (1967) in his study on the experience of San Diego residents who crossed over to Tijuana to get an abortion under sordid conditions in the clandestine clinics that then met the demands of women residing on both sides of the border. Today, it is the turn of residents in Mexico to cross over to the other side to have access to an abortion, only in this case under legal conditions that ensure acceptable hygiene, medical attention, and psychological counseling. Due to the illegal status of voluntary abortion under Mexican laws, this level of care is something that Mexican women cannot get in their own country, even in induced abortion cases that arrive at the hospital in emergency conditions.

Faced with these conditions, Mexican women who wish to have an abortion see the border as a space of opportunity to cross over to the other country where they are allowed to decide whether to have an abortion. In the United States, Mexican women find themselves pressured only by their own individual selves and their personal ideas about this controversial social and health issue. Having an abortion under these conditions is not, however, an option for all Mexican border women because it is feasible only for a privileged segment of this population. Going to the other side where they are legally allowed to have an abortion is possible only for those women who have the money, the information, and the means that are necessary to cross the border, such as the possession of a national passport with a visa or a local passport.[3] This means that the option of having a risk-free abortion is highly discriminatory on the basis of social class. This works against the vast majority of Mexican border women who do not have the resources to cross over to the other country or who do not have the money they need to pay for it. For them, the option of crossing to the other side to have access to that other social space does not exist. For these women, the option is to put their lives at risk or, at the very least, to run risks of morbidity and social stigma should they decide to terminate an unwanted pregnancy. These class differences in the practice of abortion on the border reveal how, in practice, Mexican abortion laws have a clearly discriminatory character against Mexican women with the least financial resources.

Methodological Strategy and Source of Data

The aim of this study was to carry out a descriptive analysis of voluntary induced abortions among women from different groups in the San Diego–Tijuana transborder region. The information is drawn from the clinical records of Womancare Planned Parenthood for San Diego and Riverside counties in California. This clinic carried out all of the abortions performed by Planned Parenthood in San Diego and Riverside counties over this time period. The clinic records contain information on abortions performed on 815 women during the spring and summer of 1993. The services were offered by the Womancare Clinic to women residing in San Diego as well as to women from the municipalities of Tijuana, Mexicali, Tecate, and Ensenada in Baja California, Mexico, who crossed the border to receive care. This data source is of high quality and trustworthy. The information it provides is very limited as far as the women's social and demographic characteristics are concerned, due to the institution's policy of maximum protection for patients' privacy. It does, however, present extensive data on the opinions, motives, and feelings of women regarding abortion.

Abortion among border women is a diverse phenomenon. Coexisting within the border region are population groups with different ethnic, social, and cultural characteristics. On the Mexican side of the border, it has been observed that social class, educational attainment, migrant or native status, employment status, length of time residing in the border region, and socialization in rural or urban areas are among the parameters that are of fundamental importance in terms of the social differentiation of women (Ojeda 1997). On the U.S. side of the border, Hispanic women are frequently discussed as if they were a homogenous whole, when in reality they are also a group with substantial social differentiation (Ojeda 2004). It is crucial to take into account the heterogeneity of the Hispanic population that coexists on both sides of the border, but particularly in U.S. territory.

One way of getting at this diversity among Hispanic border women is to consider where they live: that is, whether they live on the Mexican side or the U.S. side of the border. This provides a first, albeit insufficient, parameter for social variation. It is also necessary to consider other variables that are more directly linked to social and cultural aspects, having to do with the ways in which women understand and explain their social and reproductive behaviors. For the purpose of this study, border women are differentiated by the combination of their ethnicity and their sociolinguistic condition, as well as by the country in which they live. These characteristics have been shown to result in important differences in the social behavior of Latinas on the border (Hansen 1999). Ethnicity and language are individual characteristics, but they also are related to cultural aspects that influence the ways in which women think about various issues, including family planning and abortion. This in turn has an influence on the control that women have over their reproduction and, therefore, on the reasons they may have to seek an abortion and the strategies that women may adopt to deal with the emotional effects following an abortion.

In order to answer the simple question of how many Mexican women cross the border for an abortion, it is necessary to deal with one of the difficulties of counting population groups on the border. In this space, the orthodox method of using a person's address to identify her place of residence is insufficient and unreliable. Giving the address of an acquaintance who lives on the other side is a very common social practice among some inhabitants of Mexico who want to obtain some type of service in U.S. society. False addresses may be used to access public services such as schools or professional services, including health care. Having knowledge of this common custom among Mexican border people, it was necessary to consider other types of information. We decided to identify women's ethnicity and the language used to respond to a questionnaire that they were given in the clinic before and after the surgical procedure. This procedure is also used as a proxy to analyze the diversity of Hispanic border women.

Thus, the available data and the knowledge of local customs and practices on the border make it possible to make the following assumptions. First, it is assumed that the immigrant Hispanic population (the majority of Mexican origin) in the vicinity of the border in San Diego county, especially those who are newcomers, as well as the Mexican border population who are visiting or temporarily present in U.S. territory, prefer using the Spanish language to answer the written questionnaires when offered that option. Second, it is assumed that the Mexican-origin U.S. population and the Mexican immigrant women who attended school and were socialized as children and adolescents in the United States prefer to provide written information in the English language. This assumption is used in this study, as Hispanic women are divided into three groups on the basis of the language used to complete the survey.

Findings: Diverse Patterns of Abortion among Border Women

It was calculated that Mexicans made up between 15 and 31 percent of the total number of cases that received services at Womancare during the spring and summer of 1993. The lower number includes only those who reported having an address in Baja California, while the higher number results from counting the number of Hispanic border women who used Spanish to answer the written questionnaires.

Age at Abortion

The information in table 4.1 indicates that the majority of border women who had an abortion are young, between twenty and twenty-nine years of age. Despite this general characteristic, we can distinguish some variations when we compare the age patterns of the three groups included in the study: Hispanic border women who prefer to write in Spanish, Hispanic border women who prefer to write in English, and non-Hispanic women.

TABLE 4.1 Percentage of Women Having Abortions by Woman's Age, Ethnicity, and Language Choice

| | Ethnicity | | |
| | Hispanic | | Non-Hispanic |
Age (years)	Spanish-speaking	English-speaking	
14–19	5.6	11.9	6.8
20–24	25.5	28.3	28.4
25–29	28.2	42.5	40.0
30 +	40.7	17.3	24.8
Total	100.0	100.0	100.0

Source: Medical records, Womancare Clinic, Planned Parenthood, San Diego–Riverside, spring and summer 1993.

On one hand, the ones with the youngest age structure are Hispanic women who use English to communicate in writing. This group has both the highest proportion of adolescents who had an abortion (nearly twice as many abortions as the other two groups) and the lowest proportion of women thirty years and older who had abortions.

On the other hand, Hispanic women who communicate in writing in Spanish were older at the time of having an abortion than their English-writing counterparts. They include the smallest group of adolescents who aborted and the most numerous group of women thirty years and older who had abortions. Finally, the age structure for non-Hispanic women is somewhere in between the two groups of Hispanic border women.

Age at First Pregnancy

The data point to a high proportion of women in each of the groups who had their first pregnancy while still adolescents (see fig. 4.1). Approximately 53 percent of non-Hispanic women receiving abortions reported having their first pregnancy before age twenty, compared to 49 percent of Hispanic women completing the survey in English. Only 35 percent of Hispanic border women who used Spanish were under twenty when they were first pregnant. The structure of ages at the time of first pregnancy for women who had an abortion shows that Hispanic women who are most

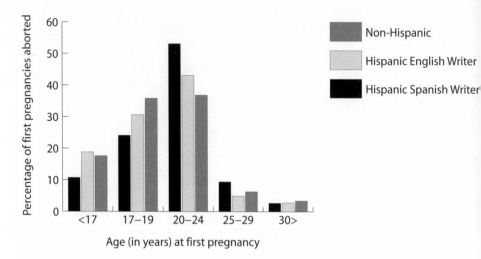

FIGURE 4.1 Abortion by women's age at first pregnancy, ethnicity, and language choice. *Source:* Medical records, Womancare Clinic, Planned Parenthood, San Diego–Riverside, spring and summer 1993.

assimilated linguistically into American society and non-Hispanic women report the highest proportion of first pregnancies in adolescence.

Figure 4.1 shows that the twenty- to twenty-four-year-old age group follows a traditional fertility curve. Among them, Hispanic border women less assimilated linguistically to American society stand out as having the highest proportion of first-time pregnancies between the ages of twenty and twenty-four. First-time pregnancies in that same age range come second among the Hispanic women writing in English. Finally, non-Hispanic women show a very different pattern of behavior: they have almost the same proportion of cases of first-time pregnancies during late adolescence (seventeen to nineteen years old) and between the ages of twenty and twenty-four.

Views about Abortion

The data in table 4.2 summarize the responses women gave to the open question: "What is your opinion about abortion?" The findings indicate the predominance of a way of thinking about abortion as a solution to a problem among women in all three groups; this type of answer accounts

TABLE 4.2 Women's Opinions about Abortion, by Ethnicity and Language Choice (percent)

| | Ethnicity | | |
| | Hispanic | | Non-Hispanic |
Opinion	Spanish-speaking	English-speaking	
A solution to a problem	48.4	42.3	48.0
A woman's right when she cannot or does not want to have a baby	29.1	34.6	39.0
Something sad or negative; feel guilty; other similar response	16.9	16.9	9.5
No response	5.6	6.2	3.5
Total	100.0	100.0	100.0

Source: Medical records, Womancare Clinic, Planned Parenthood, San Diego–Riverside, spring and summer 1993.

for more than 40 percent of the responses among each group of women. The second most frequent type of response (again, among women in all three groups) was to think of abortion as an alternative to which women have a right when they cannot or do not want to have a baby. Broadly speaking, more non-Hispanic women than Hispanic women expressed this opinion. It is interesting to note that this way of thinking is least common among Hispanic border women who used Spanish to respond to the question.

Feelings about Abortion

Despite the different views regarding abortion among women in the three groups, there is a remarkable agreement in terms of their reactions to the pregnancy that led them to the abortion clinic. Table 4.3 shows the predominance of negative reactions or feelings when the great majority of women in all three groups learned they were pregnant. The unwanted

TABLE 4.3 Women's Feelings when They Learned about Their
Pregnancy, by Ethnicity and Language Choice (percent)

| | Ethnicity | | |
| | Hispanic | | Non-Hispanic |
Feelings	Spanish-speaking	English-speaking	
Cried, shocked, threatened, crazy, sick, terrified, insecure, mad, uncomfortable	44.5	47.4	48.5
Other negative feelings	40.2	42.8	40.1
Positive feelings	15.3	9.8	11.4
Total	100.0	100.0	100.0

Source: Medical records, Womancare Clinic, Planned Parenthood, San Diego–Riverside, spring and summer 1993.

nature of the pregnancies at issue is evident in each group, as less than 20 percent of the women in all groups reported positive feelings about their pregnancies.

Motives for Abortion

The motives provided by the women for voluntarily interrupting their pregnancies show significant variation among the three groups under study. One difference among the three groups of women was the role their partner apparently had in the abortion decision. Table 4.4 shows that a higher percentage of Hispanic Spanish-writers in one way or another menioned their partner in their responses to the question: "What was the main motive that led you to make the decision to have an abortion?" Nearly one fourth of them responded that they did not want to have more children or that the abortion was a shared decision with their partner. In contrast, this type of response was given by only 13 percent of the Hispanic English-writers and by 18 percent of non-Hispanic women. Just over a quarter (28.4 percent) of Hispanic women who used Spanish

TABLE 4.4 Women's Motivations to Seek an Abortion,
by Ethnicity and Language Choice (percent)

| | Ethnicity | | |
| | Hispanic | | Non-Hispanic |
Motivation	Spanish-speaking	English-speaking	
I don't want to have more children; this is a couple's decision	24.4	12.9	18.0
This is my only option; he doesn't want the baby; I don't have a partner; economic problems; other similar reasons	28.4	24.5	15.0
I am too young to be a mom; I don't want this responsibility; I don't have time for children; other similar reasons	24.4	29.3	36.0
Health problems; previous abortion	22.8	33.3	31.0
Total	100.0	100.0	100.0

Source: Medical records, Womancare Clinic, Planned Parenthood, San Diego–Riverside, spring and summer 1993.

responded that abortion was their only option, they did not have a partner, did not have their partner's support, did not have money, or other similar reasons. Meanwhile, this type of response was given by smaller percentages of both Hispanic border women who used English and non-Hispanic women.

Another example of the different reasons for having abortions has to do with women's perceptions of themselves and the timing for having children. In this regard, there is a clear difference between the two Hispanic groups and the non-Hispanic women. Thirty-six percent of non-

TABLE 4.5 Women's Plans to Overcome Their Post-abortion Trauma, by Ethnicity and Language Choice (percent)

| | Ethnicity | | |
| | Hispanic | | Non-Hispanic |
Motivation	Spanish-speaking	English-speaking	
Talking with my partner, friends, and family; taking care of my children	15.2	33.3	37.7
Working; resting; recreational activities; personal development	47.3	35.2	38.4
I have no plans; I do not know; I have not thought about it	32.0	23.3	17.8
Psychological and/or religious assistance	5.5	8.2	6.1
Total	100.0	100.0	100.0

Source: Medical records, Womancare Clinic, Planned Parenthood, San Diego–Riverside, spring and summer 1993.

Hispanic women responded that they were not old enough to be a mother, they had no time to care for children, they did not want to assume the responsibilities of having a baby, and/or other similar reasons when asked, "Why did you decide to have an abortion?" In contrast, less than one-fourth of the women in each of the two groups of Hispanic border women gave a similar type of answer. Another type of response to the question of why they chose to have an abortion has to do with women's health problems. As is clear from table 4.4, this type of reason is important in each of the groups of women, but especially among Hispanic women that responded in English, followed closely by non-Hispanic women, with percentages of 33.3 percent and 31.0 percent, respectively. Health problems were also given as a response among Hispanic women who answered in Spanish, but to a lesser degree (in 23 percent of the cases).

Post-abortion Plans

Different scenarios are apparent in the plans women reported for dealing with the emotional effects of the post-abortion experience. In general, these scenarios may be interpreted not only as a result of women's individual preferences but also as a result of the options open to them in their respective social and cultural contexts. Table 4.5 presents the answers to the question: "What plans do you have to deal with your feelings after the abortion?" Non-Hispanic women were the most likely to report that communication with loved ones was an important post-abortion emotional recovery strategy. In addition, these same women were the least likely to report they had no plans for dealing with their post-abortion trauma. Hispanic women who were most linguistically assimilated to American society gave responses very similar to those of non-Hispanic women.

In contrast, Hispanic women who completed surveys in Spanish offer a different scenario. Fewer of them stated they had the intention of sharing their post-abortion experience with their loved ones. Also, many more women in this group reported that they did not have plans or had not thought about their emotional recuperation. Thus, in terms of plans for recovery, the data show distinct differences that could be attributed to the cultural context. English-speaking respondents showed similar patterns despite ethnic differences.

Discussion and Conclusions

The findings taken as a whole suggest the existence of various patterns of abortion among three groups of women living in the transborder context of San Diego–Tijuana. There are noticeable differences between the two groups of Hispanic border women included in the study. The linguistic writing preferences of women seem to be linked to different demographic profiles and attitudes toward abortion.

Overall, Hispanic border women most assimilated to American society show the youngest age structure at abortion. They have both the highest number of abortions during the earliest years of adolescence (younger than seventeen) and the lowest proportion of women over thirty having abortions. This group of Hispanic border women also has the highest proportion of first pregnancies occurring during adolescence. This same group of Hispanic women seems to share more attitudes toward abortion with non-Hispanic women than with Spanish-writing Hispanic women. Non-Hispanic and Hispanic English-writers show similar proportions of women who view abortion as a woman's right and adopt similar strategies for recuperation during the post-abortion phase. This situation may be explained by the fact that these two groups of women share some cultural and gender factors linked to the English language and the socialization of women in U.S. society. American society offers a social and cultural context more amenable to communication on the topic of abortion, as well as more supportive of women's reproductive rights.

Hispanic border women most assimilated to the Mexican society present a very different pattern of abortion from the other two groups. First, this group shows a highly selective demographic profile. They have the oldest age structure at abortion, with the lowest number of abortions among adolescents and the highest number of abortions by women thirty years and older. Likewise, this subgroup of border women reports the lowest number of first pregnancies in adolescence. A possible explanation for the demographic selectivity of this subgroup of Hispanic border women may reside in the fact that a large proportion of them lived in Baja California and crossed the border to have their abortion in San Diego. As mentioned previously, women crossing the border for abortions come from a select economic and social group. Only some Baja California female residents have the legal documents, economic resources, and social networks to cross for medical services.

With regard to the strategies adopted by women to recover emotionally after the abortion, Hispanic women writing in Spanish reported being the least open to communication with loved ones following the abortion. Interestingly, the partner also seemed to play a more important role in these women's decisions to abort than in the other two groups included in the study. It seems that this group of border women in some way reflects the restrictive conditions surrounding abortion that prevail in Mexico and especially in Baja California. Thus, we can say that while Mexican women who cross the border to have an abortion are able to escape the threat of jail and risks to their health, they do not necessarily escape the social punishment of having to live through an abortion and the post-abortion stage in silence and alone, just like the rest of Mexican women who decide to interrupt their unwanted pregnancies in clandestine clinics in Mexico. In both cases, women are being ideologically oppressed by the social and cultural values surrounding the restrictive abortion rights that prevail in Mexican society.

The above patterns of abortion among border women reflect not only women's individual characteristics but also the distinct cultural and social immersion of border women in the particular transborder context of San Diego–Tijuana. Each of these patterns needs to be understood in light of the cultural and social diversity that prevail among border women. For some Mexican women, crossing the border to abort represents a choice to pursue an option they do not have in their own country. For other women, abortion is seen as a basic reproductive right. And for some others, abortion is only one more event in their reproductive life cycle. The social and cultural factors associated with the women's choice to abort in each of these cases are linked in one way or another to the mosaic of opportunities offered by the U.S.–Mexico international border and the diversity and social complexity of a space where the Mexican and the American cultures are interwoven and coexist in a unique border culture.

Recent information about attitudes about family planning and abortion among women in Tijuana and San Diego indicate a more pro-choice position among younger and more-educated women (Ojeda 2003, 2004). This finding suggests that Mexican residents are crossing the border to have abortions in the clinics of San Diego in larger numbers than previously. Further research about this thorny topic is needed to study any possible changes in the diverse abortion patterns in San Diego–Tijuana and in other U.S.–Mexico border cities.

Part Two **Labor and Empowerment in the Border Region**

5 The Changing Gender Composition of the Maquiladora Workforce along the U.S.–Mexico Border

Susan Tiano

When the maquiladora program began in the mid-1960s, few but the most optimistic of its founders foresaw that it would create a major industrial corridor along the U.S.–Mexico border by century's end. And few anticipated that the maquiladoras' hiring practices would be so skewed toward recruiting female labor that maquiladora jobs would come to be stereotyped as "women's work." Women's massive influx into maquiladora jobs represented a dramatic departure from previous labor market dynamics in Mexico, where prior to the 1970s women had one of the lowest rates of formal labor force participation in the hemisphere (Tiano 1997). The scholarship that emerged during the 1980s and 1990s analyzing the composition of the maquiladora workforce and the conditions of maquiladora employment flourished during the extended period of maquiladora expansion during the late twentieth century. By contrast, little research exists to date exploring the impacts of the maquiladora industry's recent contraction, which between 2000 and 2003 led to the loss of almost one-third of a million maquiladora jobs (Hall 2002). The way in which this retrenchment has affected the gender composition of the maquiladora workforce is the focus of this chapter. Using aggregate data depicting women's and men's maquiladora employment trends, I employ propositions from the gender-and-development literature to illuminate their underlying reasons. By interpreting these trends in light of the historical record of industrialization's gendered impacts in Mexico and elsewhere, I explore whether the dynamics currently operating in the maquiladoras represent an isolated occurrence or instead parallel patterns observed in other industrializing contexts.

A common theme in the rapidly emerging globalization literature is the increasing feminization of labor, reflecting the growth of global corporations and the flexible labor regime to which their profit-maximizing strategies have contributed. Since 1974, when Richard Barnet and Ronald Muller first described the increasing global reach of transnational corporations (TNCs), much has been written either championing or criticizing corporate expansion and the globalization process it has inaugurated. With globalization has come a massive upsurge in women's employment (Cagatay and Ozler 1995; Joekes 1995; Razavi 2000), one cause of which is the preference for female labor in industries producing exports for the global economy (Pettman 1999). The feminization of the global export sector reflects the restructuring of the labor process and concomitant de-skilling of jobs to make them suitable for untrained women, whose vulnerability within gender-segregated labor markets offers them few alternatives to low-waged labor in TNC enterprises (Fussell 2000). Women are preferred both because they are less expensive to employ than men are and because their gender socialization and inexperience with labor unions presumably make them more docile and less easy to organize. In turn, women's economic need, exacerbated by economic crises, structural adjustment programs, and rising male unemployment, is propelling them into the workforce to support themselves and their families (Elson 1992). The result is an upsurge in women's economic activity throughout the world, a phenomenon that many gender scholars view as a hallmark of globalization.

In the original statement of the thesis, economist Guy Standing (1989) proposed that the feminization of labor since the 1980s reflects women's increasing employment, both absolutely and relative to men, and the erosion of working conditions such that jobs increasingly entail the insecurity, irregularity, and low wages traditionally associated with women's employment. For Standing, the feminization of labor is a double entendre reflecting both the increasingly female composition of the global labor force and the increasingly "feminized" conditions of employment for workers in the global economy. Standing coins the term "flexibilization" to describe the labor regime emerging from TNC attempts to reduce costs through subcontracting and other arrangements for avoiding the expense of a permanent workforce. In his view, flexible labor practices have transformed conditions in globalized jobs to make them more similar to those that have historically employed women, thereby feminizing the nature of work in the global economy.

While Standing leaves it to other scholars to document the erosion of global working conditions, he demonstrates labor force feminization with cross-national data showing a rise in female labor force participation, a decrease in male economic activity, and a decline in women's unemployment relative to men's in many countries throughout the world. Revisiting this issue a decade later, Standing (1999) finds that these global trends continued during the 1990s. Of the researchers who have subsequently confirmed these trends, most accept his assessment that flexibilization and the resulting feminization of work are apt to further feminize the world's workforce as globalization proceeds (Fontana et al. 1998; Fussell 2000; Joekes 1995). Thus, globalization scholars rarely consider possible forces that could slow or reverse this trend in particular contexts.

Almost two decades ago in an essay distilling central themes from the literature on women and development, I formulated a paradigm depicting three scenarios of industrialization's gendered impacts (Tiano 1986). While the paradigm reflects grand narratives that fail to account for the diversity of each woman's unique experiences and responses as active agents, in my work I have found it to be a useful ideal typical framework for conceptualizing historical and contemporary trends (Tiano 1987a, 1987b, 1990, 1994). Although each scenario reflects contrasting assumptions drawn from a specific theoretical framework, they are not mutually exclusive; rather, any or all of the three scenarios might characterize specific phases of industrialization in particular historical contexts. The integration thesis, an offshoot of modernization theory that reflects the contemporary neoliberal approach to globalization, argues that industrialization benefits women by absorbing them into the formal labor force via adequately paying jobs that increase their economic and social well-being. The exploitation thesis, an expression of socialist-feminist theory that also reflects contemporary critiques of globalization, holds that the capitalist economy takes advantage of pre-existing patriarchal relations to create a vulnerable category of low-wage women workers who are drawn en masse into insecure, poorly paying, and exploitive industrial jobs. Finally, the marginalization thesis, an offshoot of Esther Boserup's (1970) classic study of women's economic roles and the women-in-development (WID) tradition it spawned, claims that industrialization relegates women to the periphery of the labor market because patriarchal practices favor men for jobs in modern industry. Both the integration and exploitation narratives, despite their contradictory assumptions about the nature of industrial jobs, concur that women are as or more apt than men to be drawn into manufacturing. The marginalization thesis, by contrast, holds that debates over the conditions in manufacturing jobs become increasingly irrelevant for women, who are expelled from the workforce in massive numbers as industrialization proceeds.

These theoretical considerations have led me to wonder whether globalization has caused as distinctive a break from our historical past as the feminization-of-labor thesis would lead us to believe. Could it be that in our preoccupation with the forces leading to women's integration (and exploitation) within transnational firms and industries, we risk losing sight of the opposite side of the coin — the trends that expel women from the formal workforce into the ranks of the un- and underemployed? At the risk of making a generalization abstracted from historically situated contexts, I would argue that the history of industrialization shows certain regularities in women's participation in manufacturing that offer important caveats for social scientists attempting to come to grips with globalization.

Industrialization and Gender

The twentieth century witnessed a shift from industrialization models emphasizing production for domestic consumption (import-substitution industrialization or ISI) to alternative models favoring production for global markets (export-oriented industrialization or EOI). Fueled by TNC investment, EOI links regions in a manufacturing division of labor through which the labor process is geographically dispersed according to the factors of production in which regions have a comparative advantage, whether in research and design, capital-intensive manufacturing, or labor-intensive assembly of components manufactured elsewhere. The Mexican maquiladora industry was one of the earliest examples of EOI in the Western Hemisphere, emerging along the border in the 1960s when the rest of Mexico was committed to ISI and becoming two decades later the model for EOI in the rest of the country. A characteristic feature of EOI is its effect on the gender division of labor. In contrast to ISI, which primarily created jobs for male workers, EOI favors women in a pattern that harkens back to the early phases of industrialization during the late eighteenth and nineteenth centuries.

When textile manufacturing inaugurated the industrial revolution in

Western Europe and the United States, women and children constituted the bulk of the industrial workforce. As cottage industries gave way to the factory system, which encouraged the use of mechanized technologies that reduced requirements for physical size and strength (Beechey 1978), the relatively low cost of female labor became a key factor governing the gender composition of the manufacturing workforce. When child labor laws reduced the participation of children and adolescents, women's share of the workforce increased accordingly. As Louise Lamphere (1987) documents in her study of American industrialization, with the evolution of textile manufacturing the composition of the female workforce changed accordingly. Whereas in earlier epochs young single women predominated in textile manufacturing, as the industry expanded it absorbed growing proportions of older, married women, many of whom had immigrated from abroad. Yet with continuing industrialization, as metal production and other capital-intensive industries came to predominate over the light consumer goods industries, women lost their disproportionate share of the manufacturing workforce (Nash 1983).

Similarly, women were the preferred labor force during the initial stages of industrialization in Latin America (Lobato 1997; Nash 1983; Veccia 1997; Weinstein 1997). However, as the industrial sector became more capital-intensive and technologically sophisticated, men came to predominate in the durable goods industries and increased their share of jobs in textiles, apparel, and other light industries (Schmink 1986). In turn-of-the-century Mexico, when textile production was the main form of manufacturing, about 76,000 women held factory jobs; after forty years of industrial diversification, the female labor force had been reduced by half (Vaughan 1979). Similar patterns have been described for twentieth-century Brazil (Saffioti 1975; Schmink 1986).

Elsewhere (Tiano 1994), I have attributed women's declining share of industrial jobs to the dialectical interworking of capitalism, which organizes people on the basis of class relations, and patriarchy, which subordinates women to men on the basis of gender. Patriarchy is rooted in a gender division of labor that symbolically assigns men to the public sphere and women to the domestic sphere and in an attendant ideology of reproduction that defines women in terms of their roles as wives and mothers. When women enter the labor force, they are viewed, regardless of their actual domestic circumstances, as subsidiary wage earners for households supported by a male breadwinner (Beechey 1978). The image that they are merely temporary workers with minimal job commitment becomes a justification for paying them less than men are paid and for concentrating them in "female" jobs (Fernández-Kelly 1983). It also leads women to function as a surplus labor reserve, to be drawn into the labor force during periods of economic expansion and to be expelled back into the household or the informal economy during periods of economic contraction (Saffioti 1975). Class, race, and other systems of inequality mediate these dynamics to shape each woman's circumstances, which in turn reflect her agency in forging strategies of accommodation or resistance (Collins 1999). Yet in spite of the varied ways these forces manifest in particular contexts, they underlie global regularities that create gender-segregated labor markets, gender-based inequalities in wages and working conditions, and contrasting rates of female and male labor force participation.[1]

These considerations suggest two alternative scenarios of women's labor force participation in the contemporary era of global capitalist expansion. The feminization-of-labor thesis stresses women's unprecedented, large-scale incorporation into the industrial labor force under conditions of globalization. According to this perspective, the corporate imperative to maximize profits by employing the cheapest available labor has led to women's preferential recruitment by TNC manufacturing firms (as well as the increasing use of women's labor through outsourcing, subcontracting, and home-based production). The result is a qualitative change in global labor markets, reflecting an erosion of traditional impediments to women's labor force participation. The feminization-of-labor perspective has contrasting implications, depending on whether women's increasing economic activity is seen as a progressive step toward their liberation from patriarchy, as the integration thesis would have it, or as a regrettable reflection of their vulnerability within capitalist productive relations, as the exploitation thesis claims. Yet regardless of their stance about the consequences for women, proponents of the feminization-of-labor scenario concur that globalization leads to women's steadily increasing incorporation into the labor force, both within and outside of the manufacturing sector.

An alternative scenario, which is more consistent with the marginalization-of-women thesis, emphasizes the insecurity of women's recently acquired foothold within the global manufacturing workforce. This scenario stresses the vulnerability of women's economic activity to industrial restructuring and the cyclical rhythms of expansion and contraction that are endemic to the capitalist economy. While all workers are subject to the periodic oscillations that determine labor demand in boom and bust cycles, women are particularly vulnerable to economic downswings. In periods of economic contraction, men's need for employment combines with patriarchal hiring practices to funnel them into manufacturing jobs that originally absorbed a primarily female workforce. Conversely, when periods of economic expansion entail a restructuring of the manufacturing sector to include a broader range of capital-intensive industries requiring a technically skilled workforce, men are favored over women for the upgraded industrial jobs. In this scenario, the upsurge in women's economic activity during the initial stages of globalization is a temporary phase within an overall process of global capitalist expansion that will sooner or later relegate women to the margins of the industrial labor force.[2]

Is the global corporations' preference for female labor an enduring phenomenon with long-lasting implications for the gender composition of the manufacturing workforce, as the feminization-of-labor scenario implies? Or will patriarchal relations assert themselves to draw women out of the formal workforce in a way that reinforces their symbolic assignment to the domestic sphere, as the marginalization-of-women thesis would predict? A particularly apt context for considering these questions is the U.S.–Mexico border, which houses the world's largest and one of its oldest EOI programs.

Women's Employment in the Maquiladora Industry

Among the many ironies of the maquiladora program is that, although it was intended to provide jobs for men, women were preferred for assembly jobs. Initially, this angered many analysts who argued that maquiladora jobs were wasted on women (Woog 1980) and lamented that women's employment was threatening the Mexican family by eroding traditional gender roles (Tiano and Ladino 1999). The maquiladoras' hiring practices continued despite such criticism, creating in the first decade of the program a workforce in which between 80 and 90 percent of maquiladora workers were women (Fernández-Kelly 1983). Although women's proportionate representation declined somewhat over time, they continued to predominate at the end of the 1980s, when over two-thirds of maquiladora operatives were women (Sklair 1993).

In the industry's early years, most women workers were young, single, and childless. Their recruitment reflected TNC labor practices worldwide, which favored younger women because they were seen as being easier to train, less apt to organize, and unlikely to acquire the job seniority that could legitimate demands for wage increases (Fernández-Kelly 1983). My research into the hiring practices of maquiladora employers in Mexicali during the early 1980s (Tiano 1994) revealed a characteristic ideology that justified recruiting young single women. These women, employers uniformly agreed, made better workers because they did not have demanding husbands or children who could interfere with their job performance. Also, by hiring women who would work for a short period of time before quitting their jobs to marry and raise children, employers told me, they were helping shore up the Mexican family by refusing to lure married women and mothers into the labor force. As the industry expanded throughout the decade, causing employers to complain of labor shortages and rapid labor turnover, the workforce composition became more heterogeneous with the inclusion of more older married and single mothers. When I re-interviewed Mexicali maquiladora employers in 1990, I found that their hiring practices and images of the ideal worker had shifted in a manner that reflected the changing composition of the female workforce. Now they related that married mothers made better workers because they were more mature, reliable, and less apt to jump from job to job than single women, who were immature, frivolous, and more interested in finding a man than in devoting themselves to their jobs. Employers took pride in the fact that by hiring married and single mothers who needed jobs to support their children, they were helping to strengthen the Mexican family. Thus, while employers continued the patriarchal practice of defining women in terms of their reproductive roles as wives and mothers, the content of their patriarchal images had shifted to accommodate the changing nature of the maquiladora workforce and the hiring practices that had shaped its composition.

A key reason for the rapid expansion of the maquiladora industry during the 1980s was Mexico's debt crisis, which inaugurated a structural adjustment program designed to strengthen the Mexican economy. These economic policies were intended to privatize state-run enterprises, reduce government spending on domestic welfare projects, and direct the industrial sector toward export promotion (Elson 1992). These structural adjustment policies have brought incredible hardship to the Mexican population, which has endured the contraction of employment opportunities, the rising cost of goods and services, and the erosion of state-supported education, health care, and other social programs (Chant 1991). A growing empirical literature has documented the creative strategies Mexican households have formulated to survive chronic economic crises, including increased participation in the informal economy and migration to available jobs in the United States or in border or interior maquiladoras (Bene-ría 1992). The maquiladora industry's rapid expansion since the 1980s could not have occurred without a growing pool of surplus labor available for maquiladora recruitment.

As Leslie Sklair (1993) demonstrates in his analysis of maquiladora growth patterns, labor costs are the key factor regulating the pace of maquiladora investment. Even during periods of rapid expansion when maquiladora managers have complained about labor shortages and high labor turnover, they have been reluctant to raise maquiladora wages much above the legal minimum (Sklair 1993; Tiano 1994). When the debt crisis peaked in 1982, the Mexican government enacted a series of peso devaluations to attract the foreign currency to pay its growing debt. Continuing throughout the 1980s along with government-implemented minimum-wage ceilings that kept wages from rising (Cockroft 1983), the devaluations steadily eroded the real value of Mexican workers' wages. By the end of the decade, the minimum wage for maquiladora operatives, in dollar equivalents, was $0.80 per hour, about what it had been in 1970 (Sklair 1993). These trends, which continued into the 1990s, led to a dramatic rise in maquiladora investment by making Mexican workers some of the lowest paid in the world (Fussell 2000; Tiano 1994). With the added incentive of the North American Free Trade Agreement (NAFTA), which inaugurated another dramatic peso devaluation in 1995, and buoyed by the U.S. economic boom during the late 1990s, the maquiladora industry experienced record-breaking growth. In 1980, the maquiladoras employed about 120,000 workers; by 1990, their numbers had risen to over 400,000; and at its high point in 1999, some 1.3 million held maquiladora jobs (Fullerton and Barraza de Anda 2003; Sklair 1993).

Yet the first years of the twenty-first century reversed the dramatic expansion of the two preceding decades. In 2000, the United States entered a recession that dampened TNC investment in Mexico and elsewhere. Similar trends in the global economy had an analogous effect on European and Asian investment in Mexico. Even bare-bones maquiladora wages have not been sufficient to reverse the trend, which has been compounded by China's entrance into the World Trade Organization (Fullerton and Barraza de Anda 2003). Only time will tell whether the maquiladora industry's recent contraction is but a temporary downturn in its expansionary evolution or whether it will lose out to lower-wage competitors in China and elsewhere.

One possible counteractive is the restructuring that has accompanied the maquiladora industry's expansion. Since the 1980s, assembly processing has been supplemented by a growing array of firms manufacturing industrial components (Wilson 1992). As maquiladoras have diversified and become more capital intensive, they have expanded beyond the "light" industrial sectors such as apparel and electronics to incorporate a growing number of firms manufacturing automobiles and other consumer durables. Jorge Carrillo describes three distinct "generations" of maquiladoras (Carrillo and Hualde 1998). The first generation took root when TNCs were transferring to Mexico only the most labor-intensive tasks, mainly component assembly and testing. It was joined by a second generation during the 1980s, when TNCs in the electronics, automobile, and auto-parts industries began investing in manufacturing maquiladoras as a result of industrial restructuring, which accelerated in the post-NAFTA period. Carrillo sees a third generation of maquiladoras emerging, of which Ciudad Juárez–based Delphi–General Motors (GM) is prototypical. Established in 1995 as a second-generation maquiladora, it entered the third generation when GM transferred one of its research-and-development centers to Ciudad Juárez (Carrillo and Hualde 1998, 87). If other TNCs follow suit, the maquiladora industry will continue to expand even if many first-generation maquiladoras move to China or elsewhere in pursuit of ever-lower wages.

Yet a troubling sign for the maquiladora industry is the outmoded infrastructure of the border cities whose destinies are being shaped by maquiladora expansion. Mexico's economic troubles during the post-NAFTA period have accelerated migration to the border cities that offer the best employment opportunities available to many Mexican workers. The flood of migrants would have likely been larger were it not for the shortage of housing and other urban amenities.[3] Ciudad Juárez, which holds the dubious distinction of being "one of the most troubled urban areas in the Western Hemisphere" (Wright 2001, 93), may be an outlier among Mexican border cities. Yet all are experiencing the effects of rapid maquiladora expansion coupled with declining public revenues for refurbishing their eroding infrastructures.

Although the incentives that have lured firms to the border have enabled them to externalize the costs of doing business there, governmental funds for urban renovation have been insufficient to compensate for the pressure on city services resulting from rapid maquiladora expansion. A plan to raise corporate funds for investment in Ciudad Juárez's infrastructure is currently being spearheaded by a group of maquiladoras that recognize the need for urban renewal so they can make Ciudad Juárez the "Silicon Valley of Mexico" (Wright 2001, 94). Unless such attempts at civic responsibility become commonplace in border cities, the growing inadequacy of urban services could hamper continuing maquiladora investment.

Did the upsurge in maquiladora employment favor women over men, as the feminization-of-labor thesis would predict? Or did the proliferation of second-generation manufacturing maquiladoras during these expansionary years lead to the recruitment of men, as the marginalization-of-women thesis would suggest? Aggregate data on women's and men's employment trends show how the maquiladora industry's dramatic expansion and subsequent contraction have affected the gender composition of its workforce along the border.

Women's Employment in Border Maquiladoras Since 1990

The data presented in table 5.1 reflect maquiladora employment patterns in the border states of Baja California, Sonora, Chihuahua, Coahuila, and Tamaulipas from 1990 onward.

These data show the rapid growth during the 1990s of border maquiladora employment, which climbed from a little over 400,000 jobs at the decade's onset to almost a million by the decade's end. They also show

TABLE 5.1 Gender Composition of Border Maquiladora Labor Force, 1990–2003

Year	Total number of employees[1]	Change	Men	Change	Women	Change	Proportion of women
1990	402,432						
1991	413,841	0.03					
1992	443,361	0.07					
1993	465,568	0.05					
1994	500,812	0.08					
1995	545,659	0.09					
1996	617,499	0.13					
1997	729,587	0.18	358,284		371,303		50.9%
1998	805,958	0.10	402,388	0.12	403,570	0.09	50.1%
1999	887,955	0.10	451,668	0.12	436,286	0.08	49.1%
2000	998,841	0.12	510,195	0.13	488,647	0.12	48.9%
2001	930,932	−0.07	480,302	−0.06	450,630	−0.08	48.4%
2002	839,843	−0.10	438,393	−0.09	401,450	−0.11	47.8%
2003[2]	827,448	−0.01	431,700	−0.02	395,748	−0.01	47.8%

Source: Instituto Nacional de Estadística Geografía e Informática (INEGI). 2003. *Estadística de la industria maquiladoradora de exportación*. http://www.inegi.gob.mx
[1]Totals are based on yearly averages.
[2]Data for 2003 encompass period from January until October.

that maquiladora jobs proliferated more quickly in the second half of the decade, reflecting the stimulus of NAFTA and the 1995 peso devaluation. The reversal of this trend is also reflected in these data, which demonstrate a loss of 171,393 jobs between 2000 and 2003. Because the Instituto Nacional de Estadística Geografía e Informática (INEGI), the government bureau that compiles maquiladora industry data (Instituto Nacional de Estadística Geografía e Informática 2003), did not present separate data for male and female technical and administrative employees until 1997, only within the operatives category that encompasses production workers can we assess women's employment trends during the entire fourteen-year period. I have excluded these disaggregated data to simplify the table but refer to them to illuminate the trends depicted in these data.

The preferential recruitment of women that characterized the industry's early years had by 1997 given way to alternative practices that were pulling men into the workforce. That year, when job growth peaked at 18 percent, women constituted a very slight majority (50.9 percent) of maquiladora workers. By 1998, the proportions of men and women in border maquiladoras were almost equal (49.9 percent and 50.1 percent), and by 1999 men had come to occupy a majority (50.9 percent) of maquiladora jobs. Since then, women's proportionate representation in the border maquiladora labor force has shown a slow but steady decline, with women constituting less than 48 percent of the border maquiladora workforce in 2003.

During the expansionary late 1990s, men were absorbed into maquiladora jobs at higher rates than women were. Between 1998 and 1999, for example, the male workforce increased by almost 50,000, while the female workforce grew by less than 33,000. While male employment grew by 10 percent between 1997 and 2000, the growth in female employment exceeded this level only during the 1999–2000 period. Similarly, women lost ground more rapidly than men did during the turn-of-the-century contraction in maquiladora employment. In 2000, when the male workforce shrank by 6 percent, female employment declined by 8 percent. When the contraction accelerated in 2001, the female workforce dropped by 11 percent, compared to a 9 percent decline in male employment. Not until 2003, when the industry showed signs of recovering from its downturn and the erosion of maquiladora employment slowed, did the declines in women's and men's employment levels reach parity.

The disaggregated data for the operatives, technicians, and administrative employees (not shown in the table) parallel the trends for the maquiladora workforce as a whole. The proportion of women operatives steadily declined from 60 percent in 1990 to 52 percent in 2003. Similarly, women's share of skilled technical jobs dropped from 27 percent in 1997 to 25 percent in 2003, while their share of administrative jobs fell from 40 percent to 37 percent during the same period. Thus, women lost ground not only in the technical and administrative jobs in which they have traditionally been underrepresented but also in the production sector where they have historically held the lion's share of maquiladora jobs. Because production operatives constituted about 80 percent of the maquiladora workforce throughout the period, women's declining participation in production jobs accounted for much of the drop in their maquiladora employment, although their declining share of technical and administrative jobs also contributed to this trend. The steady erosion of their participation occurred in both the expansionary late 1990s and the recession that began in 2000.

Only time will tell whether the turn-of-the-century contraction was an aberration within an overall trend of maquiladora expansion, or whether it portends more frequent convulsions in the years ahead. The fact that women's share of maquiladora employment declined in both expansionary and contractionary periods suggests that the factors shaping the gender composition of the workforce operate independently of the forces that stimulate or retard maquiladora investment. These trends are more consistent with predictions of the marginalization-of-women thesis than the feminization-of-labor narrative.

Discussion

Although data on maquiladora employment trends depict changes in the gender composition of the workforce, they reveal little about the factors that have stimulated these shifts. The labor market dynamics that funnel specific population sectors into industrial jobs reflect conditions that affect the supply of potential workers in firms' applicant pools and those that shape employers' demand for workers with particular characteristics. In Mexican border cities, where the recurrent economic crises plaguing the country have forced most of the working-age population to generate income through any available means and a steady stream of migrants has augmented the economically active population, firms have generally enjoyed a plentiful supply of applicants for maquiladora employment.[4] The composition of the maquiladora workforce has thus depended on recruitment practices that reflect employers' demand for workers with specific characteristics and qualifications.

In my Mexicali-based research on maquiladora employers' images of the ideal maquiladora worker that informed their recruitment practices (Tiano 1994), I found a close fit between their hiring criteria and the composition of Mexicali's maquiladora workforce. When I began my research in the early 1980s, the overwhelming majority of workers were women. Employers consistently told me that the assembly jobs that constituted the bulk of maquiladora employment were women's jobs for which men rarely applied and were even less apt to be hired.[5] Over the course of the decade, as I noted previously, Mexicali employers' image of the ideal woman worker changed from a preference for young single women to older married or single mothers in a way that paralleled the increasing heterogeneity of the female workforce. Whether explaining their preference for younger or older women workers, their narratives were remarkably similar: their ideal worker was more reliable, more committed to her job, and thus less apt to contribute to labor turnover than her female counterpart at a contrasting life cycle stage was. Regardless of whether their hiring practices and justificatory narratives favored young or more chronologically mature women, however, it was women, rather than men, who fit employers' image of the ideal worker. The recruitment practices that reflected these hiring criteria generated a predominantly female workforce throughout the 1980s, when most maquiladoras belonged to the first generation.

As Melissa Wright (2001) convincingly demonstrates, by the late 1990s the gendered narratives that define the ideal maquiladora worker had undergone a dramatic shift. The second-generation manufacturing firms that aim to make Ciudad Juárez the "Silicon Valley of Mexico" have inaugurated a narrative that disparages women for causing rapid job turnover, which they blame for impairing Ciudad Juárez's efforts to attract investment in second-generation manufacturing firms. Wright exemplifies their discourse through a series of statements from maquiladora managers linking job turnover to women's gender roles, which closely parallel the accounts related to me by Mexicali managers. The primary difference is that while I observed a shift in the discourse over time from one that attributed irresponsibility, lack of job commitment, and high job turnover initially to older women and later to younger ones, Wright's respondents attributed these negative qualities to *all* women: "whether married or unmarried, with children or without, having too much fun or too little, turnover is linked to Mexican femininity" (Wright 2001, 103). The corollary discourse is that men demonstrate the job stability that makes them the ideal maquiladora workers. Wright's focus is the use of this discourse to exclude women from the educational and training programs that prepare workers for better-paying, more highly skilled jobs in which they are apt to remain for longer periods, thereby generating a self-fulfilling prophesy through which women are confined to turnover-reinforcing, dead-end assembly jobs. Yet she also notes its likely effect on the gender composition of the workforce when she quotes a personnel director's answer to her query about whether their attribution of high turnover to women will increase men's share of maquiladora employment: "Yes, I think so. But that is already happening. With more skilled labor, you will always have more men" (Wright 2001, 108). To the extent that this discourse and the hiring practices it reinforces are coming to characterize maquiladora investment sites beyond Ciudad Juárez, it is likely a key factor leading to the increasingly male composition of the maquiladora workforce along the border.

The marginalization-of-women narrative, with its emphasis on the interaction between capitalism and patriarchy, illuminates these trends. Unlike the feminization-of-labor thesis, which assumes that the corporate quest for cheap and docile labor is sufficient to maintain women's predominance in globalized jobs, the marginalization narrative expects patriarchal relations and ideologies to modify corporate recruitment practices and the resulting gender composition of the workforce. During EOI's initial stages, when most jobs are de-skilled and poorly paid, employers' definition of them as "women's" jobs will create a predominantly female workforce. Even if employers are willing to hire men, few will want to participate in feminized jobs within a gender-segregated workforce. The feminization-of-labor narrative accurately describes workforce composition at this stage of industrialization, when most jobs reflect the unskilled assembly labor characterizing first-generation maquiladoras. If industrialization remains exclusively devoted to assembly processing, its labor force is apt to remain feminized.[6] However, if conditions are suitable to attracting TNC investment in manufacturing, the gender composition of the workforce will become less feminized as men are differentially recruited and trained for the upgraded jobs. Men's increasing participation in skilled manufacturing positions will erode barriers to male entry into less-skilled assembly jobs, in effect masculinizing jobs that were originally defined as women's domain. The changing gender composition of the maquiladora industry, where men have increased their representation not merely as technicians, engineers, and administrators but also as production operatives, reflects this dynamic.

As Wright (2001), who has monitored this process in Ciudad Juárez, points out, women are as able as men are to receive the necessary training for skilled technical jobs, and many would wish to equip themselves with the needed skills and qualifications for the better-paying positions. However, they are generally overlooked due to patriarchal discourses that define women primarily in terms of their reproductive roles as wives and mothers and assume that their familial commitments necessarily contribute to employment instability and rapid job turnover.

While these patriarchal images are most pronounced in second-generation manufacturing maquiladoras, women's declining share of production jobs throughout the industry suggests that patriarchal discourses are also shaping hiring practices in the first-generation firms that continue to employ most maquiladora workers. The fact that women lost ground in all types of maquiladora jobs during both the expansionary period of the late 1990s and the recession of the early 2000s suggests that the forces underlying their increasing marginalization from the maquiladora industry are not a simple reflection of economic factors that condition labor supply and demand, as the feminization-of-labor narrative implies. The marginalization-of-women thesis, which stresses the role of patriarchal recruitment practices and ideologies in shaping the gender composition of the workforce, provides a more apt explanation for the decline in women's proportionate participation in the maquiladora industry. The steady decline in women's employment dominance in export-led industries along the border parallels a similar drop in their industrial participation decades earlier in central Mexico, as the industrial sphere became less labor-intensive. More generally, it reflects the changing composition of the industrial workforce in Western Europe and the United States, with the continuing evolution of their manufacturing sectors. The contemporary trends along the Mexican border appear to be repeating the historically prevalent pattern of women's marginalization from industrial employment.

Without reference to the adequacy of maquiladora working conditions and wage scales — the issue that drives the integration-exploitation debate — it is difficult to assess what their declining maquiladora participation means for border women's lives. Although this question framed my Mexicali-based research (Tiano 1987b, 1994), in the present discussion I have sidestepped it under the convenient assumption that if women are increasingly marginalized from the maquiladora workforce, the working conditions in maquiladora firms will be less and less relevant for them.

This issue may nevertheless be relevant to understanding the factors contributing to women's increasing marginalization from maquiladora employment. Most researchers agree that the conditions and wages in maquiladora jobs have not improved much in the last decade, particularly in first-generation maquiladoras (Cravey 1997; Fussell 2000; Wright 1997). Men's increasing participation in the industry does not appear to have made jobs less feminized or flexible. Guy Standing's (1989, 1999) insight about the feminization of employment conditions in export jobs that has limited their appeal to all but the most desperate workers, whether female or male, is not inconsistent with these data. The increasing masculinization of maquiladora labor described herein reflects the composition of the workforce rather than the conditions in maquiladora jobs, most of which remain highly feminized regardless of the gender of the workers who hold them. In contrast to Standing's argument that the feminization of work and the workforce go hand in hand, these considerations suggest that work feminization can also accompany trends that lead to a more masculine gender composition of the workforce.[7]

The masculinization of the border maquiladora workforce stands in contrast to what many globalization scholars apparently consider a universal link between EOI and the feminization of the global labor force. The Mexican maquiladora program's proximity to U.S. corporations and markets has imparted a distinctive cast to its evolution, promoting its rapid expansion in the post-NAFTA era and increasing its ability to attract TNC investment in manufacturing, as well as assembly processing. Also, its status as one of the world's longest-running and largest EOI programs differentiates it from other, more recently established export zones elsewhere in the world. Yet there is no reason to assume that the global processes that have shaped the maquiladora industry's evolution are dissimilar to those impacting other export zones. Indeed, Mexico's experience may herald similar changes in EOI programs in other geographical contexts as their industrialization proceeds. Whether the Mexican maquiladora industry's experience is unique, or instead prefigures similar trends in other export zones as they evolve, it demonstrates that women's participation in export-led industries is less assured than globalization and the New International Division of Labor (NIDL) scholars have previously believed.

6 The Roots of Autonomy through Work Participation in the Northern Mexico Border Region

Ana Bergareche

This chapter draws on interviews with fifty-five low-income women in Ciudad Juárez to investigate the conditions under which employment leads to autonomy. Based on my research, I argue that two factors— gender solidarity and a positive spiritual identity—contribute to women becoming autonomous through work participation. To understand autonomy better, I look specifically at women's narratives about overcoming sexual violence. The ability to overcome sexual violence is important here as it is an indicator of women's autonomy and empowerment.

Data collection took place between June 1994 and April 1997 and involved in-depth interviews and participant observation. I conducted fifty-five interviews with low-income women in the peripheral barrio known as Granjas. The study group was heterogeneous in terms of women's work trajectories and family structures. Most of the women, however, had been employed in a maquiladora at some stage. The interviews were structured as a series of life histories where the women discussed their working experiences. While answering questions about work, women talked about a broader spectrum of gender relations, including family and sexual relationships, opportunities for education and self-fulfilment, and sexual violence. One of the implications of the women's wide-ranging discussion was that work status lost its central place in the discussion of autonomy, allowing alternative variables to emerge and explain women's resistance strategies. In particular, the interviews revealed that spiritual identity and gender solidarity often shaped women's experiences of autonomy through employment.

During the last two decades, the promotion of maquiladoras has been a major focus of Mexican government policy, reinforced by the North American Free Trade Agreement (NAFTA) between the United States, Canada, and Mexico. Various elements currently constitute a threat to the further expansion of the maquiladoras, such as international competition, the low salaries, the state's inability to improve urban infrastructure, and the lack of integration between foreign investment and local industries (Expansión 1990; Pradilla and Castro García 1994). Since the turn of the century, some of these forces have reduced the number of maquiladoras, reduced the number of workers who are female, and increased unemployment in Ciudad Juárez (Quintero 1999; Staudt and Coronado 2002; Tiano, this vol.). Nevertheless, maquiladoras remain the major employer of women in Ciudad Juárez (Bayón and Rojas 1999), and maquiladora employment the driving force behind migration from the rest of Mexico to Ciudad Juárez. Many migrants have entered the maquiladora workforce upon their arrival in the city and later have found different jobs and means of economic survival.

Women's paths towards autonomy in the context of maquiladora employment are part of the restructuring of third world societies by colonialist and capitalist penetration. This restructuring has shaped gender relations, the nature of the sexual division of labor, and the social and political options open to men and women. Structural changes have been brought about by the requirements of the World Bank and the International Monetary Fund, requirements designed to deal with the debt crisis suffered by many third world countries as well as promote their incorporation into the international division of labor. In northern Mexico, such strategies have translated into massive investment in export-processing industrialization. Following the work of development scholars interested in social change (Long 1977; Moore 1965), this chapter explores the variety of responses of individuals to these structural changes. Such variety is attributed to sociocultural factors that are historically and culturally specific, a view that leads to the notion of women as active agents of their lives, regardless of whether they succeed or not in exploiting and/or resisting new opportunities (Stølen and Vaa 1991).

Contextualizing Autonomy

Autonomy constitutes a key issue in the question posed in this chapter. It is defined as an individual process that translates into women's capability to take control over their lives and to reinforce positive notions of self through a sense of power that derives from within (Kabeer 1994). A natural manifestation of this process relates to women's ability to transform their status within abusive relationships, turning from victims into autonomous women. Autonomy and empowerment go hand-in-hand, the latter constituting women's ability to use their personal autonomy in a wider social context that involves community networks and institutions. Therefore, both concepts are assumed interdependent as well as connected to wider social structures (Duarte and González 1994). Another key variable in this analysis is sexual violence, which I treat as a continuum that manifests at the physical, psychological, social, and institutional levels (Kelly 1988; Stanko 1985). Within this framework, I focus on instances of domestic violence, including marital rape and rape perpetrated by relatives, because these were the most commonly found in the study.

Women's employment patterns in Ciudad Juárez develop in relation to women's household roles as providers and reproductive agents. One of the social consequences of development in the third world is a movement of household structure away from its traditional form. Women's employment is linked to an ongoing change in household gender roles, in terms of responsibilities assigned to household members both in the productive and reproductive spheres. Previously assumed relationships, such as that between male wage-earning and household authority, are questioned and often altered as part of the dynamics of household survival. In this light, the issue of female-headed households and their significance for women's survival and well-being acquires greater significance. A large percentage of female household heads in Ciudad Juárez have reported health problems and lack of medical services. Nevertheless, female household heads in the border region seem to be better off than their counterparts in the interior are, as they enjoy less restrictive conditions and report relatively higher education levels and salaries (Howard 1994).

A superficial reading of the information above could lead to the conclusion that border women have escaped traditional stereotypes and roles to some extent. Their increased participation in the workforce and their active roles in migration and the labor process could be interpreted as a step towards gender equality. This information, however, offers only limited insight into the meanings women attribute to these experiences and the impact they have on women's well-being. For instance, B. García and de Oliveira (1994) found that although employed women often assume the material maintenance of the household, they tend to attribute the role of "provider" to their unemployed and often violent male partners, showing that women's ongoing internalization of their old roles can have a deadly impact.

Examining the symbolic aspects of women's resistance in a context of structural change can provide some clues into the paradox of women's victimization despite their material advancement. The following section explores this issue, showing some of the ways in which spiritual identity and gender solidarity become significant in women's chosen paths towards a better life, positively affecting their sense of self and therefore their identity as women and workers. Although traditional gender ideals shape women's experiences in and out of the household, the important factor for women's autonomy is the way these traditional ideals are interpreted and exercised in their daily lives. Consequently, I portray women as active agents rather than victims in the dynamics of structural change brought through foreign investment and its associated ideologies in the border region.

The view of women as agents in the development process echoes research carried out on the border during the 1980s and 1990s. This research reflects the prevalence of mixed, flexible, and experience-based attitudes towards work and concludes that workers show resistance, but the resistance is mediated by exposure to political organizations (Peña 1987; Staudt 1983; Young 1987). Devon Peña's later work in Ciudad Juárez reexamines maquiladora employment within the context of informal work organizations (Peña 1997). He identifies multiple forms of struggle and resistance through collective action and association with grassroots organizations. An interesting turn in his analysis relates to the issue of religious affiliation and to how it can contribute to women's political organizing. Similarly, research in a wider development context shows that women most often survive through collectivizing their problems, rather than privatizing them (Aptheker 1989; Blumberg 1995; Ramírez 1993; Safa 1995a; K. Ward and Pyle 1995). Women are found engaged in organizing collective meals, child-care cooperatives, and women's groups, turning daily survival into a potential path toward autonomy. These examples show that women's exercise of their choices can turn an apparently marginal arena like the domestic sphere into an instrument of collective action and personal autonomy. Consequently, focusing on the power of self highlights the possibility for women to transform external ideologies and challenging circumstances to their benefit.

Another example of turning an apparently alienating element into a redeeming one is found in religion. Religion is often described as a powerful source of gender ideology resistant to change (González de la Rocha 1994; M. Torres 1997). We can, however, find clear examples of women finding empowerment through religion. For instance, Safa (1995b) found that the role of the church was crucial in achieving social justice, as women organize in community church groups to reinforce grassroots support. Although these groups are based on traditional women's roles, they offer a base from which to challenge the existing order.

The interconnection between employment and the household has particular analytical significance, since the household is the site where bargaining takes place in women's exercise of their choices (Tiano 1994). Furthermore, the process of socialization of values and ideologies takes place in the context of the household maintenance (Selby et al. 1990). Considering sexual violence as an indicator of women's autonomy allows us to understand new dimensions of subordination, consciousness raising, and change. It is clear that conflict is significant in identifying avenues for power (Wolf 1992). Through examining the significance of the darkest aspects of conflict, such as sexual violence, we may discover not only the depths of human exploitation, but also women's capability to resist, fight, and be reborn through this experience.

The next two sections draw on my research among women workers in Ciudad Juárez to address the relationships between women's employment and their empowerment. The first section emphasizes the influence of women's gender solidarity on their resistance to traditional gender ideology. This resistance is explored through an analysis of employment, autonomy, and sexual violence. The following section follows the same approach in analyzing the influence of spiritual identity on women's resistance strategies.

Women's Paths towards Resistance: Gender Solidarity

Most women between the ages of fourteen and thirty-five (from now on referred to as younger women), as well as migrant women of all ages, use social networks created through their employment in maquiladora factories to achieve autonomy. Workplace networks may alleviate isolation and provide support that can be helpful in this process. In most cases, success resulted from taking advantage of contacts through informal work and voluntary work in non-governmental organizations (NGOs). Therefore, gender solidarity through this type of employment proves to be a valuable tool for migrant women who lack other local connections and support.

Regarding maquiladora employment, all younger women interviewed expressed that it is the most accessible job available. Therefore, they were likely to take maquiladora jobs upon arrival or when all other options have failed. When asked their interpretation of their experience as maquiladora workers, 75 percent of younger women of migrant origin reported that maquiladora employment offered them the option to establish valuable social contacts. These contacts allowed them to experience the sense of support and solidarity missing in other personal circles or at their place of origin. Consequently, it provided the opportunity to enlarge women's networks and offered a potential means towards autonomy and freedom from violence. One woman explained: "I've made friends throughout the plant, I know most people there . . . if I were to choose between working as a domestic and working in a maquiladora I would choose working in a maquiladora even though I get paid less . . . because of the atmosphere and everything, because I feel very comfortable there, I know lots of people and if I need some help, I get it."

When it comes to actually dealing with sexual violence, women's choices and the meanings they attribute to their experiences must be considered within the context of the employment options provided by structural changes. For instance, the jobs that provide women with the possibility of developing support networks are the most effective as a means towards autonomy. This is confirmed through the testimony of 90 percent of migrant women, who referred to this factor as key when confronting victimization. Women also reported that informal work and voluntary work through NGOs were the most effective settings for building networks that enhanced their autonomy. Although maquiladora employment offered the possibility for developing such networks, only a small percentage referred to them as key in finding autonomy.

Often supported by international funding institutions, NGOs provide options that enable women to transcend victimization, offering information and support on reproductive issues, AIDS prevention, and economic projects. Women in all categories had experience in these areas, proving a valuable opportunity for all, particularly those who lacked alternative resources through education and other social networks. The support received often furthered the options for women leaving abusive partners, promoting solidarity and helping them recover from the lack of self-esteem and patterns of dependence:

> He said he was going to change and I don't know what else and I went back to him, but he stayed the same . . . then as I had my children I started to work, to look for something for my children to eat, so I went with my *comadre* who sells clothes and told her I was going to help her and after that I decided to separate from him because one day he took the money I had made, he took it and spent it, so I went and told his father and mother and they said, "It's your problem." "OK," I said, "since it's my problem I'm going to solve it" . . . since I realized I didn't need him anymore and he continued drinking I thought we'd better separate, if I can work to give my children what they need, it's best to be alone.
>
> Yes, there were problems at home, my father didn't let my mother go out, but now she has changed quite a bit, she wasn't one of those people who answered back but did what she was told and not anymore, as if she has liberated, as if she's liberated from him and now she says she doesn't fear him anymore . . . and she hangs out with one of those groups from PRI and God knows what.

Women's Paths towards Resistance: Spiritual Identity

Having established the relevance of gender solidarity through certain types of employment as a means towards autonomy, I will now focus on the role of spiritual identity in this process. Among migrant women over thirty-five with low education levels, those holding positive perspectives on religion were more likely to find autonomy through work participation, especially if they had managed to reduce poverty levels. Among them, migrant women who established contact with community religious groups increased their chances of finding autonomy through work. When it came to overcoming abuse, older partnered women who could channel their spiritual beliefs towards personal growth had a greater chance to find autonomy, counteracting external limitations such as migrant origin or low education. This is confirmed when adding employment to the equation, since 95 percent of those who found autonomy through employment were older, migrant, and had low education levels.

The ability to channel spiritual beliefs into growth experiences had a positive impact on the daily lives of older migrant women with low education. They interpreted religious notions for their own benefit when it came to the material aspects of their life, including their work experience. This is illustrated by the testimony below, which refers to this woman's faith in spiritual forces as responsible for her work success. This perception may be particularly useful for women in situations of domestic violence, since their beliefs can potentially generate the strength to use material resources in achieving autonomy:

> There's something about me, I don't know how to read or write but there's something about me, when I have a problem I talk to my Father [referring to God] and it gets somehow sorted out, it really does . . . I've talked to different people and they've said that what saves me is my faith . . . "You have a lot of faith, but a lot of faith" . . . because now that we were worried about the dollars . . . "Who is going to lend me money if I have nothing?" then I got some information and that's how we started, and suddenly I got the loan here in Juárez . . . all my life I've suffered a lot anyway, but I'm very grateful to God because he's given me everything I've asked for . . . thanks to the loan I could build my own business and that's how my family survives.

In some instances, the availability of support networks and a positive spiritual identity combined in this process. One such instance was found in feminist religious groups following liberation theology, which questioned the traditional interpretation of the biblical texts. A well-known women's group in Ciudad Juárez focused on the reinterpretation of the Bible from women's standpoints, providing the means for solidarity links that may lead towards autonomy. The women who benefited from this experience were mostly older partnered women with low education and of migrant origin. The group provided them with an alternative support network that promoted consciousness raising from within their particular system of values and beliefs:

> In some places they defend women a lot, I envy those places . . . you need protection as a woman, because women are weaker and cannot defend themselves so easily . . . I now cannot get pregnant and I think that is caused by the beatings and I feel a lot of courage. . . . I feel very comfortable because you can talk about your things and it's people you trust . . . sometimes I feel depressed and I go to the meetings and feel much better, if I didn't have that group I'd probably feel trapped, because I can't tell my mum, she's a good person, but I'd hurt her.

Some women interpreted freedom from violence and the positive changes derived from it as a consequence of their spiritual faith. Those who channel such beliefs into lasting change, however, often expressed a religious identity that departed from traditional paternalistic attitudes. In such cases, women expressed their experience of growing autonomy as derived from God and referred to the way in which divine forces operated through them rather than beyond them. Younger women were less likely to have put their beliefs into practice through life-changing events such as confronting sexual violence. Older women who had managed to change their lives truly believed that God played a major part in giving them the strength to achieve real transformation. This was the case among older partnered women regardless of education level or migrant origin, showing that the relevance of spiritual identity to women's autonomy counteracts the absence of outside resources, information, and support:

> When he arrived she'd already had her operation, that's when I made my decision, I told him, "That's enough, we're going to separate, but I don't want you to come here anymore, I want to do as I want with my life and my children," when I prayed to God I asked him to give me strength not to give my children any more problems, fighting and moving from one place to another, so I said, "I have no need for this, no more."

Regarding the role of spirituality in women's experience of autonomy through work, I have shown that older women often conceptualized work opportunities as a reflection of their spiritual beliefs in God as a protector.

In exploring this issue in relation to sexual violence, I found that among older partnered women, 95 percent of migrants with low education utilized these beliefs in developing personal power. These women benefited from work as a means to overcome victimization and sexual violence in their lives. This is mostly the case when women engage in informal work and work linked to social and political movements.

The testimony of an older partnered migrant woman with little education exemplifies the role of spirituality in women's autonomy through informal work and the support of an NGO. It shows that a positively channeled spiritual identity and the options available through NGOs proved to be a valuable resource for women who otherwise lacked support systems and resources. This woman was the most successful among those in the study group in building a business from a very small loan. Her business brought her financial and emotional independence from an abusive husband, and she was able to support her daughters (who were all separated from their husbands) and grandchildren:

> When I received the loan from FEMAP [Federación Mexicana de Asociaciones Privadas], I was going through a difficult time with my husband [this woman had shared the emotional violence she had suffered throughout her relationship]. . . . but God helps me a lot [repeatedly]. . . . I couldn't believe they were giving me a loan with no interest, those young kids in FEMAP helped me a lot and I ended up being the treasurer of the first community bank . . . they cheered me up a great deal and during that time I felt free . . . after some time I gathered a little fortune . . . about $7,000 in five years, I now work about eight hours per day and earn between $200 and $300 per week.

All of the above testimonies suggest that structural change in northern Mexico has provided women with the opportunity to move into different roles from those women held in the past. Consequently, women are beginning to change their views of the world and their places in it. These changes have the potential to bring a stronger awareness of their capabilities and strengthen their sense of self. In addition, their role as workers has the potential to positively affect gender power relations, providing resources that allow women to avoid becoming victims. Women's spirituality and the availability of support networks reinforce positive attitudes about their working role. Women must, however, be open to transformation in order to take advantage of these factors. The intervening factors that generate a shift from victimization to potential autonomy are found in a strengthened sense of self and solidarity with others. Both these factors enable women to use spirituality and support networks as opportunities for growth and autonomy in many areas of their lives, including work. Life cycle and marital status are also significant factors that influence women's choices, as a sense of self and solidarity is often developed through time and in relation to other people. In the final analysis, the two intervening factors in the relationship between work and autonomy are whether women appropriate their role as workers from a strengthened sense of self and solidarity towards others.

Concluding Comments

The information presented here sheds light on strategies that can be used to strengthen women's options for autonomy. Maquiladoras and other employers could use strategies for building networks and spirituality to improve women's ability to overcome sexual violence in their lives. Such measures would also facilitate women's incorporation into the development process, while improving their productivity as workers and their general well-being. The types of work that provide the resources for women to strengthen their sense of self and solidarity can in themselves constitute a vehicle for change. Informal work and voluntary work seem to fulfill these conditions more fully than other types of work. Maquiladora employment was valued because it provided social contacts and support systems to those who were new to the labor market and/or had few or no other options. Networks established in the workplace potentially offered benefits to women who faced the decision to confront victimization in specific situations of abuse. There were, however, differences in the way specific categories of women took advantage of their resources in this area. For instance, women of migrant origin greatly benefited from the development of support systems through employment, due to their lack of other networks. In contrast, the discourse of older migrant partnered women with little education reflected the significance of their religious faith in achieving autonomy through work.

Employment would offer more support for women's autonomy if it were to facilitate women creating support networks and provide educational programs about the impact of religion and culture in their daily lives. This point is illustrated by women's positive experiences with informal employment supported by community banks and work with NGOs. These types of employment provided women with the means to achieve material independence, to question traditional gender notions (including those inherent in religious beliefs), and to exercise initiative, creativity, and leadership. All of these factors strengthen women's sense of self and promote solidarity, constituting significant elements in achieving autonomy. On the other hand, maquiladora employment offers only the possibility of developing social networks, but whether women use them to work towards autonomy depends on their other personal resources.

In exploring women's resistance strategies through employment, the evidence found reinforces the notion of women as agents of their lives, although women's paths towards autonomy show a complex, challenging, and rewarding journey. There is no doubt that women's ability to overcome victimization and gain autonomy requires a joint effort on the part of individuals and social institutions. Women's conceptualization of their role as workers is transformed through resources that can be provided by adequate employment and state policies. But most significantly, this transformation can contribute to women's greater participation in the economy and to building a better quality of life for them, their families, and future generations of workers.

7 Domestic Service and International Networks of Caring Labor

Doreen J. Mattingly

Five days a week, Rosa[1] boards a city bus that will take her to a distant wealthy neighborhood where she makes her living cleaning houses. Rosa is an undocumented immigrant from Mexico who has lived in San Diego, California, for five years; the $40 she earns each day helps to feed her three children and pay rent on her family's small apartment. Every other Tuesday, Rosa arrives at Laurie's house at 7:30 a.m., just as Laurie, her husband, and their two children are preparing to leave for school and work. Rosa works hard and fast, trying to finish in time to catch the afternoon bus that will get her home in time for dinner. Rosa's youngest child, still a baby, spends the day with Rosa's mother, who emigrated illegally from Mexico just before the baby was born. Laurie, a pharmacist, also faces a hectic day. Before work, she feeds the children breakfast, chats briefly with Rosa, confirms the children's after-school arrangements, and takes her children to school. Her husband, a teacher, picks up the children in the evening. Laurie gets home late, often with take-out food in hand, for a few hours of homework and family time before collapsing on the clean sheets Rosa has left behind.

Rosa and Laurie face many similar challenges each day. Both are working mothers trying to balance their family responsibilities with full-time jobs, and both rely on the labor of immigrant women to meet their domestic responsibilities. Laurie pays for additional labor from a host of low-wage service workers. Many of these workers, including the employees of the restaurant where she buys take-out food, the gardener who tends the yard each week, and Rosa, are immigrants from Mexico. It is an expensive strategy, but one made more affordable by the presence of immigrants willing to work for relatively low wages. Rosa also must rely on the labor of others to help with child care and housework. Unlike Laurie, however, she cannot afford to pay for this care. Nor can she turn to government programs for assistance, since she is in the United States illegally. Rosa's solution was to help her mother emigrate from Mexico so that she can care for Rosa's children and home. In both Rosa's and Laurie's households, the relations of social reproduction cross international borders. While Laurie relies on low-wage immigrant workers to meet the demands of her double day, Rosa draws on transnational family networks to access the additional caring labor she needs.

This chapter draws on in-depth interviews with immigrant domestic workers[2] and employers of domestic workers in San Diego, California, to explore two interconnected issues. First, it investigates the relationship between changes in the organization of social reproduction and women's migration. Analyses of women's international labor migration link women's international migration to changes in the demand for service workers in wealthy nations (Ehrenreich and Hochschild 2002; Momsen 1999; Truong 1996). A focus on migration for domestic service underscores the importance of changes in social reproduction — or caring labor — to flows of immigrants. Because gender divisions of labor tend to assign responsibilities for caring labor to women, changes in the way this work is done tends to influence, and be affected by, women's migration. In a rare paper on the topic, Thanh-Dam Truong (1996) argues that recent increases in female immigration, and the concentration of female immigrants in service work "point to an emerging international division of labor in reproduction" (29).

Around the world, women's emigration for domestic service is expanding in several poorer countries, including the Philippines, Sri Lanka, and Mexico (Bakan and Stasiulis 1994; Hondagneu-Sotelo 1994a; Pratt 1999; Truong 1996). International migration from low-income to high-income countries and regions has accelerated in the 1980s and 1990s, and women are a growing proportion of this flow (United Nations 2000). In the United States, as in many countries in Europe, Asia, and the Middle East, the majority of domestic workers are female immigrants from poorer countries (Ehrenreich and Hochschild 2002; Momsen 1999; Tyner 1996).

The second issue explored in this chapter is how the complex of interconnections of gender, race/ethnicity, and nationality shapes, and is shaped by, the organization of domestic service. Specifically, I examine the interconnections and hierarchies in the way that two very different groups of women manage their responsibilities for caring work. Many of these similarities result from a pervasive gender division of labor that assigns women the daily work of caring for homes and families, a category of labor known as "social reproduction." Caring labor is by and large "women's work." Feminist scholarship has paid particular attention to waged and unwaged "caring labor" or "caring work" (P. England and Folbre 1999; Himmelweit 1999), arguing that women's responsibility for caring labor (whether paid or unpaid) contributes to women's lower earnings (P. England and Folbre 1999). Although the increased paid employment of women with young children has reduced the amount of unpaid labor many women dedicate to caring for their homes and families, it has not significantly changed the gender division of caring work. Even when employed full-time, women remain responsible for most of the unpaid work of caring for their homes and families (Aitken 1998; Gregson and Lowe 1994; Hochschild 1989).

Working mothers have developed a variety of strategies for dealing with their grueling "double day" of paid work and domestic responsibilities. One important strategy is to pass on to others some of the caring work traditionally assigned to female household heads. Some women rely on the unpaid work of family members and close friends (Spain and Bianchi 1996). Research shows that daughters (Manke et al. 1994) and other female family members such as mothers and sisters (Roschelle 1997) are particularly important sources of family labor. Other women, especially those with more money, are able to pay low-wage service workers, most of whom are women, for child care, housekeeping, and food preparation. The enduring gender division of caring labor has meant that the relations of paid household work are largely relations "between women" (Rollins 1985).

Another source of caring labor is the programs of the welfare state. The U.S. safety net has always been partial in its coverage, however, distinguishing between the deserving and undeserving poor (Abramovitz 1988). In the 1990s, citizenship became an important criterion for identifying and refusing the "undeserving" and denying them benefits (Hondagneu-Sotelo 1997). Undocumented immigrants receive the fewest benefits: they are not eligible for tax-supported social services such as food stamps, welfare (formerly Aid to Families with Dependent Children, now Temporary Assistance to Needy Families), public housing assistance, or unemployment insurance. Many of these restrictions also apply to legal residents who obtained their legal status through the legalization programs of the 1986 Immigration Reform and Control Act (IRCA). Since the interviews were conducted, benefits to immigrants have been further reduced by welfare reform.[3] In addition to legal restrictions on state aid, political hostility toward immigrants has focused on their use of social services, further limiting some services and creating a climate where immigrants feel unwelcome in social service institutions. The interviews were being conducted during the campaign for California Proposition 187, which further reduced state support for undocumented immigrants.[4]

To analyze the transactions of caring labor, I conducted in-depth interviews with twenty-nine employers of domestic workers and thirty-five current and former immigrant Mexicana domestic workers in San Diego between August 1993 and May 1994.[5] Respondents were recruited through a variety of techniques. Some employers were contacted through a telephone survey conducted earlier (see Mattingly 1999a); others were found through professional women's organizations or referred by members of the Mexican immigrant community or by other respondents. Domestic workers were contacted in three ways: through referrals from key informants, by approaching women in public, and through referrals from other respondents (snowball sampling). This methodology offers some particular constraints and opportunities. Because the samples are not statistically representative of larger groups, it is impossible to generalize to the entire universe of domestic workers or their employers. In-depth interviews do, however, allow for categories and relationships to emerge from people's varied experiences rather than from preconceived ideas.

San Diego differs from other U.S. border cities in important ways. San Diego's economic structure is fairly polarized, including high-end jobs in technology-intensive sectors alongside a large pool of low-wage jobs in tourism and other services. The pronounced presence of the military and the large number of retirees from other areas contribute to the flavor of the city. While Latinos form the majority in all other border cities, they are a minority in this large metropolis, accounting for roughly a quarter of the population in 2000 (U.S. Census Bureau 2000). San Diego also has significant Asian American and African American communities and is host to new immigrants from around the world. The economic and racial-ethnic structures influence the relations of domestic work. While many employers of domestic workers in other border cities are themselves Latina and of moderate incomes (e.g., V. Ruiz 1987), there are a larger number of San Diego employers who are Anglo, wealthy, and retired.

Employers of Domestic Workers: Transactions in the Marketplace

In general, the employers interviewed had extensive networks of care that were dominated by low-wage service workers. This category includes housekeepers, gardeners, and other workers who came to their home, as well as workers at other locations, such as day-care workers and employees of restaurants and dry cleaners. As such, it is one aspect of the general commodification of care in middle-class U.S. households. Consider the title "soccer mom," which implies a form of parenting that is embedded in semi-public, fee-based organizations and institutions. It is not, however, a strategy that is available to all but rather depends on financial resources.

Table 7.1 shows the characteristics of the twenty-nine employers interviewed. Dividing the respondents based on the employment status of the woman in the household, it contains some general descriptions of the group of respondents, showing that they have above-average incomes and education. On average, the annual household income reported was over $80,000,[6] and over half of the men and women in employer households had some education beyond the bachelor's degree. The majority of households interviewed (62 percent) contained an employed woman. The table also shows that the most common type of paid household work among respondents was housecleaning. All of the respondents paid someone to clean their house. Twenty-four respondents (83 percent) employed only live-out cleaning help; the majority had their house cleaned weekly or bi-weekly. Two employed live-in child-care workers who also did the cleaning and cooking, and one of these also employed a home health-care worker for her disabled son. Two other employers paid for home health care as well as cleaning. Over four-fifths (82.7 percent) of the employers were employing a Mexican immigrant woman at the time of the interview, and all but one had employed at least one Mexicana at some point. On average, the employers interviewed paid for close to seventeen hours of domestic work each month and had employed household workers for close to ten years.

While men and older children contributed to domestic work in some

TABLE 7.1 Characteristics of Employers of Paid Household Workers

Characteristics	All (n=29)	Woman Employed (n=18)	Homemaker (n=2)	No working-age woman in home (n=9)
Type of help (number)				
Cleaning help only	24	15	2	7
In-home child care	2	2	0	0
In-home health care	3	1	0	2
Average household size	2.5	2.8	3.5	1.6
Average annual household income (U.S. dollars)	81,000	90,000	110,000	61,000
Percent of households with children under 18	41.4	55	100	0
Average number of years with paid help	9.9	9.4	14.5	10
Average hours per month of paid household help (cleaners only)	16.9	18	16	15
Percent employing Mexican female immigrant domestic worker	82.7	88.9	50.0	77.7

Source: Personal interviews, Mattingly.

houses, in most cases paid household workers replaced and supplemented women's unpaid labor. Among the twenty-two married couples interviewed, the idea of hiring a domestic worker originated with the woman in nineteen of the couples (86.3 percent), and women were primarily responsible for hiring and supervising domestic workers in eighteen couples (81.2 percent). In only four of the married households was it reported that men and women shared housework evenly before hiring a domestic worker; it is interesting to note that in two of these cases, I interviewed the husband rather than the wife. In eight other married households (36.4 percent), the respondents (all women) said that their struggles to change the gender division of household labor preceded the decision to hire cleaning help. In the remaining ten married households interviewed (45.5 percent), paid household workers took on labor that employers unproblematically considered to be "women's work." In 72 percent of the households interviewed, women's paid employment influenced the decision to hire a domestic worker. Another 16 percent of respondents told me that they had always had paid household help whether or not they (or their mothers) were employed outside the home. The decision to hire a household worker was triggered by the illness of a family member in the remaining 12 percent of employer households interviewed. Thus, for a majority of the employers interviewed, domestic work presents a solution to women's double day that alleviates pressure on the gender division of labor. Like many of the employed women I interviewed, Allison said that her time pressures caused by working and caring for her family led to the decision to hire a weekly housekeeper:

> Because I work—we both work—so it's just a displacement of time. You work all day and come home, then how do you want to spend your time? . . . I don't know how we came to the ultimate decision. Probably I screamed, said, you know, I just can't continue. Because I was a student at the time, a student and working, so it was just a practical decision at the time. It was worth it to me. It was worth it to me not to go out to dinner.

In addition to paying to have their homes cleaned, all of the dual-career employers with young children interviewed had some form of paid child care. Three of the employers interviewed had live-in child-care workers. A third household employed a babysitter three days a week. The remaining two households with preschool children took their children to family day-care providers. Three other employers had employed live-in workers at some point when their children were young. Among higher-income households, child care is only one of many paid services and programs people provide for their children. For example, employer households with school-age children, regardless of the mother's employment situation, reported complex schedules of after-school and weekend activities for their children. When I asked Rachel about the activities of her fifteen-year-old son and twelve-year-old daughter, she took a deep breath and recited the list:

> Let's see. [My daughter] takes drama classes on Saturday, and dance classes at school. She works with me on [charity] projects about once a month. She takes ice skating classes, and at school, she is on the soccer and cross-country teams. Right now, she is also taking voice and piano lessons. My son is an Eagle Scout; his father is the scoutmaster. They are very active. Right now they're away on a hiking trip. He is on the high school water polo team; that is pretty demanding. And both of them are active in the church youth group. This year [my daughter] is an acolyte at church.

The employers interviewed also paid for a number of other services. Twenty (70 percent) of the employers interviewed also employed a gardener or gardening service on a weekly or bi-weekly basis. Eighteen (62.1 percent) reported paying for other types of yard work (such as tree trimming) during the year prior to the interview, and nineteen (65.5 percent) had paid for additional cleaning services (such as having carpets or draperies cleaned). The employers interviewed (like many urban professionals) regularly paid for food preparation and service. All but two respondents (93.1 percent) reported eating out on a regular basis (the average was five times a month), and just over half (51.7 percent) reported eating take-out food for dinner at least once a month.

When the volume of paid caring labor hired for cleaning, child care, children's activities, and other services is taken as a whole, the dependence of these households on paid caring labor is quite striking. It is also interesting to note that none of the employers interviewed reported that extended family members contributed to caring labor. Indeed, two of the elderly respondents reported that they hired domestic workers because they didn't want to ask their children for help. The minimal role played by state programs is also noteworthy. The most significant form of state support is public schools, which were used by half of the respondents with school-age children (the other half sent their children to private schools). With this notable exception, state support for social reproduction was minimal in employer households.

The interviews with employers also suggested the importance of international immigration to paid household work. Most employers (75.7 percent) felt that illegal immigration made it easier to find domestic workers; the remainder said they did not know, as they had never looked for help elsewhere. Ann said, "However as far as working and having domestic help, whether they're legal or illegal, I don't know too many Americans who would do that kind of work." The interviews also revealed positive feedback effects contributing to the growth of the occupation. The more that middle-class households employ workers, and the more that immigrant workers seek employment in the occupation, the more additional middle-class households opt to "try" paying for housekeeping. Over 60 percent of the employers interviewed were not raised in homes with domestic workers. All of these first-generation employers of help told me that they had neighbors or co-workers who employed help. Even more to the point, 58.8 percent of these first-generation employers first decided to hire help at the suggestion of someone outside their home (versus 30 percent of the respondents whose parents had help). This finding is indicative of the extent that employing domestic workers has become a locally acceptable option, not just something (in the words of one employer) "that snobby rich people do."

Domestic Workers: Transactions in the Family and Community

Like many of the women who hire them to clean and provide child care, several domestic workers are also working mothers. Absent from their homes and families for much of the day, immigrant domestic workers also face a double day. In many ways, the pressures of the double day are more difficult for this group: they perform housework on both shifts, their low income makes it difficult to pay for additional caring labor, and many immigrant domestic workers are undocumented. For working mothers who live in their employer's home, their job makes it impossible to live with their families. As a result, most of the immigrant domestic workers interviewed relied on the labor of friends or family members, provided for free, for very low wages, or in exchange for room and board. Since many of the workers' family networks spanned the U.S.–Mexico border, transactions of caring labor were often international in nature.

Table 7.2 shows the characteristics of the thirty-two domestic workers

TABLE 7.2 Personal Characteristics of Domestic Workers

Characteristics	All (n=32)	Live-out (n=21)	Live-in (n=11)
Average age	33.7	37	26.9
Single, never married (percent)	25	0	72.7
Children under 6 (percent)	31.3	47.6	0
Resident alien (percent)	46.9	61.9	18.2
Average number of years in domestic service	8.5	10.0	5.5
Average number of years since last migration to U.S.	8.6	11.3	3.2
Average hourly wages (U.S. dollars)	8.02	2.72	

Source: Personal interviews, Mattingly 1999b.

interviewed, distinguishing between those employed as live-out "job workers" and those working as live-in child-care workers. Live-in domestic work tended to be done by women who were younger, did not have small children of their own, and were more recent immigrants. Live-out cleaning, on the other hand, was dominated by women with families who had been in the United States for a longer time. The table also shows the average hourly wages reported by the domestic workers. Live-out workers reported an average of over $8.00 an hour, higher than California minimum wages ($5.75 in 1994). Live-in workers, on the other hand, earned far less, although they did receive room and board in addition to wages.

The women who work in the homes of others differ from the women who employ them not only in their ethnicity, but also in their class and legal status. All but two domestic workers had annual household incomes of less than $20,000, and a majority (57.2 percent) of the domestics interviewed earned at least half of their total household income. None of the domestic workers interviewed were citizens; 53 percent of the workers interviewed were in the country illegally, and the remainder were resident aliens. Live-in work is more common among women who are undocumented immigrants, while live-out work is more common among women who are resident aliens (they possess "green cards" that make them eligible for employment).

All of the live-out workers interviewed reported that women were responsible for cooking and housework in their homes, although in some households it was not the respondent herself who did this work. None of the domestic workers reported that men made significant contributions to either cleaning or cooking, although several said that their husbands watched the children on weekends. To help them meet the dual demands of home and paid work, most of the immigrant domestic workers interviewed drew on networks of female relatives and friends. Like many of the women interviewed, Rosa did not do her own cooking and cleaning. Instead, it was done by her mother, who shares the two-bedroom apartment with Rosa, her husband, and their children. Other domestic workers reported that older daughters or other family members living with them did the cooking and housekeeping. In the homes of the immigrant domestic workers interviewed, therefore, housework and cooking are the responsibility of women, but not necessarily the domestic workers. In some cases, the work was done by another female family member, usually one less able to find employment because of her age or because she was a more recent immigrant.

Domestic workers also differed from employers in their child-care arrangements. Among the eight job workers (live-out cleaners) with preschool children, only three (37.5 percent) paid a babysitter who was not a relative. The remainder had their children cared for by relatives, often at no cost. The average payment for child care among those job workers who did pay for care was $4 per day per child. Unable to pay much for child care, the domestic workers interviewed found several different ways of accessing additional caring labor. Among the fifteen job workers with school-age children, four (26.7 percent) have family members care for their children after school and on vacations, two (13.3 percent) have left their children in Mexico, and the remaining nine (60 percent) reported that their children are at home alone after school and during school vacations. In seven of the households, preteen and teenage girls were responsible for caring for their younger siblings after school and on vacations. Given the need for additional labor in the families of immigrant workers, older children are often valued workers, rather than additional expenses. Unlike employers, few domestic workers paid for additional programs for their children. Catechism (Catholic religious education) was the most common outside activity for school-age children. Only two reported any other activities: one had a son in karate lessons and one had a daughter in a Girl Scout troop. Many reported that their older children, in addition to babysitting and helping with housework, occasionally helped them clean houses or went to work with their fathers.

Interviews with domestic workers suggest that many women migrate specifically to work in domestic service (Mattingly 1999b). Two-thirds (67.7 percent) of the domestic workers interviewed came to the United States to look for work, and almost three-fourths (73.7 percent) found jobs as live-in nannies immediately upon arrival. Three (9.7 percent) of the workers had specific jobs waiting for them when they arrived. Another nineteen (61.3 percent) already had family in San Diego who worked as domestics or gardeners and were able to help them find their first jobs. Even among those women who did not have contacts in the occupation, most knew they were likely to be cleaning houses or babysitting once they arrived in San Diego. Imelda was a schoolteacher in Mexico; she migrated to join her husband who had found construction work in San Diego. Despite her education, Imelda felt that there were no other jobs for her until she became a resident alien: "When you first arrive in the United States this [cleaning houses] is the first job you look for. When you go to the house, many people do not mind if you have no papers. Some do mind but if they had to hire another white woman they would have to pay more than $40.00."

The interviews suggest that the reliance of domestic workers and other immigrant women on female family members contributes to flows and linkages between Mexico and the United States. The interviews showed that for many immigrants, caring networks crossed international borders. Five domestic workers (15.6 percent) reported that they had helped family members immigrate illegally to live with them and care for their children. Six (18.7 percent) of the workers interviewed reported that they had left their children in Mexico when they first came; two still had children living in Mexico. Many of the immigrant domestic workers interviewed, especially single women employed as live-in caretakers, had substantial obligations for family in Mexico. Over half (56 percent) of the women interviewed sent money each month, primarily to help support their parents' households there. Those sending money sent an average of $240 each month.

The description of caring labor in the households of immigrant domestic workers makes evident the importance of female family members. Many of the networks that immigrants draw on to help with caring labor cross borders. Domestic workers with children rely on other immigrant women and girls to care for their children while they are working and, in some households, on other female family members (like Rosa's mother) to do the cooking and housework. In five of the worker households interviewed (15.6 percent), female family members were illegally helped across the border to help with caring labor. For example, Lupe, a live-out worker with two children, has had different types of arrangements throughout her children's lives. Twice, Lupe and her husband helped nieces immigrate to the United States so they could care for the children and help with the housework and cooking. Since the children have been in school, Lupe has paid friends and family members to help with child care before and after school. During the summer months, she has left them with relatives or neighbors and some days taken them to work with her. The transnational nature of networks of caring labor was further emphasized by the stories of women who left their children in Mexico with relatives. Six (18.7 percent) of the workers interviewed reported that they had left their children in Mexico when they first came, and two of the women were living apart from their children at the time of the interview. Leonora's six-year-old daughter lives with Leonora's mother in Mexico City; the wages Leonora makes cleaning houses supports them both. For the time being, Leonora is forced into the only arrangement that she can afford; bringing her mother and daughter to San Diego would be too expensive, and wages in Mexico are too low for her to meet her financial responsibilities.

Immigration, Domestic Work, and Inequality

The preceding descriptions of caring labor show that both immigrant domestic workers and their employers who have to balance children and jobs rely on the caring labor of other women. The more affluent employers interviewed relied primarily on the paid labor of low-wage workers, while the immigrant domestic workers interviewed relied largely on the unpaid or poorly paid labor of female family members. The strategies are intimately connected and interdependent. Employers are able to rely on paid labor only because the cost of that labor is lower than their own wages. Thus, the organization of social reproduction of employer households is made possible by the organization of social reproduction in the families of domestic workers. The descriptions of caring labor in the two sets of households also reveal that both strategies are based on, and contribute to, the continued international immigration of women. The demand for paid household workers attracts immigrants, and the need for unpaid caring workers in immigrant households contributes to the further immigration of women. In this respect, immigrant domestic work links social reproduction in both sets of households to global processes. The descriptions also reveal marked differences in the type and quantity of caring labor drawn on by the two groups of working mothers, differences that are particularly evident in the services they are able to provide for their children.

The interviews revealed the heightened importance of citizenship in shaping access to caring labor and in the relationships between the two groups of women. Immigration policy in the United States shapes the lives of a large pool of undocumented workers, who are employed at low wages but denied citizenship benefits. Michael Kearney argues that immigration policy in the United States is informed by a contradiction, where "[f]oreign labor is desired but the persons in whom it is embodied are not desired" (1991, 58). He goes on to argue that immigration policy can be seen as a means to separate the sites of the expenditure of labor (in the United States) and the site of its reproduction (in migrants' home countries). "Only in transnational migration," he argues, "is there national separation of the sites of production and reproduction" (1991, 59). Kearney's insightful analysis of immigration policy neglects those cases where the social reproduction of undocumented immigrants occurs in the United States, including the immigrant households discussed here. Nevertheless, he underscores the magnitude of the opposition to the social reproduction of undocumented immigrants living in the United States. For while undocumented immigrants may be acceptable in the productive sphere, their needs for assistance with social reproduction — for additional caring labor — are not seen as legitimate.

Interviews with employers of immigrant domestic workers illustrate the contradictory nature of U.S. attitudes toward undocumented immigrants. While there was near consensus among employers about the desirability of undocumented immigrants as workers, there was a diversity of opinion about who should bear the collective costs of social reproduction for people who are illegally working in a foreign country. When asked about the effects of undocumented immigration in San Diego, the most common response was the cost of providing social services, which was mentioned by twelve (41.4 percent) employers. Undoubtedly, the ongoing campaign for Proposition 187 made people more conscious about the cost of providing social services to immigrants than they would have been otherwise. Nevertheless, the opposition to the state provision of caring labor for undocumented immigrants by people who themselves rely on the caring labor of undocumented immigrants speaks volumes about the salience of citizenship as a marker of difference. For example, Joyce, who told me that her long-term domestic worker had been undocumented for many years, felt illegal immigration should be controlled. She said, "I think it causes huge drains on public services like Medicaid, Medicare, and education." What is particularly interesting is that all but one of these same respondents did not oppose the employment of illegal immigrants. This contradiction between the desirability of immigrants as a source of labor and the opposition to providing support for the social reproduction of immigrants is pivotal in marking differences in social reproduction. By invoking citizenship to constrain the purview of the state, these employers are escalating inequalities in social reproduction and further emphasizing citizenship as a legitimate marker of inequality.

Paid household work has expanded to fill the gap in caring labor created by the neoliberal policies of both the United States and the Mexican state that have cut support for the social reproduction of working mothers. In the absence of state support, both employers and domestic workers have constructed transactions of caring work that are outside of, and in many cases in violation of, the government. Instead, caring labor is increasingly organized through the market. While some portion of the growth in personal-service employment can be attributed to conspicuous consumption among the wealthy, a large portion of it is the result of changing strategies for organizing caring work. Household expenditure studies have found that women's earnings and employment status are key determining factors in households' consumption of housekeeping services and meals away from home (Cohen 1998; Oropesa 1993). Like the employers interviewed here, many women and men increasingly build their networks of caring labor in the marketplace, by directly or indirectly employing low-wage service workers. Around the world, expanding personal-service occupations, especially paid household work, hotel and restaurant work, and sexual work, are increasingly filled by immigrant women (Ehrenreich and Hochschild 2002; Truong 1996) physically removed from affluent consumers. Thus, the growing communities of immigrant workers in San Diego and other cities are in part caused by the caring strategies of more affluent residents.

The expansion of paid household workers is one aspect of the privatization of social reproduction that stems from, and contributes to, economic and social polarization (Gregson and Lowe 1994). Indeed, the strategy of paying for caring work relies on service workers earning significantly less than the people who employ them. If a woman pays as much for child care as she earns while working, there is little incentive for her to work. Employers therefore benefit from processes in Mexico and the United States that maintain a pool of low-wage workers, as these workers make it possible for them to care for their homes and families. Among the employers interviewed, 51.7 percent reported that they would be unwilling to pay more for household work. June reported that she would pay "maybe $5 more a visit. I mean, she would be making more than I would." As Gretchen pointed out, "I think if the supply of women willing to work, to clean homes for $45 a day, dried up, I don't know that the same people who could afford to pay that amount could afford to pay a lot more for the same work."

Unable to afford to pay for additional caring labor, and ineligible for most forms of government assistance, immigrant domestic workers, particularly those who are undocumented, rely instead on the free or inexpensive labor of female family members and, occasionally, friends and neighbors.

The interviews also contained evidence that reliance on family-based networks places additional constraints on women, teenage girls, and young women. Family labor is not provided completely free of charge but is part of a transaction of mutual responsibility. While there is a large literature describing and analyzing networks among immigrants, these studies often frame networks as enabling, rather than constraining women.

For example, in her study of immigrant domestic workers, Pierrette Hondagneu-Sotelo (1994b) argues that women's participation in immigrant networks influences their success as domestic workers. While my research also shows the benefits of networks for immigrant women (Mattingly 1999a), focusing on the costs and constraints embedded in family networks illuminates the relationship between family-based transactions of caring labor and inequality among women (cf. Malkin 1997). Two costs were particularly apparent in my interviews: the financial responsibility for relatives living in Mexico (discussed above) and the demands placed on the labor of girls and young women.

The caring strategy of relying on family labor pursued by many immigrant domestic workers also contributes to social polarization among women through the demands that it places on the labor of female household members, especially teenage girls and young women. Earlier in the chapter, I showed that many domestic workers rely on their daughters, some as young as twelve, for help with babysitting and housework. While this practice eliminates the expense of child care, it also places a great deal of responsibility on the shoulders of girls and young women, keeping them from studying, earning wages, or pursuing other interests. One characteristic of the system of stratified social reproduction is that it places differential value on women's work. In this hierarchy, the labor of young immigrant women has the least value. Unable to contribute by earning wages, these young women support the employment of their mothers or other female relatives by working without wages or for very low pay.

While many immigrant domestic workers come to the United States and other industrialized nations to fill jobs created by the caring strategies of more affluent families, their low incomes prohibit them from using those strategies themselves. Unable to access shrinking welfare state programs and workplace protections because of their immigrant status and the informal nature of their work, immigrant domestic workers have no choice but to rely on the caring labor of family and friends. While this strategy undoubtedly contributes in many ways to immigrant life, it also places great burdens on the working women interviewed. And although this strategy is by no means limited to women employed in domestic service, the direct links between the caring strategies of domestic workers and those of their employers make evident the relational nature of social reproduction and the role of caring labor in shaping differences among women.

Conclusions

Paid household work is one type of women-centered social relation that organizes the work of social reproduction, yet its expansion has quite different implications for the women who work in the occupation and the families who employ them. This chapter extends our understanding of the influence of paid household work on the construction and enforcement of class differences among women through the work of social reproduction. Rather than focus on differences generated through the employer-employee relationship or the structure of the labor market, I have instead analyzed the very different ways domestic workers and their employers organize the labor needed to care for their homes and families. This approach reveals how some inequalities among women are created and enforced by the resources that they are able to bring to a similar problem. It also reveals that the networks of caring labor used by both immigrant domestic workers and their employers cross international borders, suggesting the global scale of social reproduction.

Recall the stories of Rosa and Laurie that opened the chapter. Like many of the domestic workers and employers interviewed, both are working mothers who face the daily struggle of organizing labor for the social reproduction of their family members. Constrained by a gender division of labor that assigns this work to women and unable to receive much support from the state, these women must enter into transactions to access additional caring labor. The strategies they pursue are shaped by their economic class and citizenship status. Those who can afford it, such as Laurie, meet their labor needs in the marketplace, hiring workers for lower wages than they earn themselves. Lacking the money to pay for additional labor and ineligible for state support, poor immigrant women, such as Rosa, must rely on the labor of family and friends. These strategies are not independent but rather are closely connected, as one employs the other. The strategies these two groups of women use to access additional caring labor also construct and reinforce differences, as evidenced by the very different responsibilities and resources of young women in the two groups of households. The contrasting strategies for accessing caring labor also reveal the importance of citizenship in defining differences among women and their households. Of greatest importance is the influence of citizenship on households' access to state support for the social reproduction of domestic workers, which contributes to the low cost of paid caring labor and the ability of wealthier citizens to rely on paid help. The frequency with which employers evoked citizenship as a rightful marker of rights to assistance with social reproduction—even when they themselves employed undocumented domestic workers—reinforces the significance of citizenship in the material construction of racial-ethnic differences.

The interviews also reveal that the very local work of social reproduction has an international dimension. Service work can not be geographically removed from the consumers, so accessing low-wage workers from poorer countries requires that the workers migrate. In San Diego and elsewhere, the reliance of relatively affluent households on paid caring labor is made possible by the presence of immigrant women and encourages the continued migration of women. In addition, the reliance of immigrant paid household workers on the caring labor of family members emphasizes their ties to family members still in Mexico. Thus, for both immigrant domestic workers and their employers, networks of caring labor interlace the home and the world. These insights remind us of the dynamic and important role of social reproduction in the space economy and the importance of continued research into the organization of caring work in an era of globalization.

Part Three   **Activist Women Changing the Border**

8 Mexican Women's Activism in New Mexico Colonias

Rebecca Dolhinow

Women leaders are the heart of *colonia* communities and the geography of colonia communities is the geography of women's daily lives. The processes of immigrating to the United States, seeking documentation, creating a new personal community, and making a living are all played out in the practices and beliefs of everyday life. Consequently, it is through daily practices and the geography of these practices that the women in this study were produced as leaders in their U.S. colonias. Where men and women are throughout the day, their daily geographies, dictate whom they spend time with, what they have time to do, and how they share responsibilities in their homes and community.[1] In three New Mexico colonias, where this research took place, a very small and select group of women became leaders and organized their colonias to improve the conditions of their daily lives. This chapter has two primary goals: first, it analyzes the factors that dispose women to leadership more often than men in these Mexican immigrant communities; second, it examines why so few women are able to follow the path to leadership. The conclusions of this chapter are drawn from the concrete and material daily practices of leaders such as Estella, Juana, Flora, Josephina, Alicia, Esperanza, Rosa, and Marie.[2]

Colonias exist on both sides of the border, but those in the United States are a more recent development. Colonias did exist in the United States nineteen years ago when *Women on the U.S.–Mexico Border* (V. Ruiz and Tiano 1987) was published, but it is only since then that they became the focus of scholarly investigation. The colonia population on the border increased greatly in the past nineteen years, even though the development of new colonias was made illegal in the mid-1990s. Colonias are primarily immigrant communities that often lack services as basic as potable water and electricity. Colonias are usually filled with substandard housing stock, often ten- to twenty-year-old trailers and modest one- or two-room homes made from an opportunistic mix of available materials. Few colonias have wastewater systems; most homes run on overtaxed septic systems. To be federally acknowledged as a colonia, a community must be within 150 miles of the U.S.–Mexico border.[3] However, it is more than their location that makes these Mexican immigrant communities a border phenomenon. Colonias are transnational communities filled with recent Mexican immigrants, both settlers and circular migrants, with readily apparent ties to Mexican culture and traditions.

The colonias are a space in which what it means to be a Mexican in the United States is constructed. In the isolated, rural, and clearly circumscribed spaces that are the colonias, a very specific and clearly racialized space has been produced (Hill 2003; Vila 2000). Colonias are commonly referred to as Mexican communities by locals and are associated with all the racist stereotypes of "Mexicaness" on the border such as dirt, poverty, and disease. I will never forget what an acquaintance who grew up in southern New Mexico once said to me when I told him I was working in the colonias. He asked me why I would want to do that, after all they were just "piles of dirt in the desert." This was a common response from Anglos in the area, among whom this sort of geographic racism ran rampant. Yet at the same time, these were also spaces that, on a daily basis, were produced and reproduced by the women leaders this chapter chronicles. The colonias simultaneously offer new opportunities to break down and rework the common Mexican/American binaries of poverty/wealth and health/disease as women leaders and activists organize their communities to make the improvements they require and challenge these racist stereotypes.

This chapter is part of a larger project that addresses the development of colonia communities on the border in New Mexico. The three colonias in which this research took place are Los Montes, with a population of approximately thirty households; Recuerdos, with over thirty households; and Valle de Vacas, with upwards of two hundred households. All three are situated in southern New Mexico and were created in the late 1980s and early 1990s. New Mexico's colonias house the region's constantly growing population of Mexican labor upon which the area's agricultural economy relies. This research is based on eleven months of ethnographic research in three colonias with a core group of eight women leaders. The data used in this chapter were collected through participant observation techniques, field notes, and a series of four semi-structured in-depth interviews carried out over the course of the year. While I was in the colonias, I worked with several non-governmental organizations (NGOs) and interviewed NGO employees, local politicians, church workers, and activists involved in the colonias and with immigrant activism in the area. Although the majority of my time was spent with self-identified and NGO-identified leaders, I did other interviews with non-leaders. While spending time with leaders, my activities varied from agricultural field labor (picking onions) to preparing for family activities (usually cooking); a good deal of time was spent sitting around with other women and talking *chisme* (gossip).

Elsewhere I argue that through a complex set of relationships between labor supply and demand, immigration, and the growing neoliberal influence in local and national politics, colonias developed as a solution to a serious lack of affordable housing in the border region (Dolhinow 2003; see also P. Ward 1999). The economic development of the border region in the mid-twentieth century led to major movements of people from the interior of Mexico to the border (Craig 1971; Lorey 1999). When these movements were combined with the worsening Mexican economy in the 1980s, immigration to the United States increased dramatically. In response to this influx of Mexican immigrants, the United States passed the Immigration Reform and Control Act (IRCA) in 1986 and regularized the status of large numbers of previously undocumented immigrants in the border region (Nevins 2002; Staudt 1998). These new residents often found affordable housing extremely limited in the late twentieth century. As growing neoliberal influences in the United States preached the end of big government, the state pulled away from the provision of social services and the private sector and NGOs took over (Dolhinow 2005; Fraser 1993; Hart 2004; Hyatt 2001; Peck and Tickell 2002; Petras and Veltmeyer 2001; Wolch 1989). When the state did not respond to the new and greater demand for affordable housing, the private sector stepped up and developers created infrastructure-lacking colonias to house the region's Mexican working poor. In response to the substandard conditions in the colonias, NGOs were developed to organize colonia residents to improve their communities.

Moving from the particular historical and geographical juncture at which colonias developed, this chapter argues that the women who become colonia leaders are a small group able to negotiate skillfully the transnational[4] gender systems in which they live in order to create a space for their activism and leadership. "Traditional"[5] Mexican gender roles of women as caretakers and men as providers are very important in the production of political subjects in the colonias, but the transnational nature of these communities complicates gender systems and makes it impossible to simply read gender roles off family dynamics. The geographic proximity of the border's colonias to Mexico, and the frequent cross-border travels of many colonia residents, lead to a situation in which gender systems in the colonias are constantly renewed and reworked.

Although most women in the colonias share the traditional gender role of caretaker, only a few women move from the resource deprivation they experience in this role to a position of leadership from which they can make improvements in the resources of their communities. Specifically, women leaders live in households with gender systems that are more egalitarian than others or in households that function without a daily male presence. It is, of course, important to acknowledge that all of the women in my sample live individually specific lives, and it is therefore necessary to avoid making essentialist claims regarding shared qualities of womanhood or of collective identity as "women leaders." Yet my research does point to a set of common factors in the lives of colonia leaders that I argue facilitate their activism.

The Production of Subjectivities

While the central focus of this chapter is on how certain colonia women are produced as community leaders, it also discusses how women activists and outsiders describe women's activism: in particular, what they believe motivates women to become active in their colonias. Though motivations for activism and the processes that produce women as activists can be very different phenomena, they are often closely tied. The production of subjects occurs when dominant discourses, usually produced by people or institutions with power, construct frameworks in which certain behaviors, ideas, and attitudes are acceptable for some people and not for others (Butler 1999; Weedon 1987). In this way, subjects are produced who are limited in what they can and cannot do based on the discourses governing their daily practices.

The arguments presented here are based on an analysis of the daily practices of women leaders in the colonias and the meanings associated with these practices. Colonia leaders are produced as political subjects through their activism. An understanding of how subjectivities are produced is important to the arguments presented here because only a small group of women becomes leaders. Although leaders and non-leaders take part in similar daily activities, the meanings leaders assign to these activities are sufficiently different to set them apart.

Gender Roles in Colonia Households

Shortly before I arrived in New Mexico, an incident happened that, when related to me at a later date, introduced me to the complicated ways in which domestic gender relations affect women's activism in the colonias. In particular, this incident highlighted the complex relationships married leaders must negotiate in order to work with local NGOs. The board meeting of the Colonias Organizing Group (COG), the local community-organizing NGO, is held on the third Monday of every month. The COG's board is composed primarily of community leaders, most of whom are women.

Transportation to board meetings can cause problems. Most colonia households have at least one car, but that vehicle may not be running or may be needed by another family member on the night of the meeting. In order to solve the transportation dilemma, many leaders carpool. On the Monday of this particular incident, Juana and her husband Eduardo were going to give Estella a ride to the COG board meeting because she did not have a car that evening. Everyone at the COG was pleased with this solution because all too often leaders miss the board meetings and important decisions requiring a quorum must be postponed. But late that afternoon Estella called the COG director, Elena, to say she would not be able to attend the meeting. Elena later told me that she was very surprised because she had been under the impression that all the transportation problems were solved. When she asked Estella what happened to her plans to ride down with Juana and Eduardo, Estella was quiet. That was not going to work, she explained. Juana was not going to the meeting. Elena asked if Eduardo was still planning to attend, and Estella said yes, that he was. It was at this point that the director realized the awkwardness in the conversation was coming from the juxtaposition of two conflicting gender systems, hers and Estella's. Estella then explained to Elena that as a married woman, there was no way she could drive for an hour with someone else's husband. It did not matter that Eduardo and Estella's husband were close friends or that she and Juana were best friends. It simply was inappropriate, and she could not do it.

Conflicts between gender relations in the home and the demands of leadership provide a constant struggle for colonia leaders. Yet it is these very same gender relations and roles in the home that dispose women to the activism, which in turn creates these struggles. The struggle women go through on a daily basis to change their positions in domestic power relations is a theme that recurred in my interviews. According to the women themselves, family dynamics rely, for the most part, on a traditional patriarchal distribution of power. Men and women have distinct roles and responsibilities, and it is within this fixed discursive framework that colonia leaders must negotiate a space for their activism.

Since my research focused on the women leaders, and my formal interviews were with women, the discourses discussed in this chapter are primarily those used by women to describe their own actions as well as the actions of their husbands and other men in their community. My understanding of the discourses used by men to discuss gender relations was formed by observation and by interviews with the women leaders, although it also became clear that some of these discourses originated outside the colonias. While these discourses are mutually constitutive and created side by side, there is a gendered nature to their deployment as men and women call on them in different ways. It is these discourses of gender that lead women to their particular daily geographies, which, in turn, dispose women to activism more readily than men.[6]

A Father's Role

To understand better the domestic gender dynamics I observed in the colonias, I dedicated one of my formal interviews to the topic of family dynamics in general and gender roles in particular.[7] Answers to these questions support my observations and arguments regarding the importance of daily geographies in the production of women as colonia activists and leaders. While the men are gone, the women are left in the colonias to care for their families and community:

Question: What is the role of the father in the family?

I think the role of the father is to be the one who has the most authority, I mean to say they [the kids] obey him more because he has the most authority, and he is stronger because he is a man. That is the role of the father.[8] (Juana)

I think the role of the papa in the family is basically to give security to the family. [To give] support, economic support . . . the strength, he is the strongest in the house. Let's suppose that a house needs a well-made foundation. I think the father is the foundation.[9] (Marie)

I know if you were to ask this question to my mom, the role of the dad is the provider and that's basically it. And maybe they would tell you that the disciplinarian or something like that, but to me, I mean the role is provider.[10] (Alicia)

The three quotes above reveal the similarity in ideas about family structure in the homes of colonia leaders in particular, and in colonia households more generally. Fathers are disciplinarians and providers, and mothers are caretakers. All of the women I interviewed broke down domestic gender relations in similar ways. Mothers take care of the day-to-day details, and when there is trouble, the father steps in as a disciplinarian. Every answer I recorded about the family and its structure revolved around this division of family responsibilities and roles. It is interesting to note that even in families where there was no father figure present, single mothers still relied on their ex-husbands to adopt an authority role when discipline was necessary. Some single moms would call their ex-husbands and ask them to intervene when trouble with children at home became unmanageable.

A Mother's Role

If men are providers and disciplinarians, what are women?

Well, I say that the role of the mother is even greater than that of the *papá*, because if the mother does not fulfill her responsibility as a mother, well everything falls apart . . . because the man is the strength and the character and the woman is the intelligence and the wisdom.

I believe that without intelligence and without wisdom it is not possible to survive as a family. Of course, with God's will, because without God's will we are nothing, right?[11] (Marie)

Well, if the mother is too lenient with the kids, the kids do with one whatever they want. One has to also be strong of character. Because otherwise the kids are not well educated. And now if they are not well educated with what you tell them, well, that's their problem. Because one is teaching them to get ahead so they will be better in life, better than you are. And if they do not want to get ahead, that's their story.[12] (Juana)

Well, everything [is the role of the mother], wash them [kids], iron for them [kids' clothes], educate them, give them food, talk with them everyday, get them ready for school, and aside from that one also has to work, so it is hard.[13] (Flora)

As I stated earlier, the role of the mother in these families is described as that of caretaker. Mothers make sure their families are fed and dressed and ready for another day. More specifically, these quotes all point to one role, that of educator. Marie describes the mother as the one who has the intelligence and wisdom in the family, without whom the family would fall apart. Juana describes why a mother must be a bit of an authoritarian as well. Without the proper discipline, kids will take advantage of their parents and end up *mal educado*. This literally means poorly educated but in common usage means troublesome, misbehaved, and ignorant of what is right. Juana believes mothers must teach their children how to get ahead in life and how to have better lives. Helping children to achieve better lives was a common theme in my interviews with women activists. Flora's interview quite eloquently expresses the hardships of single motherhood. Not only must she fulfill all the caretaking responsibilities, she must also take on the traditionally male role of primary wage earner. Like the activist mothers Nancy Naples worked with in New York City and Philadelphia, colonia leaders see their activism as encompassing "a broad definition of actual mothering practices" (1998, 113).

Transnational Nature of Gender Roles in the Colonias

The transnational nature of colonia communities is not limited to their location on the border or their mixture of Mexican and American culture: it permeates every aspect of daily life. Sometimes this mixture of Mexican and American culture runs smoothly through daily practices, and at other times, the pressures of negotiating a culture spanning two nations becomes too much and contradictions and tensions abound. Nowhere in my research was this dynamic more pronounced than in household gender relations. The gender roles described above lay out a set of rather traditional patriarchal roles that all of the women agreed were more or less present in their homes and the homes of their neighbors. Yet many of these women are active on a daily basis in leadership roles that blur the traditional boundaries between the gender roles they themselves acknowledge. Although they describe men as the providers, these women provide their colonias with some of the most important resources that these communities otherwise would lack. I argue the transnational nature of colonias is particularly important to the negotiation of gender roles in the home and community for leaders who must reconcile the often-contradictory requirements of their roles as mothers and leaders.

The transnational nature of gender systems is manifest clearly in the variety of gender relations and roles seen in colonia families. Although the women all described the gendered division of labor in their homes in similar terms, each woman's own personal family life displayed variations on these traditional roles. For example, Josephina lived part of the year in a colonia and the other part in a small mountain village in Chihuahua. She took her first long-term trip to the United States shortly after her daughter Flora's first child was born. Since then, she has returned on a regular basis whenever Flora needed help with her children. Flora and her children were not the only attraction in the colonia of Los Montes for Josephina. She had three other daughters and eight more grandchildren spread around the colonia. Only her youngest daughter remains in Mexico. Josephina's family is truly transnational and in each of her daughter's households different gender systems exist. In Flora's home, where there was no male presence, Flora and Josephina had to provide for the family as well as assume the daily responsibilities of caretaking, while in the homes of Josephina's other daughters their husbands were the providers.

The transnational nature of Josephina's extended family characterizes the colonias quite well, as many families have members in both the United States and Mexico. Many other colonia residents live quite transnational lives, visiting relations in Mexico or simply crossing the border for shopping and socializing. The visible transnational geographies of the colonias, embodied in women like Josephina, are attended by invisible geographies that define gendered power relations in the home. In Josephina's case, she was involved in her colonia's leadership with only one of her daughters, Flora, the single mother. Her other three daughters in Los Montes were married and chose not to be active in their colonia because they did not believe their husbands would approve. Flora once commented to me on the high percentage of single mothers in colonia organizing. "The activists are 95 to 99 percent only women. Single women because those that have husbands, the husbands won't let them [be active]."[14] When I asked her why men would not let their wives be active, her answer was simple and very telling: "Because men are *machistas*, they want their women here in the house with them, they want hot food on the table."[15] But her analysis of the situation did not end there: she had obviously given it a lot more thought. "It's also a woman's fault, she gets used to it [living under her husband's control]."[16] Flora was keenly aware that her status as a single mother made her activism easier in some ways. Her sisters lived in household gender systems that were dominated by their husbands who did not approve of women's activism. The transnational nature of gender roles in the colonias is manifest differently in every household, and these differences are central to the arguments presented here on how a few women become leaders while many others do not.

In the Absence of Men

Men work 8:00 to 5:00, 9:00 to 5:00, whatever, come home, eat dinner, maybe water the trees, and go to bed. That's their role in the community.[17] (Sylvia)

For the men it's like "Okay, I'm going to work from 7:00 to 5:00, and if I work for that time, I've accomplished my role." [18] (Mario)

One of the clearest themes to emerge from my interviews was that of men's greater involvement in the "outside" world. In their role as providers, men go to work outside the colonias on a daily basis (Campbell 2003, 285). They leave the community every morning and return in the evening with their wages. Once they return from work, they are done with their responsibilities for the day. They might have to "water the trees," as Sylvia says, but they have done all the work that is required of them. Anything else they choose to do once they are home in the evening is purely recreational. Most men do not choose to take on extra responsibilities, and therefore, work on the behalf of the community falls to the women.

The same discourses dictating that men provide incomes generated outside the colonias also shape the scales at which the daily geographies of men and women are manifest. The scaling of daily life for colonia residents is closely tied to, even constituted by, gender discourses. In her discussion of the distinctions between public and private spaces, Linda McDowell acknowledges the construction of this dichotomy: "the division between the public and private, just like the distinction between geographical scales, is a socially constructed and gendered division" (McDowell 1999, 149). I would like to take this argument a step further to say that the construction of the public/private dichotomy, geographical scales, and gender discourses are all mutually constitutive. It is the dominant ideology of gender and gender roles in the colonias that dictates that men are the providers who must leave the scale of the community and enter the scale of the regional economy in order to be able to provide appropriately. Women, by contrast, play out most of their daily life at the community scale.

The absence of men during the day leads to a kind of enforced independence for women. Women leaders find it easier to be active in more "public" areas than they would if their husbands were present. It was routine for me to schedule interviews for working hours when husbands were gone and could not listen in on, or show disapproval for, my interview questions and their wives' answers. As an outsider and researcher, asking often very private questions about gender relations in the home, I acted as a bridge between the public sphere of academic research and community organizing and the private sphere of the home. Many men were clearly not comfortable with my role in their homes. The connections I drew between gender relations in the home and their wives' activism made some men nervous. These men accepted their wives' activism as long as it appeared more necessary than political and did not disrupt existing gender relations. The relationships between gender, power, and practice that our conversations raised appeared a bit too political and challenging for some husbands. For example, on several occasions Marie's husband listened in on our conversations as he got ready for his night shift at a local food-processing plant. He would accuse Marie of stirring things up in the colonia and of being too outspoken. Marie's husband had a reputation of giving NGO organizers a hard time when they came to see Marie, but he always stopped short of kicking organizers out of his house or forcing Marie to stop her activism. Many colonia women are not so lucky.

Because many colonia residents work during the day—be it in the fields, factories, or in their homes watching their children—community meetings must take place in the evening to allow the greatest number of people to attend. Most of the women I interviewed believed their partners had little desire to do anything once they got home. Husbands were not likely to want to plan or attend the community meetings necessary to make change in the colonias. Marie described her husband when he gets home from work in these terms: "Men are the head of the family and it's more comfortable to say, '*Vieja* [old lady] you take care of all of this, don't bother me I'm watching baseball, I'm watching the news, I don't want you to bother me.' And then it is the woman who has to take the initiative, make the decision to do what she believes is best to do, even if later the *Viejo* [old man] gets mad."[19]

When the men have attitudes like this, it is little wonder women do most of the community organizing. As men are produced as providers and little more, all other roles must fall to the women. "The man thinks that with work and bringing in the money he's done his part. The woman no, we are always thinking, what's better for the kids."[20] Here Estella points to the ways in which the discourses men use to define their roles limit their activity in the family as well as the community. Estella believes it is the women who think about the future of the community the most, in particular in relation to their children.

Men Who Are Always Gone

In the three colonias, only eight women, out of more than 350, self-identify as leaders. On average, each colonia has two to three women who are active in the organization of their colonia on a regular basis. Though the focus of this work is the women who do become leaders, the women who do not take part in their colonias must be acknowledged as well. The women who do not become leaders experience the same resource deprivation, discrimination, and discursive production that leaders experience, but these experiences do not lead them to become activists. The primary differences I found between activist and non-activist women were in their relationships with their partners. Two leaders in my study group, Flora and Esperanza, are single mothers whose ex-husbands live nearby but do not exert much control over the lives of their ex-wives. A third leader, Rosa, lives separately from her husband, who is in California. The rest of the women have rather egalitarian relationships with their husbands. Leaders' husbands might still occupy the traditional role of provider and authoritarian, yet they also gave their wives more room to maneuver and more respect for their personal goals than did the partners of non-leaders. This difference in gendered power relations in the home is crucial in determining which women become leaders. The few non-leaders I spoke with all requested that we meet during the day when their husbands were at work. They were worried what their husbands would say or do if they knew their wives were talking to the meddlesome *gringa*. Leaders were also aware of the important role supportive partners played in the development of their activism.

For leaders like Flora and Rosa, the absence of men in their household meant more freedom on a daily basis. Neither woman had to be home to prepare an evening meal for their husbands. Unlike the co-habiting women in my sample, Flora and Rosa's daily lives were not based on the schedules of others. They did need to prepare lunches for school-age children and be sure there was food for dinner, but they could plan meals for times that fit their schedules, and they could change plans as they pleased.

Single mothers experience activism in different ways than do married leaders. In their homes, without a regular male presence, Flora and Esperanza created different gender systems than those in most leaders' homes. In single-mother homes, women, out of necessity, must take on more of the traditionally "male" responsibilities. This greater variety of responsibilities allows women like Flora and Esperanza more room to maneuver in their roles as leaders. Flora, the heart of the organizing movement in her colonia, was the first person to whom outside organizers and county officials went when they needed help. Flora is an extreme example of the competing responsibilities colonia leaders must balance. As a single mother, she juggled both the traditional male role of provider and the domestic responsibilities of a mother and caretaker. Though balancing these two demanding roles was very difficult, it did not necessarily mean single mothers had less time or energy to be active in their colonias. The two single mothers in my sample, Flora and Esperanza, had both more responsibility and more freedom.

Doing What Comes Naturally: How Family Roles Dispose Women to Activism

Women's domestic responsibilities not only lead them to be active in their colonias but also prepare them for activism. It is possible for colonia activists to run both a household and a community at the same time because these tasks draw on a similar skill set. Several women told me if it had not been for their experiences dealing with bureaucracy in their children's schools and in health-care clinics, they would never have believed they could tackle the county's bureaucracy. As primary caretakers, these women had no choice but to learn to deal with large government institutions to get their children's citizenship paperwork, Social Security cards, and access to programs like Women, Infants, and Children (WIC). The connection between the skills learned in the home and those used to organize a community is an important way outside organizers recruit and maintain women leaders.

The COG organizers are well aware of the connections between running a household and running a community, and they actively publicize and promote these similarities when recruiting women. Mario had been a community organizer in the colonias of Doña Ana county for more than ten years. As an outside organizer, Mario was not a community leader: he was a colonia resident. Mario knew all of the women who led the colonias and worked with them on many projects. He experienced women's leadership on three levels: as a colonia resident himself, as a community organizer who recruited and trained leaders, and as the brother of an important leader. Mario often acknowledged the importance of daily life experience for colonia leaders, and he believed it was the experiences women have as mothers and problem solvers in their homes that enabled them to take on the role of leaders in their colonias. "For the women, they are prepared to deal with everything and I think that is why they spend the time on the community. Say if I have raised five children, this [leadership], this is nothing. Going to a meeting is nothing for me."[21] Mario drew on a rather stereotypical idea of motherhood in supporting his argument, yet it is important to note that this essentialization is in line with how the women often identified themselves. Raising children is all about planning. So is community organizing, a similarity that Mario recognized. Mario also realized that the social and cultural value that comes from being a mother could help dispose women to leadership. The valuable experience that Mario and the women leaders believed motherhood instills in women is crucial to understanding why it is women who take on leadership roles in the colonias. These women know if they can organize their households, then they can organize their communities by working with other women who have gained similar leadership potential from their experiences as mothers (see Gilmore 1999; Kaplan 1997).

Even women who do not choose to become leaders serve as conduits for information and contacts for outside interventions. Colonia populations can be very unstable. People come and go as migrant field labor and others return to Mexico for extended periods. County records of colonia inhabitants are often flawed because of the unstable nature of these communities. For this reason, if the county, or any organization for that matter, wants to circulate information in the colonias, they must use one of two methods. They can go door-to-door or they can call on the schools to send flyers home with the students. This second method works well because nearly every colonia household contains at least one school-age child, and the children usually give these flyers to their mothers, not their fathers, so the message ends up in the right place:

Kids come home from school with a little paper that an organization left, and they say "Look, Mom," they don't say "Look, Dad." They don't give it to the dad; they give it to the mom. And the kids are learning so much in school and educating the parents, but the first one to get the education is always the mom. It's very rare that a child will go home and say to his dad, "Look at what the teacher gave us today." It's usually the mother, so I think that is why they tend to get more involved.[22] (Sylvia)

The sharing of knowledge and education between children and mothers is very important to the dynamics of development in colonia communities.

Conclusions

How it came to be that women are the majority of leaders in the colonias is considered a matter of common sense among many NGO employees. Women are in the communities day in and day out, and in their roles as mothers and wives, they experience most intensely the resource deprivation characteristic of their colonias. These circumstances lead women to take action. This chapter has complicated these very basic, yet valid, explanations of women's activism by making necessary connections between the production of colonias as communities of Mexican working poor and the production of certain women as colonia leaders. The circumstances that led to the development of the colonias play a large role, alongside transnational gender systems, in the production of colonia leaders. Attention to the material conjuncture where multiple subjectivities are simultaneously produced is central to the work presented in this chapter.

I argue that the production of the colonias as resource-deprived, Mexican, working-poor communities on the border and the production of women activists as leaders happen simultaneously and through connections to similar local and global scale processes. In particular, the global economic restructuring that has spurred Mexican immigration to the United States, when combined with the lack of affordable housing, led to the development of colonias in which transnational gender systems and gendered power relations push women, and not men, into leadership. The results and style of the activism in which these women take part are closely tied to what discourses are available to leaders and are closely related to how leaders are produced. After losing social services such as state-sponsored affordable housing in neoliberalism's "roll back" era (Peck and Tickell 2002) during the 1980s and early 1990s, colonias are now experiencing the "roll out" phase as they are incorporated into the state's agenda through NGOs and their central role in civil society.

For Mexican immigrant women on the border, the challenges of daily life are multiplied by the resource deprivation they experience in their colonias. In response to these hardships, a small group of women become leaders who step out of their immediate communities into local politics where they fight for the improvements needed by their colonias. This research points to several important differences between women who become leaders and those who do not. Leaders are most often women who are the heads of their households or women from households with relatively egalitarian gender systems. For activism and leadership to be an option, colonia women must first identify the conditions in their colonias that they wish to change and then must make the space in their daily lives for the many responsibilities leadership entails. Few women are able to accomplish this, and those that do are quite exceptional.

9 Styles, Strategies, and Issues of Women Leaders at the Border

Irasema Coronado

My first recollection of a social activist was a petite woman from Nogales, Sonora, dressed in perpetual black, who wore a crucifix and made the rounds of bars and restaurants to collect money for her life's mission: taking in abandoned and orphaned girls. She was known as Madre Conchita, mother of all the girl orphans in the community. Madre Conchita died in 1952, but her legacy and memory still live on. El Asilo de la Madre Conchita (Madre Conchita's Orphanage) in *colonia* Buenos Aires has become an institution in the community, providing shelter and love to many children. In Mexico's northern border cities, many women have followed the same path as Madre Conchita, serving as social activists to make their communities better places to live and to help the less fortunate.

This chapter focuses on the activist roles women have played in cities along Mexico's northern border. Like women in other parts of Latin America, Mexico, and the United States, women became the principal organizers, activists, leaders, and the movers and shakers who attracted the attention of government officials to meet their needs and to deliver basic services (V. Bennett 1995; Lind 1992; Pardo 1990). During the course of my research in northern Mexico, I found more women than men work as community activists and agents of change. Inadequate urban infrastructure (such as water, sewer systems, and electricity) adversely affects and increases household work. Because women usually are in charge of the home, they are the ones most affected by the lack of basic services and are thus motivated to resolve or address these infrastructural deficiencies (V. Bennett 1995, 106). This chapter highlights women's motivations for community activism and presents three ways they work to make their communities better places to live: functioning within existing governmental and political structures, creating *asociaciones civiles* (civil associations; ACs), and working independently. Although the motives for activism transcend class differences, women's class position determines how they engage in activism.

The Setting: La Frontera Norte

Since the inception of the Mexico's Programa de Industrialización Fronteriza (Border Industrialization Program; PIF) in 1965, tens of thousands of workers from the country's interior have found their way into northern border cities. They seek the employment opportunities that accompanied the arrival of the maquiladoras: foreign-owned assembly plants that take advantage of Mexico's cheap labor. While workers drawn to these border cities usually found jobs in the maquiladoras, they were left to their own devices to find or build housing for themselves and their families. *Colonias populares*[1] emerged on the outskirts of cities because workers had limited housing options in these areas where houses were scarce, and those that were available were not affordable. Access to mortgage loans or credit in Mexico is essentially non-existent, especially for the poor.

In Mexico, the inability of local, state, and federal governments to provide basic services led to the mobilization of residents in colonias populares. People organized to make demands on the local, state, and federal governments in order to force politicians to provide basic services to the *colonia popular*. The newly arrived are called *paracaidistas*, meaning literally parachutists, or squatters. They are individuals who, from one day to the next, helped set up the infrastructure for their own particular colonia popular. This experience of daily border life magnified particularly in the late 1960s and early 1970s as workers and their families attempted to avail themselves of the basic necessities they expected from local governments. In Nogales, Sonora, long-term residents complained vehemently about the proliferation of colonias populares and accompanying negative externalities associated with the maquiladoras (Coronado 1998). Consequently, daily experience has become a harsher reality as these workers and their families, having moved north in search of better employment opportunities, frequently find themselves living in either the same or worse conditions than those they had hoped to escape. Under these conditions, female leadership has emerged.

Methodology and Research Questions

Feminist-research methodologies and an activist anthropological approach guide this work, based on the premise that feminist scholarship employs a variety of strategies for creating knowledge about women and their social worlds, often hidden from mainstream society (Hesse-Biber and Yaiser 2004, 3). By definition, feminist research is change-oriented; all feminist research has action components (Reinharz 1992, 196), a commitment to political activism and social justice (Hesse-Biber and Yaiser 2004, 3), and greater access to privileged sources of information than non-feminist ethnography. June Nash, in her foreword to *Women in Chiapas: Making History in Times of Struggle and Hope*, claims that the activist approach permits greater access to privileged sources of information than does non-feminist ethnography (2003, x).

For this work, I have drawn on my interactions with a large number of women activists on Mexico's northern border. Participant observation, formal and informal interviews, and casual conversations were part of the methodology employed over a fifteen-year period. Successful women activists along the border are highlighted for achieving certain goals. They worked to bring basic services to their colonias populares, raise awareness regarding violence against women, and engage policymakers to address environmental or health concerns.

In the past, the voices of activist women in the political arena have been denied, ignored, and even silenced in mainstream academic literature. Only a handful of studies have focused on women activists on Mexico's northern border (López Estrada, this vol.; Peña 1997; Staudt and Coronado 2002). Much border research on women focuses on the maquiladora sector (Cravey 1998; Fernández-Kelly 1983; Iglesias Prieto 1997; V. Ruiz and Tiano 1987). Scholars have also examined cross-border cooperation generally (Coronado and Padilla 2003) and specifically in the case of labor (Schmidt Camacho 1999). A recent surge in attention to violence against women in Ciudad Juárez has led to research on that topic (Portillo 2001, 2003) and on sex workers and their struggle for public space (Portillo 2003; Wright 2003), demands for justice by mothers of victims (Bejarano 2002), evolution of related women's organizations (Perez 2004), and the culture of feminicide (Monarrez 2000). Other research has focused on women in political life in Latin America (Chaney 1979; Craske 1999) and in Mexico (Barrera Bassols and Massolo 1998; Rodríguez 2003; Staudt 1998) and specifically on women in the city council in Ciudad Juárez (Hernandez 2001, 2004).

Women and Activism

Elsa Chaney's (1979) seminal work on women in Latin American politics set forth the notion that women viewed public service as an extension of household management, becoming *supermadres* (supermothers) of the nation by caring for and nurturing the citizenry as they would their own families. Women who delved into public service did so at lower levels of involvement and for limited amounts of time.

Still, women make connections between the private sphere of family and home and the public sphere of public politics. In her research with twenty-nine Latinas in Boston politics, Carol Hardy-Fanta (1997) reported that some women reported entering political activism as a slow-growing process of political consciousness; for others it was a quick *chispa* (spark) of recognition that a change was needed. She also found that Latinas drew upon family and cultural traditions and listed "helping others" as a major motivating force for their political activity. Hardy-Fanta concluded that, overall, the process of political consciousness for these Latinas is one of "making connections — between their own lives and those of others, between issues affecting them and their families in the neighborhood or community and those that affect them in the workplace" (Hardy-Fanta 1997, 233).

According to Thomas and Wilcox (1998), in the United States women are more likely than men to have entered politics from community volunteerism or women's groups. In her study of the Mothers of East Los Angeles, Mary Pardo contends that Latinas are able to transform traditional networks and resources based on family and culture into political assets (Pardo 1990). Other research has indicated that Latinas' participation in politics is due to both traditional motivations and commitment to their community (S. García and Márquez 2001).

Women report that pain, anger, and fear have served as mobilizing agents. For example, the tragic plight of the Mothers of the Disappeared demonstrates how in the midst of grief mothers organized to raise international awareness of the repressive government in Argentina (Fisher

1989). Ernesto Cortés (1993), in his Industrial Areas Foundation work in San Antonio, Texas, noted that activists usually become angry because of an injustice and then are motivated to become involved politically. In her work in Chiapas in the 1990s, Shannon Speed describes how indigenous women explained that fear of the Mexican military (which had murdered, pillaged, raped, and plundered) led them to take bold actions, blocking military incursions into their communities with their bodies, in some cases with children in their arms, in order to protect their families, their men, and crops (Speed 2003). This select body of literature uses various methodologies (including interviews, political meetings and workshops, participant observation, and testimonies of women) to demonstrate how diverse women become motivated to become involved in political activism at the border.

The following section is divided into two parts. First, I discuss women's motivations for entering the activist arena, drawing on the voices of women who participated in interviews (all of whom are identified with pseudonyms). Second, I focus on the three ways women tend to operationalize their activist work: through the existing political system, through the creation of an AC, or as independent activists.

Motivations for Activism

Border women's motivations are similar to those of activists elsewhere. The supermadre phenomenon was a shared motivating factor among women. Several of the activists stated that they felt they were the mothers of the community; they said their maternal instincts of caring and nurturing and providing for their families transcended into the community. Like the women involved in politics in other parts of Latin America, some of these border women expressed they felt like the community caretakers. "Se nos ve como la mamá de todos" (We are seen as everyone's mother), asserted Fidelina, who was indeed a grandmotherly type.

Pain, Anger, and Fear-Based Activism

Another parallel can be drawn between border women activists and the experiences of the Mothers of the Disappeared in Argentina, the anger that Cortés (1993) describes, and the fear reported by women in Chiapas.

Leticia reported she became involved and active when she was consumed with anger over a house fire in a colonia popular that killed an entire family. "Something happened; the little house started to burn in the middle of the night, some of us awoke and tried to help with buckets of water, but it was of no help. The entire family died. I realized that lack of water, fire engines, and hydrants killed those poor people." She concluded, "Por eso me movilice" (Because of that I mobilized).

Lamentably, many parallels can be drawn with the Mothers of the Disappeared in Argentina, especially in Ciudad Juárez, where women became activists when their daughters disappeared or were found raped, mutilated, and murdered. The resultant pain, anger, and desperation led them to become activists seeking justice for their daughters. This was particularly true in response to the high number of cases (over 370) of murdered and disappeared women in Ciudad Juárez and Chihuahua City (Monarrez 2000, 2002; Staudt and Coronado 2002).

Need-Based Activism — La Chispa

Women on the border also had similar experiences with women in Boston (Hardy-Fanta 1997) who recognized the need for social change. Clara, a self-described paracaidista, declared she became involved and politically active because people in her colonia did not have *tenencia de la tierra* (title to the land). Obtaining land is a particular problem for people who have journeyed to a border city, becoming squatters along with other low-income people and others seeking better lives. Squatters are usually careful to take over land that is federal government property; it is then generally easier to obtain title than if the land is privately owned. Private-land owners will not easily yield title to their land and sometimes demand compensation from the government. The title process requires involvement with a political party or lobbying a city council member. When the title is granted, a symbolic but important ceremony takes place in which government officials give the title to the family.

Without clear land title, it is unwise to demand public services because families and even entire colonias can be dislocated. Therefore, the first step is to obtain legal title and later demand basic local government services. Clara was successful obtaining title not only for her land, but also for that of thirty other paracaidista families.

Invited Activists

Entry into political activism occurred for Paula when, in the process of buying a small plot of land, paracaidistas took over her lot. She and her husband were very upset when they confronted the paracaidistas. During the course of the argument the paracaidistas, who were members of a political party, were so impressed they ended up yielding the land to Paula because she fought justly. In turn they invited her to work with their party. Although many of these activists are not part of the economic or political elite, they become part of the status quo economically, socially, culturally, and politically, finding ways to promote their causes in spite of their lack of social standing. Several Mexican politicians and activists cite "being invited to participate" as a reason for their entry into the political arena (Coronado 1998; Rodríguez 1998, 2003). Others refer to this as a selective recruitment process and sponsorship (Camp 2003).

Paula explained that "soy servidora para la persona que me necesite, no servidora pública" (I am here to serve the person who needs it, but I am not a public servant). She does not consider herself a public servant but rather a "server" of any person who needs her services. Paula claims she did not think of running for public office until someone in the party "me ofreció la candidatura" (offered me the candidacy). She emphasized launching her campaign "por la posibilidad de ayudar y hacer tanto por la gente desprotegida, a través del ejercicio del poder" (because of the possibility of helping and doing so much for the disenfranchised through the exercise of power).

The following motivating factors for entering the activist arena, as described by northern border women, are not as well developed in the existing literature: spiritual and religious activists, work-based activists, and outsourced activists. The last two may be unique to the border.

Spiritual and Religious Activists

Women on the border expressed their profound spiritual need to help others. Some women reported they felt they had a calling to help the less fortunate in their communities and that their activism was a manifestation of a spiritual need to be of service to others. Spiritual activists do not necessarily have religious linkages, though some declared they became aware of the needs in the colonias when teaching catechism to colonia children, exposing them to the community problems. Through religious work they provided medical services and food baskets to those in need. Catalina, from Ciudad Juárez, summarized her sentiments: "My mission became helping those who are in need."

One activist Catholic sister, Luz, who works with prostitutes "one at a time," explained she did not do this for recognition, or for political or economic reasons. "This is the hard work of society; we have helped women to learn to sew, sell dresses, and have provided assistance to women in jail. We also try to help mothers to better interact with their children," she noted.

Work-Based Activists

Working middle-class women, who tended to be in professional settings, became activists as they became concerned about a particular social need not being met. For example, Teresa started an organization to help people with children who are chronically ill with diseases such as leukemia or cancer. Her paid work as a hospital professional was not sufficient; she also wanted to help those who did not have access to medical care. Carmen, another professional employee of the government, said her work at the Instituto Mexicano de Seguro Social (Mexican Institute of Social Security; IMSS) introduced her to the need for day-care centers. She stated, "Through my work, though it was not really part of my job, I was able to help to document the need and fund more community day-care centers." Cecilia, a state government employee, realized more work needed to be done with gang prevention, so she lobbied for community youth programs. Through their formal employment, these three activists found ways to help their communities by garnering resources, making the necessary connections, and providing services that improved conditions.

Outsourced Activists

Outsourced activism is when an established activist sends her children or other extended family members to help with community projects, and in turn, the outsourced relative becomes involved in activist work. One activist proudly reported that her entire family was involved in activism throughout the colonia, including her children, nieces, nephews, and in-laws living with her. Her activism had a multiplier effect upon her family, a consequence in which she felt great pride. In turn, some of her family members subsequently became actively involved in their own activist campaigns. One outsourced activist, Susana, reported her involvement started only because she saw how tired and overcommitted her mother was. One day, Susana's mother had agreed to help with the organization of a *kermés* (a fundraising bazaar), and needed help. Susana explained: "I really didn't want to go because I knew it was a lot of work setting up booths and tables, but I wanted to help my mother. She asked me so I went. In the end, I became involved."

Activist Strategies and Organizations

On the border, activists tend to gravitate toward three models of activism: working within the political system, creating asociaciones civiles, and independent activism. The following examples of how women throughout the border region have been agents of change through their work illustrate these three models.

Political System Activism

In colonias populares, various important factors lead to successful activism by women. One factor is that colonias populares are usually low-income and low-resource areas with great social and infrastructural needs, where people spend an inordinate amount of time commuting to work on public transportation and spend long hours at work. They have little energy or time left over in the day to meet and strategize or to organize politically. The tremendous self-help and mutual support in colonias populares leads to community solidarity. When illness or death affects a community, people combine their resources to help afflicted families. Likewise, when building their own homes, people exchange labor and know-how among neighbors. Limited resources, energy, and time, along with limited access to telephone service and lack of awareness of public institutions, all preclude people from seeking government services on their own, creating opportunities for women to emerge as leaders in colonias populares.

Alicia, who taught catechism in her colonia, became an activist through her quest for social justice. Her parents and siblings all enjoy a sense of social esteem because of Alicia's efforts. People seek her out when they have questions regarding a government office or a neighborhood concern, or when someone is ill or dies. Alicia's knowledge of, and access to, community resources and services are highly valued. Though her family at times feels that neighbors overburden Alicia with their problems and concerns, they are proud she can help others with social services or conduct *tramites con el gobierno* (government business) because of her education and activism.

Many of the activists who work in colonias discussed how one of the first tasks that they undertake is to *crear equipo* (create a team). They begin by organizing their neighbors, taking their demand (usually only one at the beginning) to the city council, and continuing to make demands until they have been recognized and their petition or demand has been met. Eventually, these small neighborhood organizations become *comites de vecinos* (neighborhood committees) that local governments support and encourage.

The delivery of basic infrastructure to a colonia is perhaps one of the most important issues in these activists' work. For example, Carmen described her evolution into activism: "First we had water delivered in *pipas* (water pipes), then we asked for garbage pickup, and next we demanded a school. Afterwards, we pushed for public transportation and, finally, for water and sewer infrastructure." Small successes in turn allow activists to work for bigger achievements over time. Some of the reported gains include natural gas connections, public telephones, construction of a bridge, and installation of sidewalks. *Gestionar* (to diligently pursue actions that will lead one to achieve a goal), an expression used by activists, is also the ability to discern how to work and which person to approach to achieve the desired goal. In this context, gestionar means much more: knowing how to make a demand, to whom to present the demand, and how to ask for government assistance or support.

Activism through Asociaciones Civiles

By the mid 1990s, over 5,000 non-governmental organizations, including asociaciones civiles (ACs), were registered in Mexico, mostly in urban centers (Camp 2003). The rise of ACs can be attributed in part to the role women played after the 1985 Mexico City earthquake. On the northern border, environmental and labor ACs flourished prior to the ratification of

TABLE 9.1 Woman-Headed *asociaciones civiles*

Name	Place	Issues	Work
Amas de Casa de Playas de Tijuana, A.C.	Tijuana, Baja California	Environment, social, cultural	Legislative direct action, legislative education
Casa Amiga, A.C.	Ciudad Juárez, Chihuahua	Women and violence	Advocacy, legal representation
Centro de Apoyo Contra la Violencia, A.C.	Nogales, Sonora	Women and violence	Counseling, advocacy
Centro de Investigación y Solidaridad Obrera, A.C.	Ciudad Juárez, Chihuahua	Labor issues	Advocacy, worker education
Federación Mexicana de Asociaciones Privadas, FEMAP, A.C.	Ciudad Juárez, Chihuahua	Health	Delivery of health services
Nuestras Hijas de Regreso a Casa, A.C.	Ciudad Juárez, Chihuahua	Women and violence	Advocacy, family support
Organización de Comunidades Pro-Vida Digna, A.C.	Matamoros, Tamaulipas	Health, *colonia* issues	Education, delivery of health services
Proyecto Fronterizo de Educación Ambiental, A.C.	Tijuana, Baja California	Environmental	Legislative policy changes

the North American Free Trade Agreement (NAFTA), in part because of financial and moral support from U.S.–based non-governmental organizations (NGOs) that were opposed to NAFTA. Creating an AC requires knowledge, because it is a rather bureaucratic process, and money, because the services of an attorney are required. Northern border activists, either from the upper-middle class or with help from U.S.–based NGOs, are able to create their own ACs. These ACs, while affording more independence from the government, at the same time present greater challenges, especially in the state of Chihuahua, as shown in the example below (see also López Estrada, this vol.). Some ACs have been able to garner recognition and form alliances with international organizations and in some instances have been able to circumvent the government and address important issues such as labor rights, women's reproductive health concerns, and violence against women. Table 9.1 includes a list of a few of the ACs on the border headed by women.

According to television and newspaper accounts, international support of ACs, especially from women's rights organizations, is becoming an increasing problem for government officials in the state of Chihuahua, especially those working on cases of the murdered and mutilated women in Ciudad Juárez and elsewhere. State government officials have called for an investigation into the source of such funding for certain groups with AC status, especially if it comes from foreign sources. Like 501(c)3s (nonprofit organizations in the United States), ACs enjoy certain privileges; they also have responsibilities in terms of reporting their financial statements and their ability to lobby government officials is limited. The state of Chihuahua is scrutinizing local ACs that receive outside funding and recognition, which prevents the government from co-opting them, resulting in less government control of their words and actions. This is of serious concern to these ACs and their members; they fear their independence and autonomy are being challenged, especially when the government calls for audits of their books, demanding to see if they have received financial support from foreign sources.

Independent Activism

Independent activists tend to work directly with people and emulate the U.S. version of volunteerism to some extent. Olga is an independent activist who spends time at the Casa del Migrante helping people who have been deported. She translates for deported Mexicans who have lived in the United States most of their lives and now find themselves in Mexico because they have committed a deportable federal crime. These deportees speak limited Spanish, are not socialized in Mexican culture, and are forced to find employment and negotiate new legal and political systems that are alien to them. Olga does this work because she feels that it is important to help others, but she does not receive any remuneration.

Teresa can be described as an independent activist who refuses to succumb to the government or to the conditions set forth by having an AC status. She works directly with people in need, as a volunteer if necessary. She will make demands of government officials for health care, organize rallies to protest violence against women, write letters to editors of newspapers to raise awareness of water contamination, or participate in radio shows to condemn political corruption, all without compromising her independence. Financially she survives on donations. Through her actions and deeds, people on both sides of the border feel comfortable giving her money because they know that she will make good use of it. One day I witnessed her immediately take a donation to a pharmacy to buy medicine for a ten-year-old boy who was ill.

A subset of independent activists are academics who become active because of their research interests in environmental issues, human rights and immigration, indigenous communities, and other areas. Academic activists tend to serve as advocates and consultants to individual community members who need technical assistance or guidance or to emerging leaders in organizations that deal with environmental issues. Academic activists present their findings to various government officials, write articles about their causes for newspapers, help move political agendas, and make public policy recommendations. Academic activists tend to work independently of political parties and to shy away from creating ACs. They may serve as volunteer consultants to both governmental and nongovernmental organizations.

Liliana, an academic who researches indigenous communities that have moved to the northern border, also gives time, money, and expertise to the same group she studies. Without compromising her academic integrity, she works directly with the community, lobbies policymakers who are in a position to help the community, and through her research hopes to inform public policy. Independent activists are effective, though their radius of operation is seen by some as narrow and limited.

The Role of Class

Activists come from a wide variety of socioeconomic backgrounds. Some activists are very low income; nonetheless, they are able to obtain services for their colonias. Low-income activists usually depend on public transportation, a time-consuming mode of transportation. They also rely on public telephones and use cyber cafés for e-mail. Activists who work at the grassroots in colonias populares tend to come from poor families. Since many of them work, mostly in maquiladoras or in the informal sector, and at the same time care for their families, they do not have much time to organize politically or create their own organizations. It is amazing to see how many activists are able to achieve their community-based goals in spite of their limited resources.

Activists tend to demand basic services that meet immediate and practical needs. They generally do not have time to fully develop a political strategy, unlike those who create asociaciones civiles. In the Mexican political context, it is not easy to obtain AC status because it requires money, an inordinate amount of paperwork, and legal expertise to facilitate the process. Therefore, for activists who cannot formally organize, it is important to maintain links to elected officials. Activists who have not formally organized and who have had some level of success are better able to work in their communities because of their ties to politicians who in turn facilitate the delivery of basic community services and resources. It would be virtually impossible to arrange garbage collection, water and sewer infrastructure, electricity, and so forth without collaboration between activists and government officials.

These activist experiences, either through the political party structure or through the creation of asociaciones civiles, give these women confidence, experience, and connections that later serve to move their political agendas in another way. Thus, experienced and seasoned activists are able to deliver to their communities, improving the quality of life on the northern border.

Middle-class activists usually have access to private transportation. They have resources such as home telephone service and computer access.

Wealthy activists are the exception and not the rule; however, these women are able to use their own private resources to finance and create their own ACs because they have the financial resources and also are able to garner more resources to create an infrastructure for service delivery. Wealthy activists are able to earn support for their causes because they provide services to the poor, work with women, and challenge the political and economic establishment only enough to get necessary support. Health-care delivery, services to women, and helping children are relatively safe political areas where upper-class activists can engage with the support of the political and economic elite. Non-governmental organizations, such as Federación Mexicana de Asociaciones Privadas (Mexican Federation of Private Associations; FEMAP) in Ciudad Juárez, subsidize the government by providing medical services to a large segment of the population.

Class differences have determined how activists interact with others. The low-income activists take great pride in knowing how to ask and whom to ask when requesting services for their colonias. As the saying goes: *el buen pedir para el buen recibir* (knowing how to ask well allows you in turn to receive well). Many of them carefully detailed how they approached members of the city council or the mayor, and described how they presented themselves as *bien arreglada* (well-dressed) when they submitted their petition or letter. They took pride in respecting public officials and felt they were accorded greater respect when they presented themselves in a similar manner. They tended to address each other and public officials with respect, using the formal *usted* (you) rather than the familiar *tu* (you) reserved for family members and friends. They felt their demands would more likely be met if they used greater formality when presenting requests.

Not all activists use such subtleties, regardless of economic class. Some activists have used different tactics, reporting they had reverted to protests; made vocal and in some cases outrageous demands; leveraged their demands by taking press members along; and finally, *hacer un escándalo* (made a scandalous scene) as the only way authorities would ever pay attention to them. In Ciudad Juárez, low-income people who wanted title to their land camped out in front of the *presidencia municipal* (city hall) until they received the titles.

Conclusion

Mexican women on the border are like Mexican, United States, and Latin American women in general in terms of activism. Rodriguez (2003, 6) declares that "women have invariably formed the backbone of social movements and other organized forms of protest aimed at articulating demands for basic services for their neighborhoods . . . in many cases for equality and fairness from the state in the delivery of goods and services. All this political activism, both formal and informal, has transformed the role of women in the political process during the last fifteen years." It is certain that women will continue their activism for years to come.

Activists come from different backgrounds, educational levels, and different family situations and economic circumstances; however, one thing they have in common is their commitment to social justice. By *haciendo actos, mostrando los logros* (doing things and showing achievements), they show society how women, those with limited resources but possessing serious conviction, can help contribute to the evolution of democracy and social justice. These women have achieved political goals, delivered services, met demands, raised awareness, and promoted social changes. A long-time committed activist stated that her goals are achieved with *constancia, sinceridad, y amor* (consistency, sincerity, and love).

As the border industrialization program that helped develop colonias and women activists is now changing direction, women activists will likewise change gears to meet new demands. With the recent closures of many maquiladoras, workers are being laid off, hired temporarily without benefits, or are permanently losing their jobs. Community activists are responding to these changes by developing strategies to help people find work or create their own employment opportunities. Ciudad Juárez in 2002 hosted 400 maquiladoras. One year later, over 100 of the factories had closed, leaving more than 85,000 people unemployed (Coronado Moreno 2003). Clearly, activists will need to put their energies in this area as formal jobs become more scarce and uncertain. Economic needs will increase and social demands will compound. Women like Madre Conchita and the other activists must continue their political activism in the border region and beyond.

Over time, I have met countless women who have made a difference in a variety of ways, by helping members of the colonia populares gain title to land, compelling the city government to pick up the trash and provide other basic services, and addressing issues of violence against women and immigrants. Some activists work alone, others join forces with other women or organizations working on similar issues. Border women are not unlike their sisters in Latin America, other parts of Mexico, or the United States, but what sometimes sets them apart is their distance and alienation from each other.

Activists working in the region need more opportunities for collaborative work. They must unify their energies and resources in order to maximize their efficiency and efforts. The activist community on the border lacks horizontal integration. Activists in Matamoros could learn from their counterparts in Tijuana, and those in Nogales could share their experiences with those in Reynosa. What is also lamentable is that most research about community activism in northern Mexico is in English only, including my own work. More publications should be translated into Spanish and made available to community activists and residents. An effort must be made to foster unity, to strategize, and to share best practices that capitalize on the experiences of the seasoned activists on the border who have contributed so much.

IO Border Women's NGOs and Political Participation in Baja California

Silvia López Estrada

The main goal of this chapter is the analysis of female political participation through the study of the social movement of women's nongovernmental organizations (NGOs) in the Mexican state of Baja California. I address the interaction of NGOs with their counterparts in the U.S. state of California, and I focus particularly on NGOs' influence on policymaking in the border city of Tijuana.

During the 1990s, the creation of NGOs institutionalized some aspects of the feminist agenda in Latin American countries, but in the context of global feminism, it is fundamental to emphasize local differences and to interpret feminisms in light of prevalent sociohistorical and political conditions (Dietz 1990; Jelin 1994).

In this chapter, I propose that in Baja California, women's ways of doing politics are changing in response to new local geopolitics, which in part are determined by the state reform[1] that currently is in process. Because much research has focused attention on the feminist movement in Mexico City, this chapter is intended to fill the void about regional spaces using the northern border as an example. This analysis is based on empirical data from interviews with women members of NGOs and is supported by the sociological literature on women's political participation in Latin America.

The chapter begins with an overview of theoretical debates concerning feminism, non-governmental organizations, and women's political participation. I then present the methodological issues that guided this study. After offering a profile of women's NGOs in Baja California, I analyze their interaction with similar organizations in California. In the next section, I examine NGOs' influence in policymaking, using as an example the case of Tijuana's Subcommittee of Women's Affairs. In the conclusions, I discuss some of the problems and challenges that feminist NGOs included in this study face as participants in local politics.

The Social Movement of Non-governmental Organizations in Baja California

In Latin American countries like Mexico, women's mobilization has gone beyond the feminist movement: it is diverse and involves people from different social classes, rural and urban origins, and from different occupational sectors, among other factors (Lamas et al. 1995). In addition, these varied women's movements are characterized by the heterogeneity of their demands, which many times have been different from feminist demands. For example, Oliveira and Ariza (1999) distinguish three different types of female mobilizations in Mexico based on criteria of gender and age, public services demands, and human rights.

Due to the diversity of Mexican women's movements, three general varieties of feminism have developed in Mexico. Historical feminists generally included middle-class women, emphasized women's subordination, and centered their fight on domestic work, abortion, sexuality, and violence. The movement known as popular feminism, in contrast, is dominated by women from popular (low-income) sectors who face poverty and marginality and whose demands such as housing, urban services, and better living conditions are defined by their vulnerable economic situation (Espinosa 2002a; Maier 1997).

A third variety of Mexican feminism is organized through NGOs and is known as social feminism. Like historical feminism, social feminism addresses power relationships through gender analysis, but like popular feminism, it focuses its action on women of the popular sectors. These two variants of feminism also share the idea that the recognition of political and ideological differences is needed in order to elaborate a common and inclusive project (Espinosa 2002b, 33).

The development of these different sectors of Mexican feminism, as well as their encounters and disagreements, has been widely analyzed (Espinosa 2002b; C. González 2001; Gutiérrez Castañeda 2002; Lamas 1994; Mogrovejo 1992; Sánchez Olvera 2002). The different branches of the Mexican feminist movement changed as a result of these encounters, showing women's diversity, as well as the dynamism of the processes of deconstruction and construction of their identities (Espinosa 2002a; Serret 2000). While historical feminists worked to introduce a socioeconomic vision into their discourse, popular feminists tried to give a gender dimension to their demands. Social feminism had a difficult and eventually failed role as mediator between the two. However, unlike popular feminism, which dissolved for different reasons (Sánchez Olvera 2002), feminist NGOs institutionalized their movement. I will develop this issue further in the sections that follow.

Regional differences are always important. In Mexico City, where feminism had a predominantly middle-class composition, NGOs were the site of encounters between popular sectors and feminists (Lamas 1994). In Baja California, in contrast, women of the popular sectors mobilized through the urban popular movement and some middle-class women joined them, so the two groups came together before the emergence of feminist movement centered in the NGOs (López Estrada 2002).

Feminist groups in Baja California emerged from women's awareness groups,[2] and some of them went through a process that resulted in their formalization during the 1990s. Small groups first were transformed into informal civil associations, but the need for financial resources forced them to change into formal NGOs. The membership of feminist groups did not change significantly through different periods of their movement in Baja California. This is a feature that distinguishes this movement from the one in Mexico City, where feminism has diversified its leaders and composition. In some of the leaders' opinions, the loss of leaders and the lack of new members are disadvantages that may lead to the stagnation of NGOs. Despite this, the women's movement in this Mexican border state has been extremely dynamic, particularly in the past decade. Currently in Baja California, the social feminism of NGOs is often viewed as the only feminist presence. Some historical feminists in the 1990s decided to leave the movement but are still fighting women's subordination from other forums such as media, arts, and academia. These feminists do not oppose NGOs and often collaborate with them when they are asked to or through their own initiative.

Methodology

This chapter is based on information from in-depth interviews with leaders of NGOs in the municipalities of Tijuana, Mexicali, Ensenada, and Tecate.[3] I identified twenty-five NGOs that worked on reproductive and sexual rights and labor rights in those cities. From the list of twenty-five,

I selected a study group of fourteen organizations, some of which were feminist and some that identified themselves as non-feminist. In addition, I included two NGOs that work in the areas of health and whose main concern is women's overall well-being, rather than the change of women's social condition.[4]

The interviews with directors, leaders, and members of NGOs inquired about the history of the organizations; their activities, programs, and approaches; and the methodologies they develop to provide different groups of women with health-care services, legal advice, and training. In particular, I investigated the ways they worked to influence policymaking. I also interviewed public employees and attended monthly sessions of Tijuana's Subcommittee of Women's Affairs. My own participation in the subcommittee gave me a better understanding of the processes and relationships among NGOs and between them and the governmental agencies.

Women's NGOs, Political Participation, and Public Policies

The social movement of women's NGOs has had a strong presence in Baja California since the 1990s. The organizations share the goals of defending women's rights and increasing women's political participation and influence in the public sphere. A particular feature of the movement is the construction of a gender discourse with a citizenship dimension.

Liberal theory establishes an abstract concept of citizenship that defines individuals as free and equal but that in reality gives men all the attributes and privileges of freedom and equality and leaves women outside of the public sphere of politics. Because women belong to the private world, they are dependent and subordinated and are not considered public citizens (Dietz 1990; Massolo 1994, 14). Feminists criticize these conceptions and define politics as a process that includes different forms of political participation beyond public entities such as government, parliament, and political parties.

Women participate in the public sphere of politics through electoral processes and by belonging to political organizations, both formal and informal. Many studies in Latin America have documented and analyzed the specific ways of women's participation in the public sphere during the processes of democratization in the Southern Cone (Jaquette 1991; Jelin 1990) and the development of women's movements in response to the structural adjustment policies that affected most Latin American countries, including Mexico (Fernández Poncela 1995; Massolo 1994). Women's movements transformed the concept of citizenship, giving it a new meaning by centering women as political actors (Massolo 1994).

In particular, feminism has expanded the concept of politics to include everyday struggles for survival and a change in power relationships in all spheres of social life (Bystydzienski 1992; Massolo 1994, 20; Tuñón 1992, 96). Women's demands for citizenship expanded their informal means and modes of social action, diversifying the public sphere of politics (Massolo 1994; Tarrés 1998). Within everyday spaces, women establish relationships of power with public authorities, demand and negotiate resources, counteract public decisions, resist, negotiate, and exert influence (Massolo 1994, 36).

A particular form of women's participation in politics has been through their influence in policymaking, centering women's problems within the public agenda and developing alternative policies. The influence of the women's movement is expressed through the promotion of their issues and in the recognition by party and government officials of their organizations and their participation in the public sphere as political (Incháustegui 1995).

Mexican women's NGOs define their political participation mainly through their involvement in advocacy[5] and policymaking. Their main demand is to participate in the design of public policies related to violence, reproductive health,[6] and associated issues. Beyond their role as mediators between women's needs and state social policy, NGOs are constructing citizenship by working in the transformation of a legislative agenda, following campaign promises, and monitoring federal government work on international agreements. These citizen activities respond to the structure of opportunities for participation that local governments opened up (Barquet 2002).

As social and political actors, NGOs are tolerant and plural spaces created by women for resolving their specific needs through alternative models of social relationships and for representing their interests in political life. NGOs are also forums for multiple discourses and debates, training, and reflection. Sonia Alvarez (1998, 109) points out that women are diversifying their political action, and its heterogeneity is expressed in the decentralization of NGOs' practices, demands, discourses, and strategies of political mobilization. Analysts suggest that in Mexico the work of these organizations as advocates is a response to the absence of legitimacy of institutions such as the political parties (Saucedo González 1995; Tarrés 1998).

Geographical location and the political context are factors that give specificity to the social feminism of NGOs in Baja California. In terms of geography, the proximity to California has opened up a diversity of interactions between Mexican NGOs and similar organizations in U.S. cities such as San Diego and Calexico. In terms of the political context, the relationship of these NGOs with the local and regional governments is complex and subject to change over time. In Baja California, two factors have been particularly important. First, the economic and social dynamism of the last three decades has involved an ample female participation. Second, the political transformation promoted by state reform has broadened the structure of political opportunities for NGOs in the public sphere. In this way, new spaces of citizenship participation have emerged, constituting what I call an "intermediate" category between formal and informal politics. I will further illustrate this argument by discussing NGOs' participation in local politics in the city of Tijuana.

Non-governmental Organizations in Baja California

In this section, I first introduce the process of institutionalization of NGOs in Baja California, then I present the features of the NGOs included in this study. Institutionalization of NGOs and the feminist agenda has been a trend among NGOs not only in Mexico, but also throughout Latin America. In the political and cultural context of each part of the region, the identity of women's movements is created by place-specific problems and demands. Institutionalization is part of the second generation of the feminist movement, in which NGOs have been created to provide women of popular sectors with more professional services (A. Martínez and Incháustegui 1998, 179). With the financial support of various agencies, NGOs developed a new structure of social relationships with low-income women and authorities. Their main demand was to participate in the design of public policies. As a part of this process, NGOs in Baja California changed their legal status and defined their organizational structure and their goals. International agencies strongly encouraged NGOs to specialize in the services they offer to women, as well as to professionalize their members through training programs (López Estrada 2002, 211).

Profile of NGOs

Almost all the organizations included in this study were created at the end of the 1980s and the beginning of the 1990s. With the exception of two NGOs that were created in the earlier 1980s, most women's NGOs in Baja California proliferated during the 1990s, and two emerged very recently. In general, NGOs were started by middle-class professional women who offered alternative reproductive health and legal services, and training to defend the rights of specific groups of women, such as maquiladora workers and indigenous migrants. Table 10.1 shows the place and date of origin of NGOs, their intervention areas, the services they provide to women, and their financial sources. I discuss these features of NGOs in the following paragraphs.

Women's NGOs in Baja California sprang from various sources: ecclesiastical groups, as in the case of Asociación Nacional para la Superación Integral de la Mujer (National Association for the Advancement of Women), and grassroots organizations like the women's groups created during the urban popular movement of the 1970s and the maquiladora workers' fight for labor rights in the 1980s (López Estrada 2002). Some other NGOs emerged from citizens' initiatives—for example, Centro de Capacitación and Servicios Psicológicos (Center for Training and Psychological Services). Some of these groups are feminist, in that they seek larger social change in gender relations; others are concerned with women's well-being but not necessarily with changing their social condition. Some groups are part of international organizations; for example, while Fronteras Unidas (United Borders) has the support of Planned Parenthood of San Diego and the Mexican Association of Sexuality in Mexico, Patronato de Medicina Social Comunitaria (Foundation of Social Community Medicine) is linked to Project Concern International in San Diego. These groups work with funds from their central branches and adopt their goals and methodologies.

TABLE 10.1 Women's Non-governmental Organizations in Baja California

Name	Place and date of origin	Intervention areas	Services provided	Economic sources	Clientele
Alaíde Foppa*	Mexicali, 1993	Domestic violence, reproductive health, human rights	Education and training	MacArthur Foundation	General population
Asociación Mexicana para la Superación Integral de la Mujer	Tijuana, 1991	Health and nutrition, human development	Education and training on health	Membership dues	Women of popular sectors
Casa de la Mujer Factor X*	Tijuana, 1989	Labor health, reproductive health, sexuality and violence, sexual harassment, labor rights	Health services, training, legal counseling	Energy and Paper Union, McArthur Foundation	Maquiladora workers
Casa San Miguel	Tijuana, 1990	Cervical cancer	Hospice and meals for women with cancer	Donations	Poor women with cancer
Centro de Apoyo para Mujeres	Ensenada, 1994	Domestic violence	Psychological therapy, legal counseling	Membership dues	Women of popular sectors
Centro de Apoyo Terapéutico	Tijuana, 1990	Sexual violence	Psychological therapy	Donations	Low- and middle-class population
Centro de Capacitación y Servicios Psicológicos	Tijuana, 1991	Sexual diversity	Psychological services	Service fees	Women of popular and middle-class sectors

TABLE 10.1 *Continued*

Name	Place and date of origin	Intervention areas	Services provided	Economic sources	Clientele
El Lugar de la Tía Juana	Tijuana, 1990	Domestic violence	Psychological therapy, training	Service fees	Women of popular and middle-class sectors
Fronteras Unidas Pro Salud	Tijuana, 1988	Sexual and reproductive health, gender	Health services, training	Planned Parenthood	General population
Grupo Apoyo	Tijuana, 1994	Domestic violence	Psychological therapy	Municipal government	Women of popular sectors
Lilith*	Tecate, 1991	Reproductive health, domestic violence, human rights	Psychological therapy, legal counseling	Women's Foundation, Membership dues	Women of popular sectors
Mujeres por un Mundo Mejor	Mexicali, 1983	Domestic violence	Education and training	Mama Cash	Women of popular sectors
Pamsida	Tijuana, 1997	AIDS, domestic violence	Education and training	Service fees	HIV patients, women and children, general population
Patronato de Medicina Social Comunitaria*	Tijuana, 1980	Sexual and reproductive health, gender	Education and training	Project Concern International	Women of popular sectors

*These organizations belong to the Women's Network of the Peninsula of Baja California. With the exception of Casa San Miguel, Asociación Mexicana para la Superación Integral de la Mujer, Centro de Apoyo Terapéutico, and Casa de la Mujer, all of Tijuana's NGOs belong to the Subcommittee of Women's Affairs.

Those NGOs that are part of national or international organizations or that receive external funding are characterized by a more complex organization and a centralized decision-making process. They also have better infrastructure and organize their work based on plans and programs. While in fieldwork, six of the fourteen NGOs based their work on a regular budget provided by international agencies; a few others received financial support from local governments. The rest of them had no outside financial support, relying only on the low fees they charged for their services, membership dues, and donations from charity organizations. The economic situation of these organizations was fragile in general, and the competition for limited resources was one of the main problems they faced.

NGOs are characterized by differences in their specializations and intervention areas and by their size and financial resources. But some have overlapping aims that create disagreements among them, and they also compete for political resources and networks. NGOs offer low-income women health services, legal advice, and training and counseling in the areas of reproductive health, violence, and labor rights. NGOs give particular attention to poor women, and they further target the population by different age groups, occupations (like maquiladora workers), and ethnicity (such as Mixtecos). This reflects organizations' concerns about diversity and difference beyond gender.

Larger organizations have additional resources like a small library on specific topics such as reproductive health, gender, and women's labor rights. Some NGOs (Fronteras Unidas and Factor X, for example) have funding to conduct research on specific topics such as reproductive rights and workers' labor rights. For instance, Factor X organized women maquiladora workers to conduct a survey about pieceworking with the financial support of Homenet, an international home-workers' network.

Some NGOs have members who were part of the nascent women's groups in the 1970s, others who participated in the urban popular movement, and some who were part of leftist political parties. Most of the leaders developed their professional careers at the same time they were working for the organizations. These feminists constitute a resource for the movement because of their activism and experience. While the larger NGOs have part-time or full-time employees, the rest of them rely on their members' volunteer work.

Small and large organizations have different strengths. The smaller organizations have capitalized on their knowledge, information, and accumulated experience to balance their resources. For example, the Centro de Capacitación y Servicios Psicológicos has no financial funding but actively participates in seeking information, in lobbying politicians and state functionaries, and in discussing themes and strategies with major NGOs.

The most influential NGOs, however, are what Alvarez (1998, 112) calls institutional NGOs. They are characterized by specialized and professional personnel, funding from international agencies, and their use of strategic planning in providing services to women and in influencing public policies. In addition, public agencies, international foundations, and mass media distinguish them by providing support.

Institutional NGOs have been criticized for distancing themselves from popular sectors, but as Tarrés (1998, 133) argues, these NGOs are different from those of popular or civil organizations that represent a wider social base, because of their activities and structure. So as intermediaries between women's grassroots groups and local governments, the NGOs' legitimacy is not based on representation of these groups of women but instead is enhanced by their commitment to ensure that the experiences and concerns of disadvantaged or oppressed groups influence government policy agendas, processes, and outcomes.

Although some organizations try to engage their target women in programs as promoters for women's rights, in general, less-advantaged women do not belong to NGOs but are the recipients of their services and consciousness-raising efforts. In some cases, it would be difficult for these women to collaborate actively with NGOs due to the conditions of their daily lives. This is the case, for example, of battered women, who are the target populations of some NGOs.

Overall, despite the fact that not all NGOs have the same political resources, as a movement they consider themselves to be advocates with some influence in public policies and laws and to be interlocutors of public officials and mass media. NGOs take part in the debate and discussion about reproductive-health policies, domestic violence, public budget, and efficiency of municipal agencies for women's care. For NGOs, recognition by local authorities and media is not a privilege but rather the result of many years of work. Beyond their differences, NGOs are characterized by their common goals in fighting for women's rights. This unity is what makes them all a part of a genuine movement.

Issues and Methodological Approaches of NGOs

Different theoretical and ideological orientations also define the agendas and methodologies of the NGOs included in this study. Some of the organizations consider themselves feminist and others do not, but both groups of NGOs use a gender discourse in that they work in favor of women's interests. Feminist NGOs openly declare themselves as such, and they look for government recognition of their specific demands for reproductive and sexual rights. They include a gender perspective in their programs, projects, and services, as they recognize women's subordination. They also work vigorously to raise women's consciousness and promote gender equality. An example of this approach is Factor X, which worked with and for women and whose members pressed demands for women's rights and fought for women's empowerment.[7] The leaders involved women workers in their programs, recognized women's knowledge, and promoted the defense of their rights through education and training.

Non-feminist NGOs, in contrast, frequently do not explicitly include a gender perspective in their goals, but in practice they are gender conscious in their domestic violence and reproductive-health programs. Some members of these NGOs may be feminists, but others do not consider themselves as such because they think of feminism as representing hatred of men.[8] Despite such internal differences, these organizations seek to improve women's living conditions and social status. This is so, for instance, in the case of Mujeres por un Mundo Mejor (Women for a Better World) and Fronteras Unidas. Whether or not explicitly feminist, they offer alternative services defined as woman-friendly.

A third type of NGOs is non-feminist because they do not use, or may be unaware of, a gender approach to reproductive-health issues, but they do promote women's well-being. These are service organizations, sometimes related to the Catholic Church, that approach women from a humanistic stance. These NGOs rely on the volunteer work of women who do not have a professional profile but are housewives or women who belong to a religious order. This is the case with the Asociación Mexicana para la Superación Integral de la Mujer (Mexican Association for the Advancement of Women; AMSIFEM). AMSIFEM dedicates its efforts to promoting women's well-being through a program of integral education, whose main aim is to teach women home economics and to enhance their abilities in order to fulfill their socially assigned roles more efficiently, within both the family and the community. Casa San Miguel is another example of this approach. It is dedicated to providing hospice and meals to low-income women cancer patients who come from other northern cities of Mexico to get medical attention in Tijuana.

The main topics discussed and debated by NGOs in the public agenda are reproductive health and domestic violence. Although these are problems of local relevance, they owe their priority to the legitimacy gained in the national sphere as a result of the Mexican government's commitments to the agreements of international conferences and to the efforts of international agencies to promote these issues. In addition, because these problems affect women in general, it has been feasible for organizations to unify demands and proposals on these issues.

Traditional feminist issues such as abortion rights and sexuality have not been directly approached by the organizations included in this study. In part, this is due to the fact that the Partido Acción Nacional (National Action Party; PAN), a political party characterized by its conservative ideas about women's roles in society, abortion, and sexuality, currently governs Baja California. In this ideological context, it seems that NGOs are afraid of losing the spaces of influence they have gained, and so they do not engage in a direct discussion on these topics.

Only one lesbian-gay organization has been established, and the inclusion of this issue in the political agenda has not been feasible. Therefore, the groups are focusing on making sure that women get the rights they already have (e.g., abortion in the case of rape) but are not yet addressing extending rights in controversial areas such as sexual orientation or legal abortion. Regardless of the NGOs' philosophy and ideology, the methods they use in their training, as well as those used in women's care, foster women's subjectivity and emphasize introspection. In addition, those groups that recognize women's subordination and try to overcome hierarchical gender relations strongly emphasize consciousness-raising in order to strengthen women's capacity.

Binational Cooperation

The relationship between Baja California's NGOs and similar organizations in California has been built up through time. Because of the proximity of border cities such as Tijuana and Mexicali to the United States,

Mexican NGOs have been influenced by Anglo feminism and have established relationships with Californian organizations. At the same time, they have been linked to the feminist movement in central Mexico. For instance, in 1983, the feminist group Xochiquetzal organized the conference "Women's Condition and Identity," with the participation of activists from both sides of the border.

Feminists also developed a relationship with Mexican leftist parties during the 1980s and founded NGOs in Baja California with the support of organizations from Mexico City, such as Equipo Pueblo (Community Team) and Centro de Investigación y Desarrollo Humano para América Latina (Center for Human Development and Research in Latin America; CIDHAL). These groups taught Baja California feminists strategies for fund-raising, as well as how to develop community projects (López Estrada 2002). By the end of the decade, however, this relationship had broken down. The parties tried to dissolve the feminist groups, which they saw as privileging gender instead of class. Having lost their previous allies, Baja California feminists turned northward and tried to rebuild their relationships with California NGOs. Specifically, they strengthened their cross-border networks through their relationship with Womancare, a health center specializing in well-women care, gynecology exams, and birth-control and abortion services. With the support of this organization, women's groups organized self-help groups, self-cervical exams, and reproductive-health workshops. In addition, together they fought against rape in the communities of Baja California.

Mexican NGOs have continued the cross-border interaction with their colleagues in the United States. Leaders have had opportunities to participate in conferences and workshops in California to learn methods and strategies adapted for Mexican women to offer alternative health services and support therapies. For instance, Mujeres por un Mundo Mejor, an NGO from Mexicali, adapted a methodology from the Family Center of Calexico to work with victims of violence. Factor X, from Tijuana, also adapted a methodology from an NGO in San Diego to work with maquiladora workers on labor rights.

Links with U.S. organizations also provide financial assistance. Unlike the United States, Mexico lacks a philanthropical tradition, making it difficult for NGOs to gain access to financial resources. However, proximity to California gives Baja California's NGOs some advantages, such as the possibility of interacting with NGOs in the United States and obtaining financial aid and other material resources from U.S. foundations. This is due to the fact that some U.S. agencies center their attention on the consequences of economic change for women in this region.

Binational relationships between Baja California and California NGOs have been in a transition process and are taking on a new dynamism. Some binational organizations based in the United States, such as Border Health Initiative, Planned Parenthood, and Project Concern International, work in collaboration with Mexican NGOs and local governments to develop specific programs in border cities of Baja California. At present, NGOs and government agencies from Tijuana and San Diego are formalizing a binational network to fight violence against women. NGOs on both sides of the border are currently acting as mediators between the governments of California and Baja California in order to establish and formalize public policies to benefit women on both sides of the border. NGOs' roles as mediators are part of what some scholars have called citizen diplomacy (e.g., Avendaño et al. 2000).

Women's NGOs' Political Participation and Influence in Policymaking

Political mobilization of women's NGOs in Baja California takes place in a changing scenario of local public politics.[9] In the context of state reform and of the decentralization of municipal governments, other forms of participation have emerged in the last few years. I call these new forms intermediate because they are located between the formal and the informal. In these new intermediate spaces of political participation, women of different social sectors discuss public policy issues related to women's well-being and social position. I illustrate my argument here through the experience of Tijuana's Subcommittee of Women's Affairs.

The participation of local women's groups in international women's conferences, along with Mexican authorities' promise to fulfill agreements reached at the United Nations conference in Cairo on population and the United Nations conference in Beijing on women, provided the foundation for the creation of the Subcommittee of Women's Affairs. At the local level, municipal reform in Tijuana allowed the creation of subcommittees, which became new spaces for citizen participation. Similar subcommittees do not exist in the rest of the municipalities of Baja California, however. The main goals of the Subcommittee of Women's Affairs are to analyze government's public action; to participate in public decision making; and to propose and recommend alternative programs and policies in relation to women's issues. Formally, the subcommittee had no gender perspective, because it was not stated in the law. In practice, however, women's NGOs tried to integrate gender issues into the subcommittee's agenda.

Coordinated by a member of the city council, the subcommittee is composed of representatives of women's NGOs and governmental agencies. It is divided into three commissions that work on three themes: reproductive health, domestic violence, and legal issues. Each commission is composed of NGOs and public agencies specialized in these topics, and each has its own working agenda.

During the first three years, the Subcommittee of Women's Affairs was very successful, its work distinguished by efficient organization and the achievement of diverse goals. The efficiency of its work was due to the leadership of the NGO's coordinator and to the work experience of its members with local women. In addition, the NGO's relationship with mass media, and its network of relations with politicians and public employees constructed over time, contributed to the success of the first years. Among the main achievements of the subcommittee have been the creation of the Center for Women's Protection, the Battered Women's Shelter in Tijuana, the Women's Institute of Baja California, the Women's Institute of Tijuana, reforms to Baja California's adoption laws, and the creation of interinstitutional networks.

The political work done by women regarding the creation of the Women's Institute of Baja California was particularly intense.[10] NGOs participated for more than two years in the discussion and debate about the institute. The main opponents were the Catholic Church and conservative social groups. The law was passed and the institute was opened in April 2002.

As an intermediate strategy of citizens' participation in public issues, the subcommittee is limited by bureaucracy and government representatives and by the lack of resources. The subcommittee also met obstacles in trying to influence policymaking, because it lacked formal functions and did not have a clear decision-making process. NGOs can only make proposals and recommendations whose formalization follows an institutional and bureaucratic path. After all, as Tarrés (1998) notes, NGOs do not govern, but they have the right to participate in the governance process.

Political changes and public officials' lack of sensitivity to gender issues may also have affected the continuity of the subcommittee's and other NGOs' work in the commissions. In response to the lack of leadership, some organizations decided to abandon the subcommittee. Nevertheless, they continue working informally on their agenda of reproductive health and domestic violence and promoting an interinstitutional network against violence to women. As one women stated, "While the term of municipal authorities comes to an end, we will stay here."

The subcommittee enabled women's NGOs to insert the topics of reproductive health and violence into the municipal agenda. It also created a space for debate and discussion, developed some influence in policy-making, established collaboration between NGOs and public agencies, and expanded the networks of NGOs. Most important, women from NGOs acquired new skills, increased their ability to manage mass media, and learned to deal with politicians. They also learned to negotiate. For instance, when Tijuana's mayor decided to create a women's institute in the city, an influential faction of NGOs participating in the subcommittee opposed the project because they thought it was a waste of resources and that it duplicated tasks of other public agencies. But when NGO leaders realized that the mayor was resolved to open the institute regardless of public opinion, they decided to present an alternative project to the city council that was accepted and approved with minimum changes. For NGOs, the outcome represented a concession on the part of the city's mayor and demonstrated the potential long-term effects of the subcommittee.

Although NGOs were created so that feminists would gain autonomy from political parties, the organizations have learned to seek alliances, to bargain, and to come to agreements with them. The demands of women's NGOs have motivated commitment from, and solidarity with, some congressional representatives and legislators of different political parties. These local politicians supported initiatives such as the Law for Attention and Prevention to Victims of Intra-family Violence, which was recently approved by the local congress.

Conclusions

At the turn of the century, the social movement of women's NGOs in Baja California sought to influence policymaking as part of its commitment to less-advantaged women. To achieve this goal, NGOs centered their strategies on political work. As advocates, they developed novel ways of penetrating power structures and influencing policymaking through informal networks and coalitions at the local, national, and international levels.

I used the example of the Subcommittee of Women's Affairs in Tijuana to show the creative political practices that NGOs have developed in this citizen space. Difficulties continue to characterize the continuity of such political spaces, however, and in Tijuana, women's NGOs continue working in informal spaces on the construction of a gender-sensitive municipal agenda, while also working with NGOs from other cities in the state on a legislative agenda to be presented to the local congress. Above all, the intermediate character of the subcommittee continues to allow women to move in and out of this space. The subcommittee's achievements resulted in the creation of institutions, legal regulations, and programs geared towards reproductive health and domestic violence. However, in the field of cultural and ideological values, traditional ideas about women's roles in society still persist. NGOs face the ongoing challenge of promoting a new gender culture based on equity.

Despite their achievements, women's NGOs face the challenge of providing continuity to the programs and policies that they have promoted. They must also streamline the decision-making process, as well as continue to train public employees and officers in order to sensitize them about gender issues. In particular, they have to target groups such as judges and physicians that show more resistance to the gender perspective.

Thanks in part to the demands and actions of NGOs, local governments have assumed the defense and protection of women and other vulnerable groups in their discourses. Official discourses express gender equity; however, the process of incorporating gender mainstreaming in local policies has not yet been assumed by municipal authorities. Thus far, violence has been the dominant theme of women's NGOs. The groups need a more efficient use of strategic planning tools that will continue building an inclusive agenda focusing attention on local problems such as women's opportunities to access education and the labor rights of maquiladora workers, indigenous women, agricultural women workers, domestic workers, and working children.

In Baja California, NGOs are part of a transnational movement. In this context, we observe revived links between NGOs on both sides of the border. The informal work and coalitions of NGOs along the border has opened enormous possibilities for carrying out binational programs and public policies from local governments in Mexico and the United States. One of the most important efforts of NGOs' transnational coalitions along the border is influencing policies regarding domestic violence and reproductive health, which involve the increasing participation of local authorities.

Overall, NGOs in Baja California are contributing to civil society by promoting a gender dimension to public policies, institutions, and local governments and by offering vision and alternative strategies regarding gender equity.

II "Making Believe" and "Willing Partners" in Academics' Activism in the U.S.–Mexico Borderlands

Patricia Manning,
with Janice Monk and Catalina Denman

In its very essence, this chapter represents a collective endeavor. It offers one narrative, seemingly in a singular voice; however, it represents shared insights distilled from years of interactions with colleagues in research-for-action and action-based research projects, as well as significant numbers of activist friends. I am fortunate to work currently at the Southwest Institute for Research on Women (SIROW) at the University of Arizona, a center whose mission includes fostering networks of researchers engaged in socially relevant, feminist, applied research that takes into account the diversity of populations in this region. SIROW has proven a good fit for channeling my intellectual interests and professional skills into collaborative, feminist projects in keeping with my broader vision of social justice. The personal and professional fulfillment that my colleagues and I each derive from working together prompted us not only to reflect upon our own working relationships but also to consider the value in discerning the elements of successful collaborations within such a dynamic context as the border region. We see respectful collaborative processes as consistent with long-standing feminist goals of challenging hierarchical relationships, conducting research around questions that differentially impact upon women's lives, and facilitating socially transformative applications of such research.

This chapter offers my framing of some of our collective analyses of collaborative ventures—from which some findings were published previously (Denman et al. 2004; Monk et al. 2003), while the others are presented for the first time here. It is not only a chapter about some of the things we accomplished as activists and scholars along the way but, more importantly, a discussion of the elements of successful collaboration and our own experiences of building and sustaining valuable collaborative relationships in the complex U.S.–Mexico border region. I offer my thoughts as both a personal reflection and a shared analysis of three examples of successful activist collaborations that cross multiple divides within this borderland region.

The stance I take for this self-reflective analysis could be termed rigorous partiality (Clifford 1986). In the words of Rudolph and Rudolph: "Rigorous partiality recognizes and validates the situated, inflected nature of truth. Rather than denying or repressing the sociology of knowledge, rigorous partiality self-consciously acknowledges that context shapes why and how knowledge is acquired and what it is taken to mean" (Rudolph and Rudolph 2003, 682).

The two cases that serve as the basis for my analysis are the Transborder Consortium for Research and Action on Gender and Reproductive Health at the U.S.–Mexico Border and Mujer Sana~Healthy Woman; they form the core of my professional work at SIROW. Though the cases differ in their specific focus, they share a common concern for health in the broad sense of that word: that is, the well-being of marginalized groups in the border region. Each depends integrally as well upon successful collaborations among its participants.

In the following pages, I will first discuss the meaning of collaboration. After defining terms, I present my own distilled version of what we found makes for productive collaborations, including what I playfully sum up as "making believe," and "willing partners." The *doble sentido* (double meaning) implied by those phrases refers to the often-challenging contexts we work in, as competing institutional norms, political considerations, and funding realities shape the directions of our collective endeavors. Along the way, I will touch upon some of the personal context that has helped shape my current work, as I focus on the productive relationships sustained within the Transborder Consortium and Mujer Sana~Healthy Woman, by examining the various factors that allow us to continue with socially engaged educational work across multiple boundaries. Finally, I will offer some closing thoughts on facilitating sustainable, complex, collaborative relationships within such dynamic settings as the U.S.–Mexico borderlands.

Collaboration: Defining Terms and Discerning Influences

Mattessich et al. (2001) distinguish collaboration from other forms of working together, which they label cooperation and coordination, on the basis of how those arrangements differ in four key areas: their vision and relationships; their structure, division of responsibilities, and styles of communicating; their understanding of authority and accountability; and their ways of managing resources and rewards. They define collaboration as the most complex form of interaction which "is a mutually beneficial and well-defined relationship entered into by two or more organizations to achieve common goals. The relationship includes a commitment to mutual relationships and goals; a jointly developed structure and shared responsibility; mutual authority and accountability for success; and sharing of resources and rewards" (Mattessich et al. 2001, 59).

Arthur Himmelman (1996) defines a similar framework that forms a continuum of increasing levels of complexity and commitment and identifies three common barriers to working well together: dealing with time, trust, and turf. He adds another significant conceptual refinement in his discussion of the importance of power relations in decision making and ownership.

The Social Science Research Council (2000) undertook an examination of international scholarly collaboration in the context of scientific cooperation across teams of researchers and institutions from the North and the South. The SSRC identified seven criteria for evaluating such joint endeavors: agenda-setting, goals, personnel, process, institutional structure, financial responsibility, and results. In a similar vein, the Swiss Commission for Research Partnerships with Developing Countries (KFPE) (1998) proposed eleven categories for building viable research teams among disparate partners: deciding on objectives together, sharing information and developing networks, building up mutual trust, creating transparency, sharing responsibility, monitoring and evaluating the collaboration, disseminating the results, applying the results, sharing the profits equitably, increasing research capacity, and building on achievements.

While the above definitions of collaboration and the categories for building teams and evaluating activities reflect our own experiences, they can begin to sound more formulaic than process-oriented. The components of the process matter, but I do not think that there is one route, or even a particular sequence, to be followed that can ensure successful collaboration. Engaging in a sort of reflexive, critical examination of collaborative processes means attending to both the way those relationships are structured and to the sociocultural realms in which such relationships are played out, from homes and conference rooms to international encounters. In doing so, some basic considerations stood out for me as indicators of good and sustainable collaborative relationships. The following brief summary offers some insights relevant to our own experiences; it does not purport to be a comprehensive listing.

Following Himmelman's (1996) reminder, it is important for prospective co-workers to make explicit their fundamental assumptions about the kind of power dynamics within the working relationship. Even with jointly developed plans and structures and a commitment to share authority, resources, and rewards, prospective partners may be unaware of the extent to which their own criteria for fair and reasonable or customary entitlements shape their expectations for conduct within work relationships. That issue became clearer to us both in explaining our variety of experiences with similar types of partnerships and in reviewing the scholarly literature, where, from a variety of disciplinary perspectives, the assumptions around fair, reasonable, and customary dynamics were addressed in different ways.

Another issue that needs to be considered in planning a collaborative relationship involves the question of standing, given the fluidity of membership among collaborating institutions. On the one hand, in recognizing the diversity within all organizations, who represents the community in community-based organizations? Whose voice counts as the organization's? On the other hand, owing to both personnel changes and the addition or disassociation of partners, how is trust maintained among variable partners? Is the trust invested in the institutional arrangements, in the particular members only, or in some mixture of the two? It is fair to assume both that collaboration is facilitated when each organization decides its own representational structure and that trust develops between persons, although institutional ties may facilitate that relational process. While that may sound obvious, both academics and agency employees would do well to be aware of the potential bureaucratic limits on authority and autonomy based on credentials and protocols.

Positionality matters as much in applied research processes as it does elsewhere: different professional training and experience influence not only the assumptions we make and the questions we ask but also the diverse skills team members bring to approaching specific topics. Clearly, who we are, where and how we have been educated, and what roles we are called upon to play in collective ventures all matter. Nonetheless, regardless of our background, are we able or willing to temporarily surrender certain presumptions and allow for alternative sources of insight, and to what extent does that feel uncomfortable, like a breach of reason or norms? Knowing something about one another's sensitivity to the role of positionality in human relations can be helpful in preventing some of the more predictable misunderstandings among potential collaborators.

Consideration should also be given to another theme, prevalent throughout the North-South development literature around collaboration (Himmelman 1996): the importance of working to understand the issues from the perspective of the other partners in both interpersonal and interorganizational work. The ability of colleagues to adopt an empathetic stance is crucial: it prevents the kinds of misunderstandings that can impede successful outcomes, and the attention devoted to mutual understanding facilitates the trust necessary to allow partners to work around the inevitable changes and setbacks. Good communication skills — especially listening — are imperative for this as well.

Why Collaborate?

While there has been until recently relatively little in academic literature to suggest how collaborative relationships might be created, maintained, or evaluated, it is a topic of growing interest in the social sciences. In some fields, the topic is viewed as intrinsically interesting as a form of social interaction. The applied orientation of the academic fields contributing to research on collaboration make those fields likely sources of analyses of the impetus behind, and dynamics of, collaboration (Monk et al. 2003).

The impact of neoliberal politics is another factor. Cuts in public funding for programs designed to meet basic human needs and promote many social goods, coupled with the devolution of the administration of many federal programs to state and local governments (without allowing for local discretion or resources sufficient to implement them), have left localities to contend with the social consequences (Hutton and Giddens 2002; Kawachi and Kennedy 2002). Arthur Himmelman (1996) emphasizes the importance of recognizing ideological factors behind budgetary debates:

Doing more with less requires communities, organizations, and workers to lower their expectations about new funding for services and benefits while working harder to become more cost-effective and productive. In this context, collaboration is described by depoliticized technical qualities, that is, by its practical usefulness as a cost effectiveness strategy, and is used to ease the pain associated with decreased benefits and resources for human and infrastructure needs, particularly where there are high concentrations of low-income people. (1996, 24)

In essence, then, given the persistence of social needs, the shrinking public revenue bases, and diminished authority over their distribution, governments and foundations have both been instrumental in encouraging the development of collaborative strategies to address community concerns.

The politics underlying some of the push factors behind the increasing pragmatic interest in collaboration affect not only residents of the United States but also of Mexico. Much of the recent decentralization in Mexican public administration and the ideologically related movement toward the privatization of public services, including health care, were set in motion by preparations for, and the implementation of, the North American Free Trade Agreement (NAFTA). Low incomes, the lack of primary-care providers, and the high numbers of medically under- and uninsured people in the U.S. border region, as well as the ongoing decentralization and privatization of Mexican health services, are all factors likely to increase problems of access to health care, particularly among the already underserved populations. In the borderlands, university-community collaborations, volunteerism, and other forms of civic engagement act as important mediators, advocates, and providers of services for excluded and marginalized populations in such crucial areas as health (Rodríguez 1997).

Why "Making Believe" and "Willing Partners"?

Activism can take many forms, as the companion chapters in this collection demonstrate. Whatever the means of activism, what moves us there? My sense is that some form of perceived injustice, coupled with a vision of how things might be done differently, is the spur to action. The particular motivators vary with our values, abilities, and experience; however, it seems to me that some perceived remediable imbalance in the social realm has to be there to move us to act.

My continual exposure to social injustices among diverse groups, coupled with timely critical education and mentoring around those issues, strongly influenced my life's course. Through family dynamics, childhood experiences making sense of life in Okinawan villages and military bases, adolescent years spent as an uneasy neighbor to residents of U.S. urban ghettoes and migrant camps, and adult years negotiating the complex settings of the U.S.–Mexico borderlands, I was given the tools to help me understand that alternative structures were possible and that cultivating empathy and nonviolence along the way, both as means and ends, was more likely to lead to positive outcomes and meaningful relationships. Many groups and teams I have had the privilege to work with — including the Sanctuary Movement in Tucson, Arizona, Witness for Peace in Nicaragua, my activist faith community, and various regional peace and justice organizations — have been continuing sources of education in collaboration around nonviolence as a way of life and means of social change.

There are many examples of daily misery and indignities endured by large sectors of our communities in these borderlands, and I find them unconscionable in light of my experiences and my education. These conditions are both remediable and preventable, given the political will to implement more inclusive policies. Consequently, both my research and activism challenge the "making believe" that policies privileging markets are essential for social well-being and that the primary function of government is to enforce that ideology within and beyond national boundaries.

In another turn on the phrases "making believe" and "willing partners," the coercive regulations enacting neoliberal ideology cause many community-oriented groups to band together, to act "as if": as if they were able to provide services sufficient to meet the demands; as if their services were sustainable because of their public value; as if collaboration with other groups could occur smoothly and successfully because of their shared goals. That very stance, however, rooted in optimism and hope, may well be another important organizational quality that makes sustainable collaboration possible. The goodwill to create viable partnerships in spite of the formidable contextual and logistical obstacles goes a long way toward ensuring willing partners for collaborations based on shared values and visions.

Although these different experiences with activism have depended upon collaboration in diverse settings, it seems we thought that belief in the shared value of the work was the main element that would facilitate our working together. I think we simply assumed that some individuals were more gifted at working well with others, and that smooth collaboration depended largely upon personal qualities and good group chemistry. It would be years later, while working at SIROW, that I would see collaboration itself as a significant research topic for developing insight into what, beyond a shared sense of mission and helpful personalities, makes for successful collaboration.

Case Descriptions

There were not any road maps or how-to manuals that could guide us systematically through the complexities of designing and working in transborder and/or multicultural, multidisciplinary, feminist research-for-action teams with multiple objectives and diverse constituencies. Admittedly, there are many challenges involved in organizing and sustaining collaborative relationships across political, social, cultural, and disciplinary borders. In each case, making the programs work has required that we grapple over time with the predictable misunderstandings that can arise among diverse partners because of differing expectations over such areas as turf, status, goals, priorities, authority, expertise, loyalties, and institutional or regional cultures.

Team building itself became a priority, in addition to our focus on goals and objectives. In our experience, once a team has developed the organizational structure reflective of its goals and mission, aiming to work with others who share a larger vision and particular goals; who are sensitive to questions of power and authority and willing to negotiate them respectfully; who have similar criteria for equity or fairness; and who can suspend judgment, communicate well, and adopt an empathetic style of problem solving all help to ensure meaningful, sustainable collaborations.

Successful collaborations do not just happen with a certain mix of personal qualities, as if they depended mainly on good luck in finding and screening partners: they are dependent upon skills that can be worked on among willing partners. In our experience, the rewards from developing those skills needed to sustain the collaborative relationships are as significant as the tangible accomplishments from them. Each of the following case studies represents a particular embodiment of successful feminist collaborative activism in the border region and serves to illustrate some of the qualities discussed above as facilitating sustainable collaboration.

The Transborder Consortium for Research and Action on Gender and Reproductive Health at the U.S.–Mexico Border

Since 1993, Mexican and U.S. feminist scholars and community agency personnel have joined efforts in the Transborder Consortium for Research and Action on Gender and Reproductive Health[1] at the U.S.–Mexico Border (the Transborder Consortium, for short), crossing national, disciplinary, and university-community boundaries in conducting research, implementing community-based actions, and attempting to influence re-educational practices and inform public policy around community health. For several years, I have had the pleasure, and the ongoing challenge, of working through SIROW with both *socias* (trusted collaborators) and short-term colleagues involved with the Transborder Consortium.

The fundamental relationship developed over several phases revealed our intuitive understanding of some of the challenges to plan for and skills to develop among partners. While we realized the need to find common ground and to set the agenda jointly, we were prepared to encounter various complexities of culture, language, context, institutional politics, personalities, resource disparities, and conceptual and methodological understandings. That awareness was important in motivating us to seek partners with known histories of cooperative, cross-border work. Friendship networks were effective for finding and convening like-minded scholars from Mexico and the United States interested in such collaboration. Developing those initial ideas was encouraged by foundation project officers who valued the participatory action-research orientation of the proposal, seeing it as a strong point rather than a hindrance, and encouraged a collaborative structure.

Eager to make the consortium a viable model, we steered around those gendered health topics such as abortion or rape that could be sufficiently contentious to derail a new partnership, especially around its community relations. We therefore settled on a key but safer health issue: using a gender lens to approach research and action on cervical-uterine cancer and its prevention, since it is a principal cause of death among Mexican women in their reproductive years and Mexican American women in general. Each member institution of the consortium took the lead in planning one seminar relevant to the theme to which regional scholars and representatives of community health agencies were invited. These events not only expanded networks but also included brainstorming in small groups about possible future work. Through these activities, we clarified our common interests in gender/power relationships: in the importance of thinking about regional cultural constructions of masculinity as well as femininity; of diversity among women within our context; and of the significance of qualitative methods in creating contextualized understandings.

Throughout the subsequent years of consortium funding, regular communications, equal responsibility for design and implementation of the varied research and action endeavors, and equal sharing of money and resources among consortium partners set the stage for good-faith efforts in all our varied operations together. Whether we were issuing and deciding among proposals for major research grants or modest research and capacity-building activities; conducting periodic faculty development seminars; holding networking and training workshops for *promotoras* (community health outreach workers); hosting regional research conferences; or developing appropriate means of disseminating relevant findings to diverse audiences, these initial structural and procedural decisions were crucial to our ongoing successful collaboration.

Trust is built on a daily basis through mutual signs of respect. The question of trust itself was not articulated but was initially assumed, in deference to the existing relationships among some of the partners, and continuously demonstrated through attention to process. In planning for the joint seminars and future work, we made deliberate decisions about honoring cultural differences such as language preference, meeting times, and meal schedules. In face-to-face gatherings, we would follow the customs of our hosts and make accommodations as necessary for comprehension and physical comfort. Translation was always provided, either formally or informally, into both Spanish and English. Meal times would be set and announced in advance and light refreshments made available to all whose body chemistries were out of sync with their best collaborative intentions. Conference calls would be arranged by consensus as to the optimal time for all participants.

In hindsight, we can see how our gradual and respectful approach and our sharing of information, resources, and responsibilities all contributed to building trust. Lasting collaborations take time, particularly when they involve cross-cultural exchanges where less can be taken for granted and more checking in is necessary for nurturing solid relationships. However, open lines of communication, attending to processes and structures as well as products and goals, and shared resources and responsibilities were necessary but not sufficient conditions for building trust among partners in the Transborder Consortium. Milton Bennett refers to the learned ability of intercultural sensitivity as *"the construction of reality as increasingly capable of accommodating cultural difference that constitutes development"* [original italics] (1993, 24). He describes that developmental process as movement from the ethnocentric stages (denial, defense, minimization) through the ethnorelative stages (acceptance, adaptation, integration) (M. Bennett 1993, 29). While self-evaluation can be self-serving, it would seem fair to conclude that, according to Bennett's categories, the consortium fortunately included a high number of culturally adaptive and integrative personalities, who, beyond having empathy for others, "experience cultural difference as part of their normal selves" (M. Bennett 1993, 55) or relate easily "by virtue of their ability to consciously raise any assumption to a meta-level (level of self-reference)" (M. Bennett 1993, 63). Good intentions and good techniques can only go so far in paving the way for trust across political and cultural boundaries without culturally sensitive and adept participants to facilitate the exchanges that are the daily bread of collaborative endeavors.

Fortunately, our working relationships in the consortium are sound and reinforced through friendships, for there have been multiple challenges in our collaborative efforts. Different calendars and institutional requirements can be just as trying to work with as the logistical difficulties imposed by the political border. The fact that part of our work also entails funding and coordinating others' research and capacity building in diverse communities means that we are exposed to all the joys and sorrows that extended networks can produce. Human relationships can be just as likely fulfilling and harmonious as fraught with tensions that may or may not be successfully negotiated, especially when the parties involved do not have the benefit of an ongoing relationship with a reservoir of trust to draw upon. Such exchanges form part of the turf issues referred to in the literature and can leave more lasting impressions on short-term participants in joint endeavors than the actual research-based interventions. For example, institutional cultures and reward systems may present obstacles that exacerbate differences in personality styles and political or civic affiliations; disciplinary and language differences can at times be problematic, although they also may serve as spurs to new insights. Sharing financial resources and engaging community personnel in allocating and managing some of those resources via the consortium's steering committee address significant, but not all, aspects of power differentials and collegiality, since both academic institutions and community organizations are structured hierarchically around competitive criteria for evaluation.

Careful planning, systematic attention to power dynamics, open communication, a predominance of culturally adaptive and integrative personalities, and both the effort and good fortune involved in convening a group of women who are committed to a shared vision and also genuinely appreciate one another have all contributed to making a good, feminist organizational structure into a rewarding, productive collaboration.

Mujer Sana~Healthy Woman

During the process of analyzing and evaluating our collaborative experiences through the Transborder Consortium, another opportunity arose to consciously apply these insights in the development of an entirely new SIROW project. Owing largely to a combination of experience, vision, and timely efforts among colleagues in a branch of SIROW called the Services Research Office (SRO), Mujer Sana~Healthy Woman was awarded funding in late 2002 for a five-year project empowering women's preventive health.[2] Mujer Sana~Healthy Woman has three main goals: to help women caught up in alcohol and drug use to get and stay healthy by preventing their infection with HIV, STDs, Hepatitis A, B, and C, and TB; to encourage health-promoting behaviors for themselves and through their relationships (or at least in the interim to reduce harm to themselves and others); and to connect participants to comprehensive medical and social services as needed.

It, too, is a complex, collaborative, participatory action-research endeavor. Through Mujer Sana~Healthy Woman, academic professionals and program staff from four different community agencies collaborate in applying feminist methodologies and innovative, culturally informed pedagogies in working with diverse populations of substance-involved women seeking healthier lives. We do not duplicate the work of the substance-abuse counselors. Rather, the aim of our curriculum is to provide a supportive setting for women to explore personal, relational, and social issues, through a mix of experiential learning, informational exchanges, and the exploration of themes in various art forms or media across a range of cultural expressions. Our participants reflect much of the ethnic diversity of women in this border region, with participants to date self-identifying as Latina/Mexicana/Chicana/Mexican American/ Hispanic, African American/Black, Native American (from different nations), and White/Anglo/Caucasian. Since the connotations of these terms vary tremendously, all are offered in structured baseline interviews, along with a write-in "other" category, as one cluster of categories for ethnic self-identification.

Mujer Sana~Healthy Woman is a participatory action-research project in which the data come from the multiple interventions. The curriculum is designed to be experiential and interactive and to appeal to different learning styles. It balances shared information, experiences, and insights with creative and hands-on activities structured around the organizing themes for each session. The data are gathered through structured interviews administered upon enrollment and again at six- and twelve-month follow-up interviews. Each interview involves a labor-intensive process of ensuring informed consent and eliciting and recording responses to a confidential, in-depth questionnaire about personally sensitive and often painful topics. In addition, other data such as written individual questions or group brainstorming responses and session notes kept by facilitators contribute significantly to the research process. We are a staff of nine, each with specific responsibilities, but we are heavily cross-trained since the work is so interactive and service-driven.

Mujer Sana~Healthy Woman did not develop in isolation; it represents a project carefully designed with cumulative insights from earlier iterations of SIROW–SRO health-related action-research projects for women, most notably the evolving Community Outreach Project on AIDS in Southern Arizona (COPASA) for women. That institutional continuity provided the crucial foundation for designing and implementing such a complex collaboration as Mujer Sana~Healthy Woman. The existence of multiple intersecting networks of professional relationships built on trust, and an established, supportive institutional structure from which to launch Mujer Sana~Healthy Woman, made the actual implementation of a collaborative endeavor much smoother than would have otherwise been the case.

The complexity of the daily operations and the instability in our partners' client enrollments, funding sources, and the lives of the clients they serve, mean that the work rhythms are not as smooth as are the work relations. Some of the bumps in the road go with the territory of substance abuse and mental health services research. My earlier discussion about the consequences of the current political climate is also germane here for understanding some of the particular challenges our participants and agency collaborators face. Regular meetings and frequent interim communications with program representatives of those agencies help immeasurably to both prevent and solve problems together. There is contractually based transparency and predictability in the distribution of funds across sites and regular sharing of information through various means. Our solid relationship structure has proven invaluable in dealing with sensitive institutional, personnel, and client matters.

Mujer Sana~Healthy Woman and the Transborder Consortium represent very different forms of complex collaboration but serve to illustrate the importance of many of the same variables. Trusted networks reduce the uncertainties in finding potential partners and minimize the likelihood of a mismatch of interests and expertise relevant to work expectations. Once potential partners are identified, the conscious, systematic attention to process is essential: a sound feminist design, careful planning, and purposeful attention to work processes and conditions, as much as to productive requirements, all make relationships smoother and less dependent upon personal qualities. Open communication, cross training, and daily teamwork help facilitate empathy and problem solving and minimize the snap judgments and unexamined assumptions that can be divisive. Mutual accountability in decision making, the use of resources, and the sharing of rewards reinforce the incentives to collaborative work, especially where the collaborators and tasks are consistent, as they are in Mujer Sana~Healthy Woman. Part of that mutual accountability comes from the shared belief in the possibility of healthier lives for all the women participating and our common efforts to make that belief a reality, even among those clients who are struggling the most to see that process through.

The work entailed in making the Mujer Sana~Healthy Woman collaboration function smoothly represents another rewarding means of engaging in a different form of research-related activism. I will conclude with a discussion of lessons learned and insights into productive collaboration for social change.

Concluding Thoughts

I hope the reader now has some sense of the kind of engaging, fulfilling work undertaken through the Transborder Consortium and Mujer Sana~Healthy Woman and some of the factors that have made them sustainable and productive. While the day-to-day routines and missions vary tremendously between these complex endeavors, the components that explain their surprisingly smooth operations are remarkably similar. They are collaborative in the definitional sense in that they each involve well-defined, reciprocally beneficial relationships; mutually defined goals and structures of accountability; and shared responsibility, resources, and rewards (Mattessich et al. 2001). Beyond meeting the minimal criteria for collaborations, however, I believe that the common underlying ethical commitment to a more equitable sharing of resources and rewards, along with a critical feminist sensitivity to power dynamics and a preponderance of culturally adaptive and integrative personalities among the teams, are significant factors in explaining the sustainability of these endeavors. The setting of the U.S.–Mexico border adds to the logistical complexity and the demographic and cultural diversity of the communities we work with and relate to, but it does not change the nature of the work that goes into successful collaboration. If anything, that diversity is inherently rewarding for those of us who see differences and the unexpected as opportunities to learn and grow. A predisposition to assume good faith and to grant respect, and to suspend judgments while assuming reasonable explanations for others' actions, is crucial and is to some extent what is meant by being personally and culturally adept. Such a stance, reaffirmed by demonstrations of mutual trust, contributes greatly to helping us make allowances for the inevitable logistical, organizational, and culturally based challenges of working in complex settings.

Each of the cases described in this chapter is designed and implemented with an eye to the socially transformative potentials inherent in respectful, community-based work with diverse populations. These qualities represent a distillation of many of the recommendations of the KFPE (2001) and Mattessich et al. (2001): having our interactions depend heavily on developing empathy with, and an appreciation for, the perspectives of others involved; choosing and cultivating teams who share core values around the due treatment of others; maintaining open communication and articulating assumptions and expectations clearly; designing mutual accountability processes and structures; creating welcoming work environments to the extent possible; and sharing available resources equitably for the need at hand.

In essence, the intentions of the collaborating partners matter tremendously, but they are not sufficient to ensure productive and fulfilling relationships, even when implemented through sound organizational structures, adequate resources, and dedicated colleagues. Sociopolitical contexts and unique circumstances may determine the life span of even the best programs, so all the more reason to think strategically, to take great care in designing sound relationships and systems, and to act with integrity at every step. That means engaging in one sense of "making believe": that process of taking the steps needed daily to remind oneself and convince others that the work is valuable in itself. This vision of activism, one not dependent on immediate results for validation, also encourages combining sensitivity and awareness with the determination to empower others along the way, that is, "willing partners" as fellow travelers. At the level of individual investment, productive and sustainable collaborations like the Transborder Consortium and Mujer Sana~Healthy Woman — not only in the U.S.–Mexico borderlands but in any setting — also depend upon flexibility, radical respect for differences, careful attention to the sources and distribution of power, trust, open communication, and a shared vision of what is possible. The good news is that those are all learnable skills and not just the property of a lucky few.

Notes

2. The Unsettling, Gendered Consequences of Migration for Mexican Indigenous Women

1. The category "indigenous women" might be a questionable one given that it infers similarity while referring to women of distinct ethnic cultures, languages, beliefs, and everyday practices. Its validation, however, can be found in the historically subaltern designation of indigenous peoples as a "cultural Other," marginalized and impoverished through the ethnicization of exploitation. Shared gender oppression and discrimination as a "social Other," within and without indigenous cultures, also authorizes its use.

2. During our interviews, many women referred to their arranged marriages as being "sold." Their lack of fluency in Spanish, however, together with the patent challenges of intercultural communication, left me in doubt as to the etymology of the use of the word "sold." Is this indeed a term that was intentionally chosen to describe the implication of arranged marriages for women? Or is this the Spanish word used by non-indigenous society to refer to this practice? Interrogations of this sort are imperative in intercultural communication, for as Franz Fanon (1965) pointed out decades ago, subaltern societies are partially constituted by seeing their own reflection through the "eyes" (discourses) of hegemonic observance.

3. The Zapatista movement of the 1990s has placed contemporary indigenous claims for the right to collective autonomy and self-determination of Native peoples on the national political agenda. Based on the traditional laws and customs that have historically governed the internal functioning of Native communities, the idea of indigenous autonomy and self-determination could also be seen as another expression of citizenship: a citizenship that emanates from the rights and obligations accrued through belonging to a self-governing ethnic community. Traditionally, women have not had equal rights to participate in public and community affairs in most Native communities. Rather, they have been gender-excluded from community governance and responsibilities. In that sense, the actual changes in women's roles and participation in economic, social, political, and cultural aspects of extra-territorial communities indicates a gradual coming of age of female citizenship for indigenous women, both within the context of the community itself, as well as in broader, nation-state terms.

4. The few testimonies presented in this chapter are fragments of extensive

biographical narratives of twenty-eight indigenous women of different ages, ethnicities, and places of origin, presently residing in Baja California, Mexico, or in California, U.S.A. Most of these women are Mixtecs from Oaxaca; however, one is Purépecha from Michoacán, one is Huichol from Nayarit, and two are Chinantec and Triqui women from Oaxaca. The research for the construction of these biographies was done over a six-year period, involving three distinct studies. The initial project focused on the relationship between indigenous immigrant women and environment. The second was a research-action project geared toward preventing uterine cancer in indigenous immigrant women. The third was also a research-action project linked to education for the prevention of HIV–AIDS among indigenous (im)migrants. Some very rich narratives also emerged from a two-day workshop on ethnicity, migration, and discrimination, with the participation of indigenous immigrant women residing in both Californias, organized by the Oficina en Apoyo de los Pueblos Indígenas (Office of Indigenous Affairs linked to the Mexican President's office) and El Colegio de la Frontera Norte in December 2001 in Tijuana, Baja California.

5. Globalization is not as yet a fully defined sociological category. It implies different things to different people. However, most authors agree that it refers to a more intense phase of international economic integration, a multisited productive model, and greater world awareness as a result of technological advances in cybernetics, communications, and the use of mass media. It has been called "late-modernity" by Anthony Giddens (2003) and "des-modernity" by Alain Touraine (1997), while many social analysts from the ex-colonies of Latin America, Asia, and Africa insist that it is simply a reformulation of colonialism.

6. Oaxaca, the state with the largest indigenous population, registers approximately 150,000 people emigrating annually, while one-third of its 3,200,000 total population temporarily or permanently resides in other states or countries (Ruiz Garcia 2002).

7. Peasant economies are known to also employ women's workforce in agricultural tasks such as planting, weeding, and reaping. In most traditional Mexican societies, however, these are periodic events during work-intensive seasons, rather than a constant norm. Male labor, on the other hand, is hardly ever applied to reproductive tasks, such as housework or child care.

8. For Native Mexican communities, territory refers to the geography of cultural origin, the geo-ecological context of culture, the historical space where collective life evolved, the location of beginning and lineage, and the spatial delimitation of cultural specificity. Extensive contemporary migration documents the reorganization of identity and belonging in extra-territorial locations. The concept of trans-territoriality references the cultural, economic, social, political, and affective ties cultivated between hometown and settlement communities by emigrants. Trans-territoriality can stretch over national borders, thus constituting transnational communities that share a single cultural heart.

9. The indigenous diaspora has expanded to all urban and agro-industrial regions in Mexico, extending in the northern part of the continent from Alaska and Canada to

New York, Oregon, Washington, North Carolina, Texas, Wyoming, Arizona, Georgia, Nevada, California, and Florida, among other locations.

10. In indigenous communities of origin, gender socialization begins very early. The specialization that patterns girls into women by puberty begins around the age of five. Young girls begin to forge their way toward womanhood by helping their mothers collect firewood, carry water, herd sheep, wash dishes and clothes, water patio plants, and care for younger siblings by strapping them to their backs with traditional rebozos. Between the ages of eight and twelve, girls gradually learn to make tortillas, sew, embroider, do beadwork, and cook. By the time their bodies are transformed by the hormonal changes of puberty, the social process that shapes them into cultural representations of femininity has been completed. In peasant economies, children are seen as an active part of the family workforce, and work is a prime training ground for gendering society.

11. The reorganization of family and local, hometown production as a result of male emigration, and its impact on gender roles and relations, is not the focus of the present chapter. However, Maria Eugenia D'Aubeterre Buznego (2000) deals with the theme at length.

12. The concept of "permanent immigration" or "permanent residency" can be problematic when speaking of indigenous communities. Studies have stressed the elasticity of indigenous immigration. Even after years of permanent residency in extraterritorial localities, families frequently return for long periods of time to offer different forms of community service (*téquio*, *mayordomías*, or public office) in order to preserve the collective recognition, community citizenship, and the right to land use. Often, families return permanently once children are raised and the older years are approaching.

13. "Liquid" is the term that indigenous farm workers use in reference to pesticides.

14. Indigenous cultures are articulated by values entrenched in the pulse of the collective. Individuality has traditionally been a relative notion always mediated by group necessities, in contrast with highly industrialized societies, where it is the prime existential paragon. Surely, one of the cultural aspects that call for deeper examination is the effect of growing claims for individuality on collective cultural paradigms.

15. I use the term "ethnicized," as Saskia Sassen (1998, 87) uses the term "racialized," to refer to the association and exploitation of specific ethnic (or racial) groups within particular labor slots. This process is one of the defining characteristics of globalization. Though these groups of people, generally immigrants, are fully incorporated into the global informational economy, they appear to be tangential, and even marginalized from it. Analyzing the same phenomena, Sassen terms it "the ethnic economy" (1998, 87).

16. It is interesting to observe how first-generation indigenous immigrant families in Baja California tend to rearticulate the extended family in spatial arrangements that differ from those of hometowns. In receiving communities, even families with grown children that immigrated as nuclear units build two- and three-story structures to accommodate different generations. Frequently in these extended domestic

arrangements, adult male children assume patriarchal authority. All the older women I have interviewed, however, affirm that they have accrued significant economic and social capital in the family with age.

17. Poverty restricts economic autonomy, generally requiring the collaboration of various family members in economic survival strategies geared to just making ends meet. Nonetheless, the power of entitlement has important implications for women in shaping notions of self and self-value.

18. "Uses and customs" is a colloquial reference to historical, socially recognized, accepted, and applied values, practices, and regulations that order and reproduce indigenous community life.

19. Speaking of these intercultural contentions, a young Triqui woman law student stated:

> In the communities in Oaxaca, traditional law doesn't protect girls that are married-off while still children. Here they put the guy in jail and wait until the girl turns eighteen. The men are surprised. They think that it's discrimination against our culture. We even have relatives in jail for rape. My father is a moral leader of our community, and he's against arranging marriages with young girls. I think that we should leave that custom in the past, because it is really only discrimination among our own people.

3. Women's Daily Mobility at the U.S.–Mexico Border

1. The literature of the border is vast and growing. A few of the important works that describe the changing significance of the U.S.–Mexico border include Andreas and Biersteker 2003; Arreola and Curtis 1993; Dunn 1996; Herzog 1990; Heyman 1991; House 1982; O. Martínez 1994; Nevins 2002; Vila 2003a; and Weeks and Ham-Chande 1992.

2. The Homeland Security Act of 2002 abolished the Immigration and Naturalization Service (INS) and transferred its functions and operations into the new Department of Homeland Security (DHS). The INS is now U.S. Citizenship and Immigration Services (USCIS) and the Border Patrol is U.S. Customs and Border Protection (CBP), both within DHS.

3. See, for example, http://apps.cbp.gov/bwt/; http://www.borderlineups .com/; http://www.bythorborder.com/cgi-bin/english/traffic/index.cgi; http:// www.highway401.com/. Some websites offer real-time cameras trained on the border so users can watch the traffic. See, for example, http://www.telnor.com/telnor/cfm/ homeGaritas.cfm.

4. Abortion in a Transborder Context

1. The case is that of a thirteen-year-old girl who was raped and became pregnant; with the support of her parents, she sought to have an abortion under the terms of the

Mexican law. Although she met all the legal requirements, her right to an abortion was denied by state health authorities in Baja California, who put up bureaucratic red tape, and by the social and psychological pressure of activists from that state's pro-life group.

2. The cost of an abortion in Planned Parenthood's clinics at San Diego is between $350 and $408, depending on a patient's income. This is less than what it costs to have an abortion under high-risk conditions at clandestine clinics in Mexico, where the cost is approximately between $500 and $1,500 (2003 prices).

3. "Local passport" is what Mexican border inhabitants call the visa issued by the U.S. government to some Mexican border residents who have met certain requirements regarding personal identification and address. It allows holders to travel twenty-five miles into U.S. territory.

5. The Changing Gender Composition of the Maquiladora Workforce along the U.S.–Mexico Border

1. Danish economist Esther Boserup (1970) was one of the first to present cross-national data on women's labor force participation. Although subsequent critiques of her work emphasized the tendency of aggregate census data to underestimate women's actual economic activity (Benería and Sen 1981), the patterns Boserup documented have been corroborated in subsequent studies. Of all the world's regions in 1970, women had the lowest economic activity rates in northern Africa, where only 10 percent of adult women were in the formal labor force, as well as western Asia (13 percent), southern Asia (24 percent), and Latin America (28 percent). While women's employment rates increased in three of the four regions during the next two decades (to 17 percent, 21 percent, 23 percent, and 32 percent respectively), they continued to lag behind the rest of the world, where women's labor force participation rates ranged between 40 percent and 60 percent in 1990 (United Nations 1991). Even in nations with relatively high rates of female labor force participation, however, women's rates have not reached parity with men's rates.

2. A decade ago, I speculated that:

Export-processing industrialization may seem to depart from the pattern of women's marginalization from modern manufacturing. Women's large-scale absorption into the manufacturing labor force contrasts with the typical trend under ISI (import-substitution industrialization), which replaces women with machines and skilled male labor. As long as TNCs (transnational corporations) continue to relocate their labor-intensive operations to the third world, women may continue to constitute the bulk of their workforce. Yet it is also possible that women's predominance in export manufacturing is a temporary phenomenon. As export-oriented industries become more capital intensive or more diverse in their composition, the demand for female labor may diminish. Even if these industries continue in the present, labor-intensive form, the gender composition of the labor force may change because of state intervention (or other factors). (Tiano 1994, 4)

3. As Gustavo Elizondo, Ciudad Juárez's mayor, lamented to the *New York Times*, "[W]e have no way to provide water, sewage, and sanitation for all the people who come to work. . . . Every year we get poorer and poorer even though we create more and more wealth" (quoted by Wright 2001, 93).

4. Much has been written about the seeming paradox of high job turnover and apparent labor shortages in a context of rapid in-migration and rising unemployment. In my Mexicali-based research (Tiano 1994), I found support for Sklair's (1993, 179) claim that "there is no real labor shortage . . . [although] . . . an artificial labor shortage has been unintentionally created by the industry being reluctant to pay decent wages."

5. As Kathryn Kopinak's (1996) research on maquiladora job advertisements in Sonora demonstrates, the fact that most job openings specified female applicants shows that employers played a significant role in the feminization of first-generation maquiladora jobs.

6. Puerto Rico's export-processing sector, which has remained almost exclusively devoted to garment and other types of component assembly during the half century of its existence, exemplifies this situation. Its labor force has remained feminized despite considerable male unemployment on the island, leading to a situation in which women have much better employment options than men. For a discussion of how this has affected Puerto Rican households, see Safa 1995a.

7. Leslie Salzinger (1997) describes another way that the docility stereotype has become disassociated with women's preferential maquiladora recruitment. As women workers in Ciudad Juárez have become more militant and less apt to show the docility traditionally associated with femininity, employers have hired more young men. While male recruitment is in part a response to the shortage of young women willing to work in maquiladoras, it also reflects a discursive reconstruction of docility as less a female trait than a desired feature of both men and women workers.

7. Domestic Service and International Networks of Caring Labor

Author's Note: This chapter was excerpted from "The home and the world: Domestic service and international networks of caring labor," *Annals of the Association of American Geographers* 91(2): 370–86. Research for this chapter was partially supported by the National Science Foundation (SES 9304771).

1. Like all names used in this chapter, "Rosa" is a pseudonym.

2. In this chapter, "paid household work" and "domestic service" are used synonymously to describe cleaning, child care, and elder care performed for wages in the homes of employers.

3. Welfare benefits for documented immigrants, also known as resident aliens, were dramatically reduced by the Personal Responsibility and Work Opportunity Reconciliation Act of 1996 (Hing 1998; Wheeler 1996). A sweeping welfare reform bill that ended a federal commitment to provide even a minimal level of assistance to America's poorest, the act claimed a savings of $53.4 billion, 44 percent of which resulted from

eliminating coverage for immigrants (Hing 1998). The original act barred both documented and undocumented immigrants from receiving Supplemental Security Income (SSI) and food stamps. The act also barred documented immigrants from receiving any federal means-tested assistance for a period of five years after entry, authorized states to pass laws denying legal immigrants' access to several state-administered federal programs, and required sponsors for family-based immigrant visas to prove their financial ability to support applicants (Wheeler 1996). An outcry against these cuts led to a re-reform of welfare laws in the 1997 budget agreement, at which time most disability and health benefits were restored to legal immigrants who were in the country and covered before the initial legislation (Hing 1998). Despite these changes, welfare reform in the United States severely curtailed the social and economic safety net available to immigrants.

4. The proposition prohibited undocumented immigrants from attending the state's public educational system and required that tax-supported social service providers screen all applicants for legal status. Shortly after the referendum, a federal judge issued an injunction against most aspects of the proposition, although the screening of applicants and the prohibition banning attendance at public higher education were permitted (Schnaiberg 1995).

5. I also conducted a telephone survey of a geographically representative random sample of five hundred households living in the city of San Diego. The goal of the survey was to determine the extent of domestic work in the city, its geographic distribution, the characteristics of households who employ domestic workers, and the characteristics of the workers that they employ (for details see Mattingly 1999a).

6. This number is probably low because the highest income category was "$100,000 and over."

8. Mexican Women's Activism in New Mexico Colonias

1. For an introduction to how daily practices are spatialized and how these daily geographies are gendered, see Domosh and Seager 2001; Massey 1994; McDowell 1999; Mitchell 2000.

2. I would like to thank the women leaders of the *colonias* without whom there would not be a chapter. Their vision and dedication are inspiring and their courage to stand up and fight for what they think is rightfully theirs is phenomenal. All the names used in this chapter are pseudonyms: this is true for leaders, organizers, and NGOs. I believe this is necessary to protect these brave women who already risk so much by challenging unscrupulous developers, racist neighbors, and powerful government bureaucracies.

3. The U.S. government definition of a colonia is any identifiable community in the U.S.–Mexico border regions of Arizona, New Mexico, and Texas that is determined to be a colonia on the basis of objective criteria, including lack of potable water, inadequate sewage systems, and a shortage of decent, safe, and sanitary housing. This defini-

tion comes from the U.S. Office of Housing and Urban Development (HUD) and is important because much of the federal money available for improvements in colonias is distributed based on these criteria. This definition is important also because of what it does not say. The federal definition describes only the absence of services and infrastructure and, by highlighting these negative aspects of colonias life, reinforces the discrimination many colonia residents experience. On more than one occasion while I was working in the colonias, I heard a non-colonia resident describe the colonias as "the third world in our backyard." Discriminatory behavior towards the colonias was, and is, not uncommon, yet colonia residents are fiercely devoted to their communities.

4. For a more detailed discussion of transnationalism, see Glick-Schiller et al. 1992.

5. "Traditional" is a very complex and slippery term. One person's tradition might be another's exception. But, nonetheless, it is used by many to describe the patriarchal nuclear family composed of a father, mother, and children. This is how I use the term here because the women in my study sample employed the term in this way.

6. Because of the gendered structuring of daily geographies in the colonias, my presence during the day meant I interacted mostly with women. As a result, I use women's remarks and comments on men's behavior. Observations of men's behaviors and attitudes provided by women are based in the same discourses that, in part, generate the men's behavior. My limited observations of men's activities support the women's commentaries, as do the statements of outside organizers with whom I worked.

7. The questions I used in this interview were very simple. I acknowledge that they might have elicited less complex answers than more nuanced questions would have. What I wanted to get at was the rather stereotypical answers that make up the discourses I observed the women employing. Because I have a great deal of daily ethnographic detail on the very same gender relations the women discussed in the interviews, I can reconcile these two, often conflicting, sources into a more realistically complex whole.

8. Interview #4 Juana (12/07/00)
9. Interview #4 Marie (11/29/00)
10. Interview #4 Alicia (12/12/00)
11. Interview #4 Marie (11/29/00)
12. Interview #4 Juana (12/07/00)
13. Interview #4 Flora (12/06/00)
14. Field notes Flora (6/19/01)
15. Field notes Flora (6/19/01)
16. Field notes Flora (6/19/01)
17. Interview #1 Sylvia (11/10/00)
18. Interview #1 Mario (12/05/00)
19. Interview #3 Marie (11/02/00)
20. Interview #3 Estella (10/30/00)
21. Interview #1 Mario (12/05/00)
22. Interview #1 Sylvia (11/10/00)

9. Styles, Strategies, and Issues of Women Leaders at the Border

1. Based on my research experiences in both U.S. and Mexican *colonias*, I offer the following explanation of the term *colonia*. In the United States the word is used to describe a poor residential area, or neighborhood, where individuals or families, lacking financial resources, have collected to set up a makeshift-to-permanent residential style, often self-built in areas adjacent to and/or often just beyond city limits, having little to no provided infrastructure such as water, electricity, and access to public transportation. Along Mexico's northern border, however, the term *colonia* has many more variations; indeed, the term has the same meaning as *neighborhood* does in the United States. Thus, northern Mexican neighborhoods, or colonias, span the gamut from rich to poor, full infrastructure and services to none, and with many neighborhoods falling in between those extremes. The term *colonia popular* is used throughout Mexico to refer to an unplanned housing area that does not have urban services. It is also a code word for a poor residential area.

10. Border Women's NGOs and Political Participation in Baja California

Author's Note: I thank the interdisciplinary Women's Studies Program at El Colegio de México for its financial support to carry out this research.

1. The term *state reform* makes reference to reformation of the Mexican Constitution and secondary laws, but, importantly, the state reform involves transformation of rules and political attitudes. Supporters of the state reform claim it is part of the democratic transition in Latin American countries.

2. Espinosa (2002b, 17) defines these as "small groups where women reconstructed and shared their personal histories and critically analyzed the personal experience of being women."

3. During my fieldwork, I did not find any NGOs in Rosarito, a recently created *municipio*, but NGOs from Tijuana have created some community centers there.

4. These NGOs are Casa San Miguel and Asociación Mexicana para la Superación Integral de la Mujer. See table 10.1.

5. In the context of Latin American countries, Miller (2000, 3) defines advocacy as "initiatives and campaigns directed to influence the political sphere, not only in policies and laws, but in power systems, decision-making processes that may include the formal legal system, government, public sector. . . ." This set of strategies has the goal of eliminating gender inequity and other forms of social exclusion.

6. In Mexico, the NGOs' role in the conceptualization of reproductive health has been extremely important (González Montes 1999).

7. Unfortunately, Factor X closed its doors in 2004 because of internal differences among their members. Some of them joined other organizations in order to continue the work they were doing with maquiladora workers.

8. Women's resistances to feminism are also present in other regions. Espinosa (2002b, 24) argues that popular women in Mexico City did not want to be called feminists; even when they participate in gender reflections, they preferred to talk about "women's problems."

9. These transformations resulted from the creation of the Committees for Planning of Municipal Development through federal and state legislation. Through these subcommittees, social actors get closer to decision-making processes. It was not a radical change, but it was novel in terms of social representation (Guillén López 2001, 87–89).

10. Women's institutes were created as a response of Mexican government to the demand of international agencies for introducing gender mainstreaming in public planning and policymaking. In 2000, President Fox opened the National Women's Institute, and since then, most states have created their own institutes, sometimes with the support of women's NGOs, as in the case of Baja California. Historical feminists, which some consider to be part of an isolated movement, claim the autonomy of the movement and have strongly criticized the feminist NGOs for participating in the National Women's Institute and the state institutes. While some scholars think that feminist participation in these institutions is a loss for the movement, other scholars consider it to be a chance for NGOs to influence policymaking from inside. In general, the state institutes face difficulties as a result of the small budgets assigned by the governments and the absence of sensitivity about the gender perspective in planning and policymaking. Although there have been some successful experiences of feminists and academics collaborating with the institutes as employees, some of these women have quit their jobs, feeling deceived by bureaucracy and power games.

11. "Making Believe" and "Willing Partners" in Academics' Activism in the U.S.-Mexico Borderlands

1. The consortium initially focused on gender and reproductive health but has subsequently broadened its orientation to "gender and health."

2. SIROW–SRO colleagues Rosi Andrade, Sally Stevens, Bridget Murphey, and Barbara Estrada, in consultation with the lead author, are the primary architects and authors of the participatory-action research design for Mujer Sana~Healthy Woman, funded by the Center for Substance Abuse Treatment of the Substance Abuse Mental Health Services Agency/SAMHSA).

Bibliography

Abramovitz, Mimi. 1988. *Regulating the Lives of Women: Social Welfare Policy from Colonial Times to the Present*. Boston: South End Press.

Ackelson, Jason. 2003. Directions in border security research. *Social Science Journal* 40(4): 573–81.

Aitken, Stuart. 1998. *Family Fantasies and Community Space*. New Brunswick, NJ: Rutgers University Press.

Alegría, Tito. 1990. Ciudad y trasmigración en la frontera de México con los Estados Unidos. *Frontera Norte* 2(4): 7–38.

Alonzo, Ana María. 1995. *Thread of Blood: Colonialism, Revolution, and Gender on Mexico's Northern Frontier*. Tucson: University of Arizona Press.

Alvarez, Sonia. 1998. Los feminismos latinoamericanos de globalizan en los noventa: Retos para un nuevo milenio. In *Género y cultura en America Latina*, edited by María Luisa Tarrés, 89–133. Mexico City: El Colegio de México.

Andreas, Peter. 2003. A tale of two borders: The U.S.–Canada and U.S.–Mexico lines after 9-11. In *The Rebordering of North America: Integration and Exclusion in a New Security Context*, edited by Peter Andreas and Thomas J. Biersteker, 1–23. New York: Routledge.

Andreas, Peter, and Thomas J. Biersteker, eds. 2003. *The Rebordering of North America: Integration and Exclusion in a New Security Context*. New York: Routledge.

Andreas, Peter, and Timothy Snyder, eds. 2000. *The Wall around the West: State Borders and Immigration Controls in North America and Europe*. Lanham, MD: Rowman & Littlefield.

Anzaldúa, Gloria. 1987. *Borderlands/La frontera*. San Francisco: Aunt Lute Books.

Aptheker, Bettina. 1989. *Tapestries of Life: Women's Work, Women's Consciousness, and the Meaning of Daily Experience*. Amherst: University of Massachusetts Press.

Araya, María José. 2003. *Un acercamiento a las encuestas sobre el uso del tiempo con orientación de género*. United Nations, Division of Social Development, CEPAL. Women and Development Series, No. 50. Santiago, Chile: United Nations.

Arizona-Mexico Commission. 2004. *Border Issues*. http://www.azmc.org/index.asp?from=borderissues (accessed May 26, 2005).

Arizpe, Lourdes. 1975. *Indígenas de la ciudad de México: El caso de las Marías*. Mexico City: Secretaría de Educación Pública.

Arreola, Daniel D., and James R. Curtis. 1993. *The Mexican Border Cities: Landscape Anatomy and Place Personality.* Tucson: University of Arizona Press.

Avendaño, Rosa María, José A. Moreno, and Enrique Riego. 2000. Las ONG en la frontera Baja California–California: Un acercamiento al estudio de la diplomacia ciudadana. *Estudios Fronterizos* 1(1): 89–135.

Baden, Sally. 1997. Recession and structural adjustment's impact on women's work in selected developing countries. In *Promoting Gender Equality at Work: Turning Vision into Reality*, edited by Eugenia Date-Bah, 24–58. London: Zed Books & International Labour Organisation.

Bakan, Abigail, and Daiva Stasiulis. 1994. Foreign domestic worker policy in Canada and the social boundaries of modern citizenship. *Science and Society* 58(1): 7–33.

Ball, Donald W. 1967. An abortion clinic ethnography. *Social Problems,* 13: 293–301.

Barnet, Richard, and Ronald Muller. 1974. *Global Reach: The Power of the Multinational Corporations.* New York: Simon and Schuster.

Barquet, Mercedes. 2002. Sobre el género en las políticas públicas: Actores y contexto. In *Estudios sobre las mujeres y las relaciones de género en México: Aportes desde diversas disciplinas*, edited by Elena Urrutia, 345–76. Mexico City: Programa Interdisciplinario de Estudios de la Mujer, El Colegio de México.

Barrera Bassols, Dalia, and Alejandra Massolo. 1998. *Mujeres que gobiernan municipios: Experiencias, aportes y retos.* Mexico City: Programa Interdisciplinario de Estudios de la Mujer, El Colegio de México.

Bayón, Christina, and Georgina Rojas. 1999. Mujeres, familias y trabajo en la frontera México–Estados Unidos. In *Reducing Vulnerability among Families in the Mexico and U.S. Border Region*, edited by Peter M. Ward, 37–46. Mexico City: University of Texas System and Desarrollo Integral de la Familia (DIF) Nacional.

Beechey, Veronica. 1978. Women and production: A critical analysis of some sociological theories of women's work. In *Feminism and Materialism*, edited by Annette Kuhn and Ann Marie Wolpe, 155–97. London: Routledge & Kegan Paul.

Bejarano, Cynthia. 2002. Las super madres de Latino America: Transforming Motherhood and Contesting State Violence Through Subversive Icons. *Frontiers: A Journal of Women Studies* 23(1): 126–50.

Benería, Lourdes. 1992. The Mexican debt crisis: Restructuring the economy and the household. In *Unequal Burden: Economic Crises, Persistent Poverty, and Women's Work*, edited by Lourdes Benería and Shelly Feldman, 83–104. Boulder, CO: Westview Press.

Benería, Lourdes, and Gita Sen. 1981. Accumulation, reproduction, and women's role in economic development: Boserup revisited. *Signs* 7(2): 279–98.

Bennett, Milton J. 1993. Towards ethnorelativism: A developmental model of intercultural sensitivity. In *Education for the Intercultural Experience*, edited by R. Michael Paige, 21–71. Yarmouth, ME: Intercultural Press.

Bennett, Vivienne. 1995. *The Politics of Water: Urban Protest, Gender and Power in Monterrey, Mexico.* Pittsburgh: University of Pittsburgh Press.

Besserer, Federico. 1999. Sentimientos (in)apropiados de las mujeres migrantes: Hacia una nueva ciudadanía. In *Migración y relación de género en México*, edited by Dalia Barrera Bassols and Cristina Oehmichen Bazán, 317–88. Grupo Interdisciplinario Sobre Mujer, Trabajo y Pobreza A. C., Instituto de Investigaciones Antropológicas. Mexico City: Universidad Nacional Autónoma de México.

Bhabha, Homi. 1994. *The Location of Culture*. New York: Routledge.

Blumberg, Rae. 1995. Gender, microenterprise, performance, and power. Case studies from the Dominican Republic, Ecuador, Guatemala, and Swaziland. In *Women in the Latin American Development Process*, edited by Christine E. Bose and Edna Acosta-Belén, 194–225. Philadelphia: Temple University Press.

Bondi, Liz. 1993. Gender and geography: Crossing boundaries. *Progress in Human Geography* 17: 241–46.

Border Governors' Conference. 2002. *U.S.–Mexico Border States: September 11 Border Impact Report*. Austin: Texas Department of Agriculture. http://www.agr.state.tx.us/border/activities/iga_911_border_impact.htm (accessed May 26, 2005).

Border Trade Alliance. 2003. Policy Issues Surrounding Department of Homeland Security Implementation. White Paper. Phoenix, AZ: The Border Trade Alliance. http://www.thebta.org (accessed March 24, 2004).

Boserup, Esther. 1970. *Women and Economic Development*. New York: Saint Martins.

Bustos, Sergio. 2004. Scanners Added at Borders: Devices Won't Screen Everyone. *Arizona Republic*, April 19. http://www.azcentral.com/arizonarepublic (accessed May 26, 2005).

Butler, Judith. 1999. *Gender Trouble: Feminism and the Subversion of Identity*. New York: Routledge.

Bystydzienski, Jill M. 1992. *Women Transforming Politics: Worldwide Strategies for Empowerment*. Indianapolis: Indiana University Press.

Cagatay, Nilufer, and Sule Ozler. 1995. Feminization of the labor force: The effects of long-term development and structural adjustment. *World Development* 23(11): 1883–94.

Camp, Rod. 2003. *Politics in Mexico: The Democratic Transformation*. 4th ed. Oxford: Oxford University Press.

Campbell, Howard. 2003. The U.S. census 2000 and 'colonias' along the U.S.–Mexico border: An anthropological approach. In *Dígame!: Policy and Politics on the Texas Border*, edited by Christine Brenner, Irasema Coronado, and Dennis Soden, 275–94. Dubuque, IA: Kendall Hunt.

Carrillo, Jorge, and Alfredo Hualde. 1998. Third generation maquiladoras: The Delphi–General Motors case. *Journal of Borderlands Studies* 13(1): 79–97.

Castillo, Debra A., María Gudelia Rangel Gómez, and Bonnie Delgado. 1999. Border lives: prostitute women in Tijuana. *Signs* 24(2): 387–422.

Castillo, Debra A., and María Socorro Tabuenca Córdoba. 2002. *Border Women: Writing from La Frontera*. Minneapolis: University of Minnesota Press.

Chaney, Elsa. 1979. *Supermadre: Women in Politics in Latin America*. Austin: University of Texas Press.

Chang, Grace. 2000. *Disposable Domestics: Immigrant Women Workers in the Global Economy*. Cambridge: South End Press.

Chant, Sylvia. 1991. *Women and Survival in Mexican Cities: Perspectives on Gender, Labor Markets, and Low Income Households*. Manchester: Manchester University Press.

Christensen, Kathleen. 1993. Eliminating the journey to work: Home-based work across the life course of women in the United States. In *Full Circles: Geographies of Women over the Life Course*, edited by Cindi Katz and Janice Monk, 55–87. New York: Routledge.

Clifford, James. 1986. Introduction: Partial truths. In *Writing Culture: The Poetics and Politics of Ethnography*, edited by James Clifford and George Marcus, 1–26. Berkeley: University of California Press.

Cockroft, James. 1983. *Mexico: Class Formation, Capital Accumulation, and the State*. New York: Monthly Review Press.

Cohen, Philip N. 1998. Replacing housework in the service economy: Gender, class, and race-ethnicity in service spending. *Gender and Society* 12(2): 219–31.

Collins, Patricia Hill. 1999. Producing the mothers of the nation: Race, class, and contemporary U.S. population policies. In *Women, Citizenship, and Difference*, edited by Nira Yuval-Davis and Pnina Werbner, 118–29. London: Zed Books.

Coronado, Irasema. 1998. *Who Governs in a Binational Context? The Role of Transnational Political Elites*. Ph.D. dissertation, Department of Political Science, University of Arizona.

Coronado, Irasema, and Hector Padilla. 2003. Texas-Mexico cross-border relations. In *Dígame!: Policy and Politics on the Texas Border*, edited by Christine Brenner, Irasema Coronado, and Dennis Soden, 357–73. Dubuque, IA: Kendall Hunt.

Coronado Moreno, Martin. 2003. Comercio e industria registran año negativo localmente. In *Diario de Juárez Suplemento Especial Anuario*, edited by Bertha Ramirez, 21. Ciudad Juárez, Mexico: Chihuahua.

Cortés, Ernesto. 1993. Reweaving the fabric: The iron rule and the IAF strategy for dealing with poverty through power and politics. In *Interwoven Destinies: Cities and the Nation*, edited by Henry Cisneros, 294–319. New York: W.W. Norton.

Cortez, Richard. 2003. *Open Letter to Honorable Tom Ridge, Secretary of Homeland Security*. Phoenix, AZ: Border Trade Alliance. http://www.thebta.org (accessed May 26, 2005).

Craig, Richard B. 1971. *The Bracero Program: Interest Groups and Foreign Policy*. Austin: University of Texas Press.

Craske, Nikki. 1999. *Women and Politics in Latin America*. Oxford: Polity Press.

Cravey, Altha. 1998. *Women and Work in Mexico's Maquiladoras*. Lanham, MD: Rowman and Littlefield.

———. 1997. The politics of reproduction: Households in the Mexican industrial transition. *Economic Geography* 73(2): 166–86.

D'Aubeterre Buznego, María Eugenia. 2000. *El pogo de la nova: Matrimonio, vida conyugal y practices transnacionales en San Miguel Acuexcomal, Puebla*. Zamora, Michoacán: El Colegio de Michoacán; Puebla, Puebla: Instituto de Ciencias Sociales y Humanas, Benemérita Universidad Autónoma de Puebla.

de Keijzer, Benno. 1997. La masculinidad como factor de riesgo. In *Género y violencia*, edited by Inés Martínez de Castro, 49–70. Hermosillo, Sonora: El Colegio de Sonora, Secretaría de Salud Pública del Estado de Sonora.

Denman, Catalina, Janice Monk, and Norma Ojeda de la Peña, eds. 2004. *Compartiendo historias de fronteras: Cuerpos, géneros, generaciones, y salud*. Hermosillo, Sonora: El Colegio de Sonora.

Department of Homeland Security (DHS) website. n.d. http://www.dhs.gov (accessed May 26, 2005).

Dietz, Mary G. 1990. El contexto es lo que cuenta: Feminismo y teorias de la ciudadanía. *Debate feminista* 1: 114–42.

Dolhinow, Rebecca. 2005. Caught in the middle: The state, NGOs, and the limits to grassroots organizing along the U.S.–Mexico border. *Antipode* 37(3): 558–580.

———. 2003. *Borderlands Justice: Women's Community Activism in the Colonias of Doña Ana County, New Mexico*. Ph.D. dissertation, Department of Geography, University of California, Berkeley.

Domosh, Mona, and Joni Seager. 2001. *Putting Women in Place: Feminist Geographers Make Sense of the World*. New York: Guilford.

Duarte, Patricia, and Gerardo González. 1994. *La lucha contra la violencia de género en México: De Nairobi a Beijing, 1985–1995*. Mexico City: COVAC.

Dunn, Timothy J. 1996. *The Militarization of the U.S.–Mexico Border 1978–1992: Low-Intensity Doctrine Comes Home*. Austin: Center for Mexican American Studies, University of Texas at Austin.

Ehrenreich, Barbara, and Arlie Russell Hochschild, eds. 2002. *Global Woman, Nannies, Maids, and Sex Workers in the New Economy*. New York: Metropolitan Books.

Elson, Diane. 1992. From survival strategies to transformation strategies: Women's needs and structural adjustment. In *Unequal Burden: Economic Crises, Persistent Poverty, and Women's Work*, edited by Lourdes Benería and Shelly Feldman, 26–48. Boulder, CO: Westview Press.

England, Kim V.L. 1993. Changing suburbs, changing women: Geographic perspectives on suburban women and suburbanization. *Frontiers* 14(1): 24–43.

England, Paula, and Nancy Folbre. 1999. The cost of caring. *Annals of the American Academy of Political and Social Science* 561(1): 39–51.

Espinosa, Gisela. 2002a. Rezagos y los retos para el feminismo y los movimientos de mujeres. In *Feminismo en México. Revisión histórico crítica del siglo que termina*, edited by Griselda Gutiérrez Castañeda, 157–72. Mexico City: Colección Libros del PUEG, Universidad Nacional Autónoma de México.

———. 2002b. Ciudadanía y feminismo popular. In *Democracia y luchas de género: La construcción de un nuevo campo teórico y político*, edited by Griselda Gutiérrez Castañeda, 15–46. Mexico City: Colección Libros del PUEG, Universidad Nacional Autónoma de México.

Expansión. 1990. *Frontera norte. Las maquiladoras frente a la integración [The northern border. The maquiladoras in the face of integration]*. 552(22), October 24.

Falcón, Sylvanna. 2001. Rape as a weapon of war: advancing human rights for women at the U.S.–Mexico border. *Social Justice* 28(2): 31–50.

Fanon, Franz. 1965. *Los condenados de la tierra*. Mexico City: Fondo de Cultura Económica.

Fernández Poncela, Ana. 1995. *Participación política. Las mujeres en México al final del milenio*. Mexico City: Programa Interdisciplinario de Estudios de la Mujer, El Colegio de México.

Fernández-Kelly, María Patricia. 1983. *For We Are Sold I and My People: Women and Industry in Mexico's Frontier*. New York: University of New York Press.

Fisher, Jo. 1989. *Mothers of the Disappeared*. Cambridge: South End Press.

Flora, Maria Sagrario. 1994. Work intensity and time use: What do women do when there aren't enough hours in a day? In *Color, Class and Country: Experiences of Gender*, edited by Gay Young and Bette J. Dickerson, 168–81. London: Zed Books.

Fontana, Marzia, Susan Joekes, and Rachel Masika. 1998. *Global Trade Expansion and Liberalization: Gender Issues and Impacts*. Department for International Development (DFID), Report no. 42. Brighton, UK: Institute of Development Studies.

Fraser, Nancy. 1993. Clintonism, welfare, and the antisocial wage: The emergence of a neoliberal political imaginary. *Rethinking Marxism* 6(1): 9–23.

Fregoso, Rosa Linda. 2003. *Mexicana Encounters: The Making of Social Identities on the Borderlands*. Berkeley: University of California Press.

Fullerton, Thomas, and Martha Patricia Barraza de Anda. 2003. Maquiladora prospects in the global environment. *Texas Business Review* (October 1): 1–5. Austin: Bureau of Business Research, University of Texas at Austin.

Fussell, Elizabeth. 2000. Making labor flexible: The recomposition of Tijuana's maquiladora female labor force. *Feminist Economics* 6(3): 59–79.

García, Brígida, and Orlandina de Oliveira. 1994. Trabajo y familia en la investigación sociodemografica de México. In *La Población en el Desarrollo Contemporáneo de México*, edited by Francisco Alba and Gustavo Cabrera, 251–279. Mexico City: Centro de Estudios Demográficos y de Desarrollo Urbano, El Colegio de México.

García, Sonia R., and Marisela Márquez. 2001. Motivational and attitudinal factors amongst Latinas in U.S. electoral politics. *National Women's Studies Association Journal* 13(2): 112–22.

Giddens, Anthony. 2003. *Runaway World: How Globalization Is Reshaping Our Lives*. New York: Routledge.

Gilmore, R. W. 1999. You have dislodged a boulder: Mothers and prisoners in the post Keynesian California landscape. *Transforming Anthropology* 8: 12–38.

Glick-Schiller, Nina, Linda Basch, and Christiana Blanc-Szanton. 1992. Transnationalism: A new analytic framework for understanding migration. *Annals of the New York Academy of Sciences* 645: 25–52.

González, Cristina. 2001. *Autonomía y alianzas: El movimiento feminista en la ciudad de México, 1976–1986*. Mexico City: Colección Libros del PUEG, Universidad Nacional Autónoma de México.

González, Deen J. 1999. *Refusing the Favor: The Spanish American Women of Santa Fe*. New York: Oxford University Press.

González, Norma. 2001. *I Am My Language: Discourses of Women and Children on the Borderlands*. Tucson: University of Arizona Press.

González de la Rocha, Mercedes. 1994. *The Resources of Poverty: Women and Survival in a Mexican City*. Cambridge: Blackwell.

González Montes, Soledad. 1999. *Las organizaciones no gubernamentales mexicanas y la salud reproductiva*. Mexico City: El Colegio de México.

Gordon, Linda. 1999. *The Great Arizona Orphan Abduction*. Cambridge: Harvard University Press.

Grasmuck, Sherri, and Patricia Pessar. 1991. *Between Two Islands: Dominican International Migration*. Berkeley: University of California Press.

Gregson, Nicky, and Michelle Lowe. 1994. *Servicing the Middle Classes: Class, Gender, and Waged Work in Contemporary Britain*. New York: Routledge.

Guillén López, Tonatiuh. 2001. Gobernabilidad y gestión local en México: El caso de Tijuana, B.C. 1989–1997. In *Transición política y democracia municipal en México y Colombia*, edited by Martha Schteingart and Emilio Duhau, 39–106. Mexico City: Editorial Porrúa.

Gutiérrez Castañeda, Griselda, ed. 2002. *Feminismo en México. Revisión histórico-crítica del siglo que termina*. Mexico City: Colección Libros del PUEG, Universidad Nacional Autónoma de México.

Hall, Kevin. 2002. Jobs at risk in Mexico: Foreign companies looking elsewhere for cheaper labor. *Hispanic Vista*. http://latinobeat.net/html/051302mex.htm (accessed May 26, 2005).

Hansen, Ellen. 1999. The difference a line makes: Women's lives in Douglas, Arizona and Agua Prieta, Sonora. In *Life, Death, and In-Between on the U.S.–Mexico Border: Así es la vida*, edited by Martha Oehmke Loustaunau and Mary Sánchez-Bane, 77–94. Westport, CT: Bergin & Garvey.

Hanson, Susan, and Geraldine Pratt. 1995. *Gender, Work and Space*. New York: Routledge.

Hardy-Fanta, Carol. 1997. Latina women and political consciousness: La chispa que prende. In *Women Transforming Politics: An Alternative Reader*, edited by Cathy Cohen, Kathleen Jones, and Joan Tronto, 223–37. New York: New York Press.

Harris, Nigel. 1995. *The New Untouchables: Immigration and the New World Worker*. New York: St. Martin's Press.

Hart, Gillian. 2004. Geography and development: Critical ethnographies. *Progress in Human Geography* 28(1): 91–100.

Hernandez, Elsa Patricia. 2004. Las regidoras en el municipio de Juárez: Elites discriminadas? In *Cambio politico y participación ciudadana en Ciudad Juárez*, edited by Hector Padilla, 161–210. Ciudad Juárez, Mexico: Universidad Autónoma de Ciudad Juárez.

———. 2001. *La participación política de las mujeres en el gobierno local: El caso de las regidoras de Juárez, 1980–2001*. Master's thesis, Universidad Autónoma de Ciudad Juárez.

Herzog, Lawrence A. 1990. *Where North Meets South: Cities, Space, and Politics on the U.S.–Mexico Border*. Austin: Center for Mexican American Studies, University of Texas.

Hesse-Biber, Sharlene Nagy, and Michelle Yaiser, eds. 2004. *Feminist Perspectives on Social Research*. Oxford: Oxford University Press.

Heyman, Josiah McC. 1991. *Life and Labor on the Border: Working People of Northeastern Sonora, Mexico, 1886–1986*. Tucson: University of Arizona Press.

Hicks, Emily D. 1991. *Border Writing: The Multidimensional Text*. Minneapolis: University of Minnesota Press.

Hill, Sarah. 2003. Metaphoric enrichment and material poverty: The making of 'colonias.' In *Ethnography at the Border*, edited by Pablo Vila, 141–65. Minneapolis: University of Minnesota Press.

Himmelman, Arthur Turovh. 1996. On the theory and practice of transformational collaboration: From social service to social justice. In *Creating Collaborative Advantage*, edited by Chris Huxham, 19–43. London: Sage Publishers.

Himmelweit, Susan. 1999. Caring Labor. *Annals of the American Academy of Political and Social Science* 561: 27–38.

Hing, Bill O. 1998. Don't give me your tired, your poor: Conflicted immigrant stories and welfare reform. *Harvard Civil Rights–Civil Liberties Law Review* 33(1): 159–82.

Hochschild, Arlie. 1989. *The Second Shift*. New York: Viking.

Hondagneu-Sotelo, Pierrette. 1997. Working 'without papers' in the United States: Toward the integration of legal status in frameworks of race, class, and gender. In *Women and Work: Exploring Race, Ethnicity, and Class*, edited by Elizabeth Higginbotham and Mary Romero, 101–25. Thousand Oaks, CA: Sage Publications.

———. 1994a. *Gendered Transitions: Mexican Experiences of Migration*. Berkeley: University of California Press.

———. 1994b. Regulating the unregulated? Domestic workers' social networks. *Social Problems* 41(1): 50–64.

House, John W. 1982. *Frontier on the Rio Grande: A Political Geography of Development and Social Deprivation*. New York: Oxford University Press.

Howard, Cheryl. 1994. Female heads of households in Ciudad Juárez. In *Policy Recommendations for Managing the El Paso–Juárez Metropolitan Area*, edited by Samuel Schmidt and David Lorey. El Paso: El Paso Community Foundation and Center for Inter-American and Border Studies, University of Texas at El Paso. http://www.municipiodenogales.org/1936.htm (accessed May 26, 2005).

Huntington, Samuel. 1998. *El choque de civilizaciones y la reconfiguración del orden mundial*. Buenos Aires: Paidos.

Hurtado, Albert L. 1999. *Intimate Frontiers: Sex, Gender, and Culture in Old California*. Albuquerque: University of New Mexico Press.

Hutton, Will, and Anthony Giddens, eds. 2002. *Global Capitalism*. New York: The New Press.

Hyatt, Susan. 2001. From citizen to volunteer: Neoliberal governance and the erasure of poverty. In *The New Poverty Studies: The Ethnography of Power, Politics, and Impoverished People in the United States*, edited by Judith Goode and Jeff Maskovsky, 201–35. New York: New York University Press.

Iglesias Prieto, Norma. 1997. *The Beautiful Flowers of the Maquiladora: Life Histories of Women Workers in Tijuana*. Austin: University of Texas Press. [Published in Spanish in 1985 as *La flor más bella de la maquiladora: Historias de vida de la mujer obrera en Tijuana, B.C.N.* Mexico City: Secretaría de Educación Pública, Centro de Estudios Fronterizos.]

Incháustegui, Teresa. 1995. Participación política y políticas públicas: Cómo hacer el vínculo en el caso de las mujeres? In *Participación política: Las mujeres en México al final del milenio*, edited by Ana Fernández Poncela, 121–24. Mexico City: Programa Interdisciplinario de Estudios de la Mujer, El Colegio de México.

Instituto Nacional de Estadística Geografía e Informática. 2003. *Estadística de la industria maquiladora de exportacion 1990–2002*. Aguascalientes, Mexico: Instituto Nacional de Estadística Geografía e Informática.

Jaquette, Jane S. 1991. *The Women's Movement in Latin America: Feminism and the Transition to Democracy*. Boulder, CO: Westview Press.

Jelin, Elizabeth. 1994. ¿Ciudadanía emergente o exclusión? Movimientos sociales y ONG en los años noventa. *Revista Mexicana de Sociología* 54(4): 91–106.

———, ed. 1990. *Women and Social Change in Latin America*. London: Zed Books.

Joekes, Susan. 1995. *Trade-related Employment for Women in Industry and Services in Developing Countries*. Occasional paper, no. 5. Geneva: United Nations Research Institute for Social Development.

Kabeer, Naila. 1994. *Reversed Realities: Gender Hierarchies in Development Thought*. London: Verso.

Kaplan, Temma. 1997. *Crazy for Democracy: Women in Grassroots Movements*. New York: Routledge.

Kawachi, Ichiro, and Bruce P. Kennedy. 2002. *The Health of Nations: Why Inequality Is Harmful to Your Health*. New York: The New Press.

Kearney, Michael. 1995. The local and the global: The anthropology of globalization and transnationalism. *Annual Review of Anthropology* 24: 547–65.

———. 1991. Borders and boundaries of state and self at the end of empire. *Journal of Historical Sociology* 4(1): 52–74.

Kelly, Liz. 1988. *Surviving Sexual Violence*. Cambridge: Polity Press.

KFPE. *See* Swiss Commission for Research Partnerships with Developing Countries.

Kibria, Nazli. 1993. *The Family Tightrope: The Changing Lives of Vietnamese-Americans*. Princeton: Princeton University Press.

Kiy, Richard, and Naoko Kada. 2004. *Blurred Borders: Transboundary Issues and Solutions in the San Diego/Tijuana Border Region*. San Diego: International Community Foundation.

Kopinak, Kathryn. 1996. *Desert Capitalism*. Tucson: University of Arizona Press.

Lamas, Marta. 1994. Algunas características del movimiento feminista en Ciudad de México. In *Mujeres y participación política: Avances y desafíos en América Latina*, edited by Magdalena León, 143–65. Bogotá, Colombia: Tercer Mundo Editores.

Lamas, Marta, Alicia Martínez, and María Luisa Tarrés. 1995. Building bridges: The growth of popular feminism in Mexico. In *The Challenge of Local Feminisms*, edited by Amrita Basu with C. Elizabeth McGrory, 324–50. Boulder, CO: Westview Press.

Lamphere, Louise. 1987. *From Working Daughters to Working Mothers: Immigrant Women in a New England Community*. Ithaca, NY: Cornell University Press.

Lind, Amy Conger. 1992. Power, gender, and development: Popular women's organizations and the politics of needs in Ecuador. In *The Making of Social Movements in Latin America*, edited by Arturo Escobar and Sonia E. Alvarez, 134–49. Boulder, CO: Westview Press.

Lobato, Mirta Jaida. 1997. Women workers in the 'Cathedrals of Corned Beef': Structure and subjectivity in the Argentine meatpacking industry. In *The Gendered Worlds of Latin American Women Workers: From Household and Factory to the Union Hall and Ballot Box*, edited by John French and Daniel James, 53–71. Durham, NC: Duke University Press.

Long, Norman. 1977. *An Introduction to the Sociology of Rural Development*. London: Tavistock.

López Estrada, Silvia. 2002. Las organizaciones no gubernamentales feministas en Baja California. In *Baja California: Escenarios del nuevo milenio*, edited by Tonatiuh Guillén, 203–29. Mexico City: Universidad Nacional Autónoma de México.

Lorey, David E. 1999. *The U.S–Mexican Border in the Twentieth Century*. Wilmington, DE: Scholarly Resources Inc.

Luibhéid, Eithne. 2002. *Entry Denied: Controlling Sexuality at the Border*. Minneapolis: University of Minnesota Press.

Mahler, Sarah J. 2003. Engendering transnational migration: A case study of Salvadorans. In *Gender and U.S. Immigration: Contemporary Trends*, edited by Pierrette Hondagneu-Sotelo, 287–316. Berkeley: University of California Press.

Maier, Elizabeth. 1997. *Dilemas de los feminismos latinoamericanos: Cuaderno de trabajo*. Tijuana, Mexico: El Colegio de la Frontera Norte.

Malkin, Victoria. 1997. *Reproduction of Gender Relations in the Mexican Migrant Community of New Rochelle, New York*. Paper presented at the Colóquio de Antropología e História Regional, Michoacán, Mexico, October 1–2.

Manke, Beth, Brenda Seery, Ann Crouter, and Susan McHale. 1994. The three corners of domestic labor: Mothers', fathers', and children's weekday and weekend housework. *Journal of Marriage and the Family* 56: 657–68.

Marchand, Marianne H. 2002. Engendering globalization in an era of transnational capital: new cross-border alliances and strategies of resistance in a post–NAFTA Mexico. In *Feminist Post-Development Thought: Rethinking Modernity, Postcolonialism, and Representation*, edited by Kriemild Saunders, 105–19. New York: Zed Books.

Martinez, Alicia, and Teresa Incháustegui. 1998. Feminist policies in contemporary Mexico: Strategies and viability. In *Women's Participation in Mexican Political Life*, edited by Victoria E. Rodríguez, 179–92. Boulder, CO: Westview Press.

Martínez, Oscar J. 1997. Border people and their cultural roles: The case of the U.S.–Mexican borderlands. In *Borders and Border Regions in Europe and North America*, edited by Paul Ganster, Alan Seedler, James Scott, and Wolf Dieter-Eberwein, 293–98. San Diego: San Diego State University Press.

———. 1994. *Border People: Life and Society in the U.S.–Mexico Borderlands*. Tucson: University of Arizona Press.

———. 1988. *Troublesome Border*. Tucson: University of Arizona Press.

Massey, Doreen. 1994. *Space, Place, and Gender*. Minneapolis: University of Minnesota Press.

Massolo, Alejandra. 1994. *Los medios y los modos: Participación política y acción colectiva de las mujeres*. Mexico City: El Colegio de México.

Mattessich, Paul W., Marta Murray-Close, and Barbara R. Monsey with the Wilder Research Center. 2001. *Collaboration: What Makes It Work*. 2nd ed. St. Paul, MN: Amherst H. Wilder Foundation.

Mattingly, Doreen J. 1999a. Job search, social networks, and local labor market dynamics: The case of paid household work in San Diego, California. *Urban Geography* 20(1): 46–74.

———. 1999b. Making maids: U.S. immigration policy and immigrant domestic workers. In *Gender, Migration, and Domestic Service*, edited by Janet Momson, 62–80. New York: Routledge.

McCaughan, Edward J. 1993. Mexico's long crisis: Toward new regimes of accumulation and domination. *Latin America Perspectives* 20(3): 6–31.

McDowell, Linda. 1999. *Gender, Identity and Place: Understanding Feminist Geographies*. Minneapolis: University of Minnesota Press.

Miller, Valerie. 2000. *Desafíos y lecciones de la incidencia política: Interrogantes e implicaciones para programas de acción, capacitación y apoyo financiero*. Paper presented at the Regional Meeting on Advocacy, Training and Financial Support, Antigua, Guatemala, October 13–14.

Mitchell, Donald. 2000. *Cultural Geography: A Critical Introduction*. Malden, MA: Blackwell.

Mogrovejo, Norma. 1992. Movimiento urbano y feminismo popular en la ciudad de México. In *Mujeres y ciudades: Participación social, vivienda y vida cotidiana*, edited by Alejandra Massolo, 59–96. Mexico City: El Colegio de México.

Momsen, Janet Henshall, ed. 1999. *Gender, Migration, and Domestic Service*. New York: Routledge.

Monarrez, Julia E. 2002. Feminicidio sexual serial en Ciudad Juarez: 1993–2001. *Debate Feminista* 13(25): 297–305.

———. 2000. La cultura del feminicido en Ciudad Juarez, 1993–1999. *Frontera Norte* 23(12): 87–117.

Monk, Janice, Patricia Manning, and Catalina Denman. 2003. Working together: Feminist perspectives on collaborative research and action. *ACME: An International E-Journal for Critical Geographers* 2(1): 91–106.

Moore, Wilbur E. 1965. *The Impact of Industry*. Englewood Cliffs, NJ: Prentice-Hall.

Naples, Nancy. 2002. Changing the terms. In *Women's Activism and Globalization: Linking Local Struggles and Transnational Politics*, edited by Nancy A. Naples and Manisha Desai, 3–14. New York: Routledge.

———. 1998. *Grassroots Warriors: Activist Mothering, Community Work, and the War on Poverty*. New York: Routledge.

Nash, June. 2003. Foreword. In *Women of Chiapas Making History in Times of Struggle and Hope*, edited by Christine Eber and Christine Kovic, ix–xv. New York: Routledge.

———. 1983. The impact of the changing international division of labor on different sectors of the labor force. In *Women, Men, and the International Division of Labor*, edited by June Nash and María Patricia Fernández-Kelly, 3–38. Albany, NY: SUNY Press.

Nathanson, Charles E., and Julio Lampell. 2001. *Solving Our Border Crossing Problem in an Era of Terrorism*. Briefing paper prepared for San Diego Dialogue's Forum *Fronterizo* series. San Diego: University of California. http://www.sandiegodialogue.org (accessed May 26, 2005).

Nevins, Joseph. 2002. *Operation Gatekeeper: The Rise of the 'Illegal Alien' and the Making of the U.S.–Mexico Boundary*. New York: Routledge.

Ojeda, Norma. 2004. What do California Latinas and Mexicanas in Baja California think about family planning and abortion? In *The Two Californias Binational Survey Findings*. San Diego: San Diego State University; El Colegio de la Frontera Norte; Planned Parenthood. March 2004. (mimeograph)

———. 2003. *¿Qué piensan las mujeres en Baja California acerca de la planificación familiar y el aborto? Hallazgos de una encuesta*. Mexico City: El Colegio de la Frontera Norte.

———. 1997. Algunas contradicciones en el perfil sociodemográfico de las mujeres en la frontera norte de México. In *Cuadernos de trabajo*, 4–6, No. DTS-2. Mexico City: El Colegio de la Frontera Norte.

———. 1994. Familias transfronterizas en Tijuana: Migración y trabajo internacional. In *Familias transfronterizas en Tijuana–San Diego: Dos estudios complementarios*, edited by Norma Ojeda and Silvia López, 11–42. Mexico City: El Colegio de la Frontera Norte.

Oliveira, Orlandina, and Marina Ariza. 1999. *Un recorrido por los estudios de género en México: Consideraciones sobre áreas prioritarias*. Paper presented at the Gender and Development Workshop, CIID/IDRC, Montevideo, Uruguay, September 6–7.

Oropesa, R. Salvador. 1993. Using the service economy to relieve the double burden: Female labor force participation and service purchases. *Journal of Family Issues* 14(3): 438–73.

Ortíz-González, Victor. 2004. *El Paso: Local Frontiers at a Global Crossroads*. Minneapolis: University of Minnesota Press.

Pardo, Mary. 1990. Mexican American women grassroots community activists: 'Mothers of East Los Angeles.' *Frontiers: A Journal of Women Studies* 11(1): 1–7.

Pavlakovic, Vera K., and Hak-Hoon Kim. 1990. Outshopping by maquila employees: Implications for Arizona's border communities. *Arizona Review* 38(1): 9–16.

Peck, Jamie, and Adam Tickell. 2002. Neoliberalizing space. *Antipode* 34(2): 380–404.

Peña, Devon G. 1997. *The Terror of the Machine: Technology, Work, Gender, and Ecology at the U.S.–Mexico Border*. Austin: Center for Mexican American Studies, University of Texas.

———. 1987. Tortuosidad: Shop floor struggles of female maquiladora workers. In

Women on the U.S.–Mexico Border: Responses to Change, edited by Vicki L. Ruiz and Susan Tiano, 129–54. Boston: Allen and Unwin.

Perez, Martha Estela. 2004. La coordinadora en pro de los derechos de la mujer: Una lucha de mujeres por mujeres? In *Cambio político y participación ciudadana en Ciudad Juárez*, edited by Hector Padilla, 211–44. Ciudad Juárez, Mexico: Universidad Autónoma de Ciudad Juárez.

Pessar, Patricia R., and Sarah J. Mahler. 2003. International migration: Bringing gender in. *International Migration Review* 37(3): 812–29.

Petras, James F., and Henry Veltmeyer. 2001. *Globalization Unmasked: Imperialism in the 21st Century*. London: Zed Books.

Pettman, Jan Jindy. 1999. Globalization and the gendered politics of citizenship. In *Women, Citizenship and Difference*, edited by Nira Yuval-Davis and Pnina Werbner, 207–20. London: Zed Books.

Pick, James B., W. James Hettrick, Nanda Viswanathan, and Elliot Ellsworth. 2001. *Binationality in the U.S.–Mexican Border Twin Cities*. Executive Summary Final Report to the Ford Foundation. Redlands, CA: University of Redlands. (mimeograph)

Poniatowska, Elena. 2000. *Las mil y una: La herida de Paulina*. Mexico City: Plaza y Janes México.

Pope, Cindy. 2001. Babies and borderlands: Factors influencing Sonoran women's decision to seek prenatal care in Southern Arizona. In *Geographies of Women's Health*, edited by Sarah L. McLafferty, Isabel Dyck, and Nancy D. Lewis, 143–58. New York: Routledge.

Portillo, Lourdes, producer and director. 2001. *Señorita Extraviada*. New York: Women Make Movies.

———. 2003. Filming *Señorita Extraviada*. *Aztlan* 28(2): 229–34.

Pradilla, Emilia, and Cecilia Castro García. 1994. *Las fronteras de la maquila*. Mexico City: Frontera Norte, Territorios.

Pratt, Geraldine. 1999. From registered nurse to registered nanny: Discursive geographies of Filipina domestic workers in Vancouver, B.C. *Economic Geography* 75(3): 215–36.

Pratt, Geraldine, and Susan Hanson. 1991. Time, space and the occupational segregation of women: A critique of human capital theory. *Geoforum* 22:149–57.

Price, Patricia. 2004. *Dry Place: Landscapes of Belonging and Exclusion*. Minneapolis: University of Minnesota Press.

Quintero, Cirila. 1999. Condiciones laborales y sindicales en las maquiladoras y sus implicaciones para la familia. In *Colonias and Public Policy in Texas and México: Urbanization by Stealth*, edited by Peter M. Ward, 47–51. Austin: University of Texas Press.

Ramírez, Luz de Socorro. 1993. La crisis económica y las respuestas de las mujeres a través de las organizaciones de sobrevivencia. In *La mujer Latinoamericana ante el reto del siglo XXI*, edited by María Pilar Pérez Cantó and Marta Elena Casaús Arzú,

247–65. IX Jornadas de Investigación Interdisciplinaria sobre la Mujer. Madrid: Instituto Universitario de Estudios de la Mujer, Ediciones de la Universidad Autónoma de Madrid.

Razavi, Shahra. 2000. Export-oriented employment, poverty, and gender: Contested accounts. In *Gendered Poverty and Well-Being*, edited by Shahra Razavi, 239–68. Maiden, MA: Blackwell.

Reinharz, Shulamit. 1992. *Feminist Methods in Social Research*. Oxford: Oxford University Press.

Rey, Joel R., Steven E. Polzin, and Stacey G. Bricka. 1995. An assessment of the potential saturation in men's travel. In *Nationwide Personal Transportation Survey*. 1990 NPTS Report Series, Demographic Special Reports, 1-1-1-63. Washington, DC: Federal Highway Administration, U.S. Department of Transportation.

Rodríguez, Victoria. 2003. *Women in Contemporary Mexican Politics*. Austin: University of Texas Press.

———, ed. 1998. *Women's Participation in Mexican Political Life*. Boulder, CO: Westview Press.

———. 1997. *Decentralization in Mexico: From reforma municipal to solidaridad to nuevo federalismo*. Boulder, CO: Westview Press.

Rollins, Judith. 1985. *Between Women: Domestics and Their Employers*. Philadelphia: Temple University Press.

Roschelle, Anne R. 1997. *No More Kin: Exploring Race, Class and Gender in Family Networks*. Thousand Oaks, CA: Sage Publications.

Rosenbloom, Sandra. 1995. Travel by women. In *Nationwide Personal Transportation Survey*. 1990 NPTS Report Series, Demographic Special Reports, 2-1-2-57. Washington, DC: Federal Highway Administration, U.S. Department of Transportation.

———. 1993. Women's travel patterns at various stages of their lives. In *Full Circles: Geographies of Women over the Life Course*, edited by Cindi Katz and Janice Monk, 208–42. New York: Routledge.

Rudolph, Lloyd I., and Susanne Hoeber Rudolph. 2003. Engaging subjective knowledge: How Amar Singh's diary narratives of and by the self explain identity formation. *Perspectives on Politics* 1(4): 681–94.

Ruiz, Olivia. 1998. Visiting the mother country: Border-crossing as a cultural practice. In *The U.S.–Mexico Border: Transcending Divisions, Contesting Identities*, edited by David Spener and Kathleen Staudt, 105–20. Boulder, CO: Lynne Rienner Publishers.

Ruiz, Vicki. 1987. By the day or the week: Mexicana domestic workers in El Paso. In *Women on the U.S.–México Border: Responses to Change*, edited by Vicki L. Ruiz and Susan Tiano, 61–76. Boston: Allen and Unwin.

Ruiz, Vicki L., and Susan Tiano, eds. 1987. *Women on the U.S.–Mexico Border: Responses to Change*. Boston: Allen and Unwin.

Ruiz Garcia, Aída. 2002. *Migración oaxaqueña, una aproximación a la realidad*. Oaxaca, Mexico: Coordinación Estatal de Atención al Migrante Oaxaqueño.

Safa, Helen. 1995a. *The Myth of the Male Breadwinner: Women and Industrialization in the Caribbean*. Boulder, CO: Westview Press.

———. 1995b. Gender implications of export-led industrialization in the Caribbean basin. In *Engendering Wealth and Well-Being*, edited by Rae Lesser Blumberg, Cathy A. Rakowski, Irene Tinker, and Michael Monteón, 89–112. Boulder, CO: Westview Press.

Saffioti, Heleieth I.B. 1975. Female labor and capitalism in the United States and Brazil. In *Women Cross-Culturally: Change and Challenge*, edited by Ruby Rohrilich-Leavitt, 59–94. The Hague: Mouton.

Saint-Germain, Michelle A. 1998. Re-presenting the public interest on the U.S.–Mexico border. In *The U.S.–Mexico Border: Transcending Divisions, Contesting Identities*, edited by David Spener and Kathleen Staudt, 59–81. Boulder, CO: Lynne Reinner Publishers.

Saldívar, José David. 1997. *Border Matters: Remapping American Cultural Studies*. Berkeley: University of California Press.

Salvídar-Hull, Sonia. 2000. *Feminism on the Border: Chicana Gender Politics and Literature*. Berkeley: University of California Press.

Salzinger, Leslie. 2003. *Genders in Production: Making Workers in Mexico's Global Factories*. Berkeley: University of California Press.

———. 1997. From high heels to swathed bodies: Gendered meanings under production in Mexico's export processing industry. *Feminist Studies* 23(3): 549–74.

San Ysidro Chamber of Commerce. n.d. *Border Crossing*. http://www.sanysidrochamber.org/border.php (accessed May 26, 2005).

Sánchez Olvera, Alma Rosa. 2002. *El feminismo Mexicano ante el movimiento urbano popular: Dos expresiones de lucha de género, 1970–1985*. Mexico City: Universidad Nacional Autónoma de México, Campus Acatlán.

Sassen, Saskia. 1998. *Globalization and Its Discontents*. New York: The New York Press.

Saucedo González, Irma. 1995. Apuntes para la elaboración de una propuesta de participación política feminista. In *Participación política: Las mujeres en México al final del milenio*, edited by Anna M. Fernández Poncela, 125–36. Mexico City: Programa Interdisciplinario de Estudios de la Mujer, El Colegio de México.

Schmidt Camacho, Alicia. 1999. On the borders of solidarity: Race and gender contradictions in the 'New Voice' platform of the AFL-CIO. *Social Justice* 26(3): 79–102.

Schmink, Marianne. 1986. Women and industrial development in Brazil. In *Women and Change in Latin America*, edited by June Nash and Helen Safa, 136–64. South Hadley, MA: Bergin and Garvey.

Schnaiberg, Lynn. 1995. Judge rejects Prop. 187 bans on Calif. services. *Education Week*. 15(13): 13–18. 29 November 1995.

Selby, Henry A., Arthur D. Murphy, and Stephen A. Lorenzen. 1990. *The Mexican Urban Household*. Austin: University of Texas Press.

Serret, Estela. 2000. El feminismo mexicano de cara al siglo XXI. *El Cotidiano* 16(100): 42–51.

Sklair, Leslie. 1993. *Assembling for Development: The Maquila Industry in Mexico and The*

United States. San Diego: Center for U.S.–Mexican Studies, University of California at San Diego.

Social Science Research Council. 2000. *International Scholarly Collaboration: Lessons from the Past*. A Report of the Social Science Research Council Inter-Regional Group on International Scholarly Collaboration, Vol. 3. New York: Social Science Research Council.

Social Science Research Laboratory, San Diego State University. 2001. *Survey of California Latina Attitudes Regarding Family Planning Issues*. Research Report to Planned Parenthood Affiliates of California Incorporated. San Diego: The Social Science Research Laboratory of San Diego State University. (mimeograph)

Solórzano-Torres, Rosalía. 1987. Female Mexican immigrants in San Diego county. In *Women on the U.S.–Mexico Border: Responses to Change*, edited by Vicki L. Ruiz and Susan Tiano, 41–59. Boston: Allen and Unwin.

Spagat, Elliot. 2005. Border's Fast Lane Turns Slow. *The Sacramento Union*, May 9. http://www.sacunion.com (accessed October 1, 2005).

Spain, Daphne, and Suzanne M. Bianchi. 1996. *Balancing Act: Motherhood, Marriage, and Employment among American Women*. New York: Sage.

Speed, Shannon. 2003. Actions speak louder than words: Indigenous women and gendered resistance in the wake of Acteal. In *Women of Chiapas Making History in Times of Struggle and Hope*, edited by Christine Eber and Christine Kovic, 67–96. New York: Routledge.

Spener, David, and Kathleen Staudt. 1998. Conclusion: Rebordering. In *The U.S.–Mexico Border: Transcending Divisions, Contesting Identities*, edited by David Spener and Kathleen Staudt, 233–57. Boulder, CO: Lynne Rienner Publishers.

Standing, Guy. 1999. Global feminization through flexible labor: A theme revisited. *World Development* 27(3): 583–602.

———. 1989. Global feminization through flexible labor. *World Development* 17(7): 1077–95.

Stanko, Elizabeth Anne. 1985. *Intimate Intrusions: Women's Experience of Male Violence*. London: Routledge.

Staudt, Kathleen A. 1998. *Free Trade?: Informal Economies at the U.S.–México Border*. Philadelphia: University of Philadelphia Press.

———. 1983. Economic change and ideological lag in households of maquila workers in Ciudad Juárez. In *The Social Ecology and Economic Development of Ciudad Juarez*, edited by Gay Young, 97–120. Boulder, CO: Westview Press.

Staudt, Kathleen A., and Irasema Coronado. 2002. *Fronteras no mas: Toward Social Justice at the U.S.–Mexico Border*. New York: Palgrave Press.

Stølen, Kristi Anne, and Mariken Vaa. 1991. *Gender and Change in Developing Countries*. London: Norwegian University Press.

Swiss Commission for Research Partnerships with Developing Countries (KFPE). 2001. *Enhancing Research Capacity in Developing and Transition Countries*. Bern: KPFE Secretariat.

———. 1998. *Guidelines for Research in Partnership with Developing Countries*. 2nd ed. Bern: KFPE Secretariat.

Tarrés, María Luisa. 1998. De la identidad al espacio público: Las organizaciones no gubernamentales de mujeres en México. In *Organizaciones civiles y públicas en México y Centroamérica*, edited by José Luis Méndez, 101–33 . Mexico City: Porrúa Editores.

Thomas, Sue, and Clyde Wilcox. 1998. *Women and Elective Office: Past, Present and Future*. Oxford: Oxford University Press.

Tiano, Susan. 1997. The role of women. In *Understanding Contemporary Latin America*, edited by Richard Hillman, 237–70. Boulder: Lynne Rienner Publishers.

———. 1994. *Patriarchy on the Line: Labor, Gender, and Ideology in the Mexican Maquila Industry*. Philadelphia: Temple University Press.

———. 1990. Women workers in the electronics and garment industries: Who assembles in Mexicali maquilas? *Review of Latin American Studies* 3(1): 63–82.

———. 1987a. Gender, work, and world capitalism: Third world women's role in development. In *Analyzing Gender: A Handbook for Social Science Research*, edited by Beth Hess and Myra Marx Ferree, 216–43. Newbury Park, CA: Sage Press.

———. 1987b. Maquiladoras in Mexicali: Integration or exploitation? In *Women on the U.S.–México Border: Responses to Change*, edited by Vicki L. Ruiz and Susan Tiano, 77–102. Boston: Allen and Unwin.

———. 1986. Women and industrial development in Latin America. *Latin American Research Review* 21: 157–70.

Tiano, Susan, and Carolina Ladino. 1999. Dating, mating, and motherhood: Identity construction among Mexican maquila workers. *Environment and Planning A* 31: 305–25.

Torres, Marta 1997. *Espacios familiares: Ámbitos de sobrevivencia y solidaridad*. Mexico City: Programa Universitario de Estudios de Género, Consejo Nacional de Población, Desarrollo Integral de la Familia, Universidad Nacional Autónoma de México, and Universidad Autónoma Metropolitana.

Touraine, Alain. 1997. ¿Podremos vivir juntos? *Fondo de Cultura Económica*. Mexico City.

Tribe, Laurence H. 1990. *Abortion: The Clash of Absolutes*. New York: W.W. Norton.

Truong, Thanh-Dam. 1996. Gender, international migration and social reproduction: Implications for theory, policy, research, and networking. *Asian and Pacific Migration Theory* 5(1): 27–52.

Tuñón, Esperanza. 1992. Women's struggles for empowerment in Mexico. In *Women Transforming Politics: Worldwide Strategies for Empowerment*, edited by Jill M. Bystydzienski, 95–107. Bloomington and Indianapolis: Indiana University Press.

Turf, Luke. 2004. SENTRI May Speed Car Crossings at the Border. *Tucson Citizen*, May 6. http://www.tucsoncitizen.com (accessed May 26, 2005).

Tyner, James A. 1996. The gendering of Philippine international migration. *Professional Geographer* 48(8): 405–16.

United Nations. 2000. *The World's Women 2000: Trends and Statistics*. Social Statistics and Indicators, Series K, No. 16. New York: United Nations.

———. 1991. *The World's Women 1970–1990: Trends and Statistics*. Statistics and Statistical Methods Publications, Series K, No. 8. New York: United Nations.

U.S. Census Bureau. 2000. Table DP1, Profile of General Characteristics, San Diego

City, California. http://censtats.census.gov/data/CA/1600666000.pdf (accessed May 26, 2005).

Vaughan, Mary. 1979. Women, class, and education in Mexico, 1880–1928. In *Women in Latin America*, edited by Eleanor Leacock Burke, 63–80. Riverside, CA: Latin American Perspectives.

Veccia, Theresa. 1997. 'My duty as a woman': Gender ideology, work, and working-class women's lives in Sao Paulo, Brazil, 1900–1950. In *The Gendered Worlds of Latin American Women Workers: From Household and Factory to the Union Hall and Ballot Box*, edited by John French and Daniel James, 100–146. Durham, NC: Duke University Press.

Velasco Ortiz, M. Laura. 2002. El regreso de la comunidad: Migración indígena y agentes etnicos: Los mixtecos en la frontera México–Estados Unidos. Mexico City: El Colegio de México, Centro de Estudios Sociológicos, El Colegio de la Frontera Norte.

Velez-Ibáñez, Carlos G. 1996. *Border Visions: Mexican Cultures of the Southwest United States*. Tucson: University of Arizona Press.

Vila, Pablo, ed. 2003a. *Ethnography at the Border.* Minneapolis: University of Minnesota Press.

———. 2003b. Gender and the overlapping of region, nation, and ethnicity on the U.S.–Mexico border. In *Ethnography at the Border*, edited by Pablo Vila, 73–104. Minneapolis: University of Minnesota Press.

———. 2000. *Crossing Borders, Reinforcing Borders: Social Categories, Metaphors, and Narrative Identities on the U.S.–Mexico Frontier*. Austin: University of Texas Press.

Ward, Kathryn B., and Jean L. Pyle. 1995. Gender, industrialization, transnational corporations, and development: An overview of trends and patterns. In *Women and the Latin American Development Process*, edited by Christine E. Bose and Edna Acosta-Belén, 37–64. Philadelphia: Temple University Press.

Ward, Peter M. 1999. *Colonias and Public Policy in Texas and Mexico: Urbanization by Stealth*. Austin: University of Texas Press.

Warner, Judith. 1995. Time allocation. In *Gender and Agricultural Development: Surveying the Field*, edited by Helen Henderson with Ellen Hansen, 12–17. Tucson: University of Arizona Press.

Waterman, Shaun. 2003. Biometric Borders Coming. *The Washington Times*, October 28. http://www.washingtontimes.com (accessed May 26, 2005).

Weedon, Chris. 1987. *Feminist Practice and Poststructuralist Theory*. New York: Basil Blackwell.

Weeks, John R., and Roberto Ham-Chande. 1992. *Demographic Dynamics of the U.S.–Mexico Border*. El Paso: Texas Western Press, University of Texas at El Paso.

Weinstein, Barbara. 1997. Unskilled worker, skilled housewife: Constructing the working-class woman in Sao Paulo, Brazil. In *The Gendered Worlds of Latin American Women Workers: From Household and Factory to the Union Hall and Ballot Box*, edited by John French and Daniel James, 72–99. Durham, NC: Duke University Press.

Wheeler, Charles. 1996. The new alien restrictions on public benefits: The full impact remains uncertain. *Interpreter Releases* 73: 1245.

Wilson, Patricia. 1992. *Exports and Local Development: Mexico's New Maquiladoras*. Austin: University of Texas Press.

Wolch, Jennifer R. 1989. The shadow state: Transformations in the voluntary sector. In *The Power of Geography*, edited by Jennifer Wolch and Michael Dear, 197–221. Boston: Hyman.

Wolf, Diane L. 1992. *Factory Daughters: Gender, Household Dynamics and Rural Industrialization in Java*. Berkeley: University of California Press.

Woog, Mario. 1980. *El programa mexicano de maquiladoras*. Guadalajara, Mexico: Instituto de Estudios Sociales, Universidad de Guadalajara Press.

Wright, Melissa. 2003. The politics of relocation: Gender, nationality, and value in a Mexican maquiladora. In *Ethnography at the Border*, edited by Pablo Vila, 23–45. Minneapolis: University of Minnesota Press.

———. 2001. Feminine villains, masculine heroes, and the reproduction of Ciudad Juárez. *Social Text 69* 19(4): 93–113.

———. 1997. Crossing the factory frontier: Gender, place, and power in a Mexican maquiladora. *Antipode* 29(3): 278–302.

Young, Gay. 1987. Gender identification and working-class solidarity among maquila workers in Ciudad Juárez: Stereotypes and realities. In *Women on the U.S.–Mexico Border: Responses to Change*, edited by Vicki L. Ruiz and Susan Tiano, 105–28. Boston: Allen and Unwin.

Zavella, Patricia. 2002. Engendering transnationalism in food processing: Peripheral vision on both sides of the U.S.–Mexican border. In *Transnational Latina/o Communities: Politics, Processes, and Cultures*, edited by Carlos G. Vélez-Ibáñez and Anna Sampaio, with Manolo González-Estay, 225–45. Lanham, MD: Rowman & Littlefield.

About the Contributors

Ana Bergareche is a professor and researcher at the Universidad de Guadalajara with a Ph.D. in gender and development from the University of London (London School of Economics). The author has conducted research on women's autonomy through work participation in Ciudad Juárez, focusing on gender power relations in the area of sexual violence. She is now engaged in a project on sex tourism in Puerto Vallarta, Mexico, focusing on the processes of empowerment and victimization derived from sex work in an international context.

Irasema Coronado is an assistant professor of political science and academic advisor of the Center for Inter-American and Border Studies at the University of Texas at El Paso. She is co-author of *Fronteras no mas: Toward Social Justice at the U.S.–Mexico Border* and co-editor of *Dígame!: Policy and Politics on the Texas Border*. She has received a Border Fulbright to research and teach at the Universidad Autónoma de Ciudad Juárez. Her research interests include environmental and gender issues on the border.

Catalina A. Denman is an anthropologist, senior professor-researcher and current president at El Colegio de Sonora. She conducts research on working women, border health collaboration, and reproductive health. She is also a Mexican partner with the University of Arizona TIES project on the public-health workforce and co-coordinator, with Janice Monk of the University of Arizona, of the Transborder Consortium for Research and Action on Gender and Reproductive Health at the U.S.–Mexico Border. She has authored numerous books, chapters, and articles on these subjects, as well as on qualitative methodology.

Rebecca Dolhinow is an assistant professor of women's studies at California State University, Fullerton. Her contribution to this book is part of a larger ethnographic study of the relationship between non-governmental organizations, the state, and immigrant women's activism on the U.S.–Mexico border. She is currently working on a project that focuses on young women's activism in Southern California.

Ellen R. Hansen is an associate professor of geography at Emporia State University. She received her Ph.D. from the University of Arizona in Tucson. She lived at the U.S.–Mexico border in Douglas, Arizona, where she conducted research on women's lives, focusing on issues of daily mobility. She has also researched household migration decision making in Mexico. Her current research interests involve Mexican women in the maquiladora industry, and closer to home, how we can use oral histories to examine how memory shapes our knowledge of place.

Silvia López Estrada is a researcher and professor in the Department of Population Studies, El Colegio de la Frontera Norte (COLEF) in Tijuana. A sociologist, her research focuses on work, family, and gender; and female political participation, gender, and public policies. She is the author of many articles on these topics. A member of the National System of Researchers in Mexico, she also belongs to the Board of Advisors of the Woman's Institute of Baja California.

Elizabeth Maier is a researcher and professor at El Colegio de la Frontera Norte (COLEF) in Tijuana, specializing in women's studies in Mexico. She is also a visiting professor at San Diego State University's Center for Latin American Studies. Bilingual and bicultural, she has a Ph.D. in Latin American Studies from the Universidad Autónoma de México (UNAM). During the past years, she has focused her work on identity themes related to the experience of indigenous women immigrants on the border region between the Californias. Her most recent project rests on a community-based AIDS education, research-action methodology for that population. She is the author of many books, chapters, and articles on gender-related themes. As co-chair of the Gender and Feminist Studies Section of the Latin American Studies Association, she is preparing a compendium for the United Nations Development Fund for Women.

Patricia Manning is the associate project director for the Southwest Institute for Research on Women's multifaceted Transborder Health Consortium and project coordinator for Mujer Sana~Healthy Woman. She is a political scientist specializing in comparative politics, of Latin America in particular, public policy, and civic advocacy and activism. She has extensive experience working for non-profits and community groups in Mexico and Central America; during the 1980s, she lived in Nicaragua and worked with various peace, solidarity, and human rights organizations. She has also worked with organizations dedicated to immigrant rights, mental health advocacy, women's health among underserved populations, prison reform, and nonviolent social change.

Doreen J. Mattingly is an associate professor of women's studies at San Diego State University. She received a Ph.D. in geography from Clark University. She has published on the topics of domestic work, immigration, urban politics, feminist research methods, and parent participation in public schools. She is beginning a new research project on women's employment in call centers in India.

Janice Monk is a professor of geography and regional development and a research social scientist emerita in Women's Studies at the University of Arizona, where she directed the Southwest Institute for Research on Women for over two decades. She has co-authored or co-edited an array of books and written more than eighty chapters and articles on feminist geography, the history of women in geography, and faculty and curriculum development in women's studies and international studies. Her awards include the Lifetime Career Achievement Award from the Association of American Geographers, which she has also served as president.

Norma Ojeda is an associate professor of sociology and Chicana/Chicano Studies at San Diego State University. She is also an adjunct researcher at El Colegio de la Frontera Norte (COLEF) in Tijuana, Mexico. Dr. Ojeda has held several academic positions at COLEF and at the Universidad Autónoma de México. She has a Ph.D. in sociology from the University of Texas at Austin and a master's in demography from El Colegio de México. She has authored more than twenty refereed articles published in prestigious academic journals in Latin America, Europe, and the United States, as well as books, including *Family, Gender and Reproductive Health in Mexico*. Her areas of research are family, gender, and women's reproductive health in Mexico and among Latinas in the U.S.–Mexico international border region.

Susan Tiano is a professor of sociology at the University of New Mexico. She received her Ph.D. from Brown University in 1979, with a substantive concentration in comparative sociology. Her research focus is the U.S.–Mexico border, where she spent over two decades studying sociocultural, demographic, and economic issues affecting the Mexican maquiladora industry and its labor force. Her publications include *Women on the U.S.–Mexico Border: Responses to Change*, with Vicki L. Ruiz (1987) and *Patriarchy on the Line: Labor, Gender, and Ideology in the Mexican Maquila Industry* (1994).

Index

abortion, 53–69; attitudes about, 62–63; legal status of, 54–55; motives for, 64–67

action research, 185, 189–92

activism, 5; academic, 154–55, 178–93; church-based, 95; community, 13–14, 25–28, 34–35, 93–94, 135–41, 142–43; feminist, 185–86; independent, 146, 150, 155; by Mexican women, 125–41; motivations for, 146–50; political, 143, 145–46; spiritual, 12, 148–49

agency, women's, 3–11, 25, 28, 78, 92, 94

asociaciones civiles, 150–58, 166–67

autonomy, 11–12, 19, 33–34, 91–102, 153

Border Industrialization Program (BIP), 5, 37, 143, 157

Bracero Program, 21–22

children and childcare, 23, 35, 36, 94, 99, 103–4, 108–15, 132; as outsourced activists, 149–50; effects of, on abortion decisions, 63–66; effects of, on women's activism, 138–40, 142; effects of, on women's mobility, 36, 38–40, 42–46, 52; effects of, on women's work, 24, 80, 87, 97, 104–5, 133; social significance of, 19, 30, 136; working, 23, 77, 107, 114

chispa, 145, 147

citizenship, 31, 32, 35, 105, 116–17, 120–21; and women's rights, 162–63

class, 36, 52, 77–78, 111–12, 120; and access to abortion, 58–59; and activism, 143, 149, 153, 155–56, 160–61, 171; discrimination by, 58; polarization, 118–19

collaboration, 178–93; binational, 171–73, 177, 186–92

colonias populares, 13–14, 125–41, 142–44, 150–56

community organizing, 34, 93, 125–41, 142–58, 183, 192–93; immigrant, 25

cross-border elements: commuters, 6, 56; cooperation, 144; illegal, 7; mobility, 36–38, 47–52; networks, 172–73, 186–88

culture, border, 8, 37, 41, 53–58, 126, 133; diversity, 4, 20, 34, 53, 186, 188–90; gender roles, and, 34, 46, 68–69, 92, 176, 187; indigenous, 19, 33–34; practices, 26–27, 41

domestic violence, 19, 31–34, 98–99, 144, 152, 170–77

education, 91, 97–98, 102, 140, 170; activism and, 151, 157, 179, 184; impact of immigrants on, 117; migrants and, 19, 29–30, 32–34; mobility and, 36; sexual, 27

empowerment, 8–16, 28, 170, 189, 193; labor and, 91, 93, 95; migration and, 35; religion and, 95
export-oriented industrialization (EOI), 5–6, 76–79, 88–90

families: activism and, 145, 149–50; gender roles in, 23–25, 34–35, 79–80, 91, 103, 128, 130–32, 138–41, 170–71; migrant, 24–27; mobility and, 36–52; networks, 104; patriarchal, 19, 130; planning, 27, 28, 34, 59, 69; structure of, 56, 91, 147; survival strategies of, 32, 35, 98; unpaid labor in, 13, 28–29, 43, 105, 110–11, 113–16, 119–21
feminism, 75, 98–99, 105, 144, 159, 189–92; Mexican, 15, 160–77; NGOs and, 159–77; popular, 160–61; religion and, 98; social, 161
feminist scholarship, 3, 7–8, 52, 105, 144; methodologies in, 178, 186, 190–92
feminization of labor force, 6, 12, 73–79, 83, 86–90

globalization, 5, 11, 21, 90; labor and, 73–74, 78–79, 121; migration and, 20; neoliberalism and, 75
grassroots organizations, 94, 165, 169

health and health care, 9, 23, 81, 93, 107, 108, 144, 152, 172; abortion and, 65–66, 68; activism, 144, 152–56, 162–63, 165–68, 176–77; border, 11, 15, 48, 173; poverty and, 26; reproductive, 53–55, 57, 153, 169, 170–72, 174–75, 179, 186–92

identity, 8, 55; ethnic, 35; gender, 19, 26–27, 33, 128; migration and, 20–22, 34; spiritual, 91, 94–95, 97–101
immigration, 5, 56, 127, 140; activism and, 154; indigenous, 19–35; labor, 34, 104, 111, 115–17; policy, 38; undocumented, 7, 38, 103–6, 111–13, 116–48
Immigration Reform and Control Act (IRCA), 106, 127
indigenous peoples, activism among, 154, 165; and women, 19–35, 146, 177

journey to work, 39–40, 42–44

land: activism and, 147–48, 156; privatization of, 21; title to (tenencia de la tierra), 147, 157–58

maquiladoras: activism and, 165, 166, 168, 172; autonomy in, 91–102; employment, 6, 8–9, 12, 29, 51, 91, 143–45, 155, 157; gender composition in, 73–90; industry, 6, 40–41, 73–90; mobility of employees, 43–44, 50
marriage, 19; arranged, 27, 30–34, 56
maternity: abortion and, 66; as motivation for activism, 137–40, 144–46; employment and, 80, 87, 89, 105, 111; gender roles and, 131–32, 133; identity, 34, 77; mobility and, 47, 52
mobility: abortion-related, 57–58; cross-border, 47–51; daily, 9–11, 36–52; national security and, 37–38, 49–51
Mothers of the Disappeared (Argentina), 146–47
Mujer Sana~Healthy Woman, 179, 189–92

neoliberalism, 16, 140
networks: cross-border, 111, 114–15, 120, 172; family, 104, 111–13, 118; migrant, 22–23, 119–21; social, 48, 56, 68; women's, 23–26, 93–102, 145, 168

non-governmental organizations
(NGOs), 96, 98, 100, 101, 159–77;
methodologies of, 170–71
North American Free Trade Agreement
(NAFTA), 6–7, 37, 81–84, 90–91,
153, 180

paracaidistas, 143, 147–48
patriarchy, 19, 28–29, 75–80, 88–90,
130, 133
population patterns at the border, 5, 37,
53, 56, 59, 125–26, 139
poverty, 11, 21–29, 97, 126, 160; marriage and, 32
Proposition 187, 106, 117

religion: gender roles and, 95–97; poverty and, 97
reproduction, 22, 34, 77; sexual, 53, 56,
59
resistance, 8, 22, 35, 78, 91, 94–102
Ruiz, Vicki, and Susan Tiano, 8, 125,
144

service sector workers, 7, 103–21
sexual violence, 91–96, 99–101
social justice, 9, 178, 184; activism and,
144, 146–47, 150, 157; church and,
95
social reproduction, 7, 13, 104–5, 110,
116–21
social welfare, 21, 81, 105, 119
spiritual identity, 91, 94–101; as form of
resistance, 97–101
squatters, 143, 147

strategies: activist, 150–55, 157, 164,
172, 176–77; for resistance, 91, 95,
101–2; for survival, 35, 41, 78, 81, 93,
105, 115–16, 120
Structural Adjustment Policies, 7, 74,
80–81, 163
structural change, 3, 13–14, 56, 94–96,
140; impact of, on women, 13, 74,
79, 92, 100
supermadres, 145–47

Tiano, Susan, and Vicki Ruiz, 8, 125,
144
Transborder Consortium for Research
and Action at the U.S.–Mexico Border, 179, 186–89
transnational elements: activism, 15,
177; communities, 13, 126–28;
cooperation, 15; corporations, 74,
76; economy, 6, 13; gender roles,
133–41; immigration, 32–33, 116;
networks, 104
transportation, 36, 39–52, 129, 150;
activism and, 150–51, 155

United Nations, 173

violence against women, 152–54, 158,
160, 163, 166–69, 170–77

welfare reform, 7, 106
workers: domestic, 22, 26, 29, 104–21;
household, 105–11, 116–18, 120–21,
142